BLACK MOSES

ALSO BY CALEB GAYLE

We Refuse to Forget

BLACK MOSES

A SAGA
OF AMBITION
and the
FIGHT FOR
A BLACK STATE

Caleb Gayle

RIVERHEAD BOOKS
NEW YORK
2025

RIVERHEAD BOOKS
An imprint of Penguin Random House LLC
1745 Broadway, New York, NY 10019
penguinrandomhouse.com

BOOK DESIGN BY MEIGHAN CAVANAUGH

Library of Congress Control Number: 2024057614
ISBN 9780593543795 (hardcover)
ISBN 9780593543818 (ebook)

Printed in the United States of America
1st Printing

The authorized representative in the EU for product safety and
compliance is Penguin Random House Ireland, Morrison
Chambers, 32 Nassau Street, Dublin D02 YH68,
Ireland, https://eu-contact.penguin.ie.

To Peanut, to Ash,

and to the fam who made me.

CONTENTS

PART III

Taking the (Un)Promised Land

Cast of Characters

MAIN CHARACTERS

Edward Preston McCabe: Leader who promoted Black migration and colonization of Oklahoma.

Abram Thompson Hall, Jr.: Journalist, best friend of Edward McCabe and co-organizer of Nicodemus, Kansas.

William Lewis Eagleson: McCabe's close friend and supporter in colonization efforts in Kansas and Oklahoma and organizer of the Oklahoma Immigration Association.

ABOLITIONISTS AND ACTIVISTS

John Brown: Radical abolitionist known for his anti-slavery actions.

Anthony Burns: Fugitive formerly enslaved man whose trial fueled varied levels of support for abolitionism in New England.

Frederick Douglass: Prominent abolitionist and orator.

Henry Highland Garnet: Black minister and radical abolitionist from Troy, New York.

Samuel Howe: Abolitionist and advocate for the blind.

Charles Henry Langston: Abolitionist and advocate for Black expansion in the West.

John Mercer Langston: Lawyer, abolitionist, political leader whom McCabe admired, and namesake for Langston, Oklahoma.

Chief Alfred Sam: Pan-Africanist who requested McCabe's assistance to relocate Black Oklahomans to Africa.

Charlton Tandy: St. Louis–based lawyer, activist, and advocate for Exodusters.

POLITICAL LEADERS

David Atchison: Pro-slavery advocate and U.S. senator (1843–1855).

Blanche Bruce: First Black U.S. senator (Mississippi) to serve a full term (1875–1881).

Benjamin Butler: Failed Union general and Radical Republican congressman (1867–1875, 1877–1879) and governor of Massachusetts (1883–1884).

Charles Curtis: Vice president (1929–1933) and U.S. senator from Kansas (1915–1929) who, as a member of Congress, intensified the impact of the Dawes Act through the passage of the Curtis Act.

Henry Dawes: U.S. senator from Massachusetts (1875–1893) known for the Dawes Act and its subsequent commission.

Ulysses S. Grant: Eighteenth U.S. president (1869–1877).

Benjamin Harrison: Twenty-third U.S. president (1889–1893).

Charles Haskell: First governor of Oklahoma (1907–1911).

T. W. Henderson: Failed Black Republican nominee for lieutenant governor of Kansas.

James Henry Lane: U.S. senator from Kansas (1861–1866) who proposed a Black colony in Texas.

Abraham Lincoln: Sixteenth U.S. president (1861–1865).

Preston Plumb: U.S. senator from Kansas (1877–1891) and supporter of McCabe's Black state plan.

Samuel C. Pomeroy: U.S. senator from Kansas (1861–1873).

Andrew Reeder: First governor of Kansas Territory (1854–1855).

John Pierce St. John: Governor of Kansas, prohibitionist, and advocate for the Black relocation to Kansas as refugees.

Alexander H. Stephens: Governor of Georgia and vice president of the Confederacy (1862–1865).

James Milton Turner: First Black person to serve in the U.S. diplomatic corps, U.S. minister to Liberia (1871–1878).

Daniel Voorhees: U.S. senator from Indiana (1877–1897) who organized a sham Senate investigation of the Exoduster movement.

Charles Lawrence Robinson: First governor of Kansas (1861–1863), and free-state leader.

Theodore Roosevelt: Twenty-sixth U.S. president (1901–1909), involved in Oklahoma's statehood issues.

Wilson Shannon: Pro-slavery advocate and second governor of Kansas Territory (1855–1856).

George Washington Steele: First governor of Oklahoma Territory (1890–1891).

John Whitfield: Pro-slavery advocate and delegate from Kansas Territory to the U.S. Congress.

RELIGIOUS FIGURES

Rev. W. B. Avery: Co-organizer of the Parsons, Kansas, Convention of Colored Men (1882).

Rev. L. Fulbright: Religious leader in Black migration and antagonist to McCabe's leadership in Kansas.

Abram Thompson Hall, Sr.: Father of Abram T. Hall, Jr., and co-founder of Quinn Chapel AME in Chicago.

Rev. W. C. Jackson: AME Church leader supporting Black migration to Kansas.

Rev. Horace James: Army chaplain and superintendent of freedmen's affairs in North Carolina.

Rev. Jonathan Lee: Religious leader in colonization movement.

"PHILANTHROPISTS" AND INVESTORS

Paul Forbes: Financier and diplomat who helped finance the botched "Cow Island" colonization scheme.

Leonard Jerome: Financier and philanthropist who helped finance the botched "Cow Island" colonization scheme, and Winston Churchill's maternal grandfather.

Bernard Kock: Import-export broker and leader of botched "Cow Island" colonization scheme.

Amos Lawrence: Massachusetts philanthropist supporting anti-slavery settlers in Kansas.

Eli Thayer: Founder of the New England Emigrant Aid Company, U.S. representative from Massachusetts (1857–1861).

Charles Tuckerman: Financier and diplomat who helped finance the botched "Cow Island" colonization scheme.

EARLY SETTLERS IN KANSAS {INCLUDING EXODUSTERS}

Lulu Sadler Craig: Exoduster and writer who chronicled early life in Nicodemus, Kansas.

Charles Dow: Free-state settler whose murder is considered the beginning of the "Bleeding Kansas" period.

Willina Hickman: An Exoduster who especially disliked her advent to Nicodemus, Kansas.

Curtis Pollard: Reconstruction-era Louisiana legislator and Exoduster.

Emma Williams: Exoduster who was among the first to arrive in Nicodemus after traveling from the South while pregnant; direct ancestor of present town historian Angela Bates.

CRITICS AND OPPONENTS

Frank Coleman: Supposed murderer of Charles Dow.

John Paul Jones: Oklahoma Territory–based Black critic of McCabe and the Black state effort.

Colonel Charles Suttle: Slave owner in Virginia involved in the Anthony Burns case.

MODERN-DAY KEEPERS OF ALL-BLACK TOWN HISTORY

Angela Bates: Founder of and former president of the Nicodemus Historical Society.

Mary Boyles: Leader in preserving Black historical sites in Langston, Oklahoma.

Michael Boyles: Mayor of Langston, Oklahoma.

Karen Ekuban: Advocate for Oklahoma's Black-town history, especially Boley, Oklahoma.

BLACK MOSES

"Nigger Talk"

W e will have a new party, that of negro supremacy in at least one State, with negro State and county officers, and negro Senators and Representatives in Congress," said a young but seasoned Black politician, Edward Preston McCabe, in 1891. With the Pyrrhic advances of Reconstruction after the Civil War becoming a memory, and Black people attacked and disempowered across the United States—both South *and* North—McCabe was promising something that sounded impossible, but it wasn't. Indeed, that's why the reporter to whom McCabe was talking had come all the way from Minnesota to Oklahoma Territory in the first place. Even as America's western frontier was on the precipice of being overrun, this reporter had come to witness a run on the land. Claiming that land was the first step toward a better life for thousands of Black people, the forty-year-old McCabe was known—sometimes derisively—as "the One Who Would Be the Moses."

◄►

At noon on September 22, 1891, along the borders of the Indian Territory, rifles were fired, pistols went off, cannons blazed, all signaling the official start of the new opening of Oklahoma Territory to settlement. With that, lands that had previously been granted *permanently* by the U.S. government to several Indigenous nations including the Sac and Fox, the Iowa, the Shawnee, and the Potawatomi were now declared free to whoever could grab them and, crucially, to hold them against all others. The night before, some twenty-five thousand people—Black, white, and Indigenous—huddled at the borders of Native lands. Poor whites from across the country hoped that Oklahoma would be another iteration of an America that would favor them. Black families left the harsh conditions of the Jim Crow South as well as the North and bordering states to grab at a hope that felt tactile. Citizens of Indigenous nations watched as newcomers made their lands sites of fulfilling dreams of building their personal fortunes.

The tens of thousands at the border waited with anticipation and a sense of opportunity for a once-in-a-lifetime chance articulated in simple, transactional terms: Whether rich or poor or something in between, all could run and ride to find land. Stake their ground. Develop their land and stay on it for five years. If they did, that land, 160 acres in total, would be theirs. That land would be their stake in tomorrow.

This was actually the second land run into Oklahoma. But this only increased the anticipation—and the danger. As much land as might have been freely available, the twenty-five thousand people at the border were pitted against each other, and accidents proliferated almost as soon as the first gun fired. One woman, named Miss Daisy (no last name), from Arkansas, fell off a horse and landed headfirst on a rock, splitting open her skull. A reporter learned from couriers from New Orleans that no one immediately stopped to help her because stopping would sacrifice their chances at the land. It wasn't until much later that a friend picked up her trampled body, most of which had become part of the earth that horses and the wheels of covered wagons had trampled across, carrying anxious Boomers—

predominantly white settlers who believed that these lands were made primarily for them to settle. Prairie fires sent smoke into the air as these "new lands . . . were burning brightly, filling the air with smoke of a peculiar odor." Some claimed that "some of the fires were started to drive men off claims"—that is, arson was used to evict competitors for the land—"while others were started by men hunting for section stones," stones and markers placed at intervals to demarcate plots. People were busy beginning again.

Unlike the actual shots fired at noon, McCabe's was aimed directly at the image of America. His shot came from his vision of Negro supremacy, for a part of the United States to be occupied and colonized by and for Black people. It was this idea that ensured that McCabe and the people he led were targeted even before the land run began.

Many Black people seeking a new life out west were called "Exodusters," because they took inspiration from the Hebrews' escape from slavery in Egypt in the book of Exodus to build a new promised land of their own. Yet, for some, the name was a slur—white people mocking Black people, many of them formerly enslaved, who traveled west from the South with nothing but the dust on their clothes and the tools they were told to bring by McCabe to build their own utopia. Even these people, it seemed, posed a threat to the white people aggrieved at the direction the country had taken since Emancipation. Which is why before the rifles fired, McCabe and his Black Exodusters were already being sized up for murder.

The day of the land run began, for McCabe, almost as usual. He spent much of it doing state business on behalf of the territory's governor as treasurer. This meant riding between Guthrie, the capital of the territory, and his home of Langston, the de facto Black capital. McCabe had already attracted a number of Black people to move there: Estimates range from a low of barely a thousand to more than twenty thousand, both by supporters of McCabe's efforts and those trying to scare nearby white settlers about the looming threat of *too many* Black people. But on this day, McCabe's all-too-typical ride to Guthrie was met by assailants.

On the northern line of the land run, near the Kansas border, Black people had been harassed by white gunmen—newspapers called them "cowboys"—simply for wanting to settle the same land that white settlers desired. Reportedly an argument broke out between them. The Black people were so badly wounded that they couldn't complete the land run. Even though he was only four miles south of his own Black town of Langston, McCabe was in danger of being attacked. The night before the run, another set of white cowboys fired warning shots at McCabe's best friend and co-conspirator in the movement for Black colonization of Oklahoma, William Eagleson, and roughed up Eagleson's friends in Langston. Now, if they shot down McCabe, it would become the third unprovoked reported killing of a Black man in two days.

The three cowboys who greeted McCabe were white. And in Mc-Cabe, these men saw not a man on his way to work, but an impediment to achieving their promised land.

In no uncertain terms, they told McCabe, who was unarmed, to go away—where to didn't much matter—only to be disappointed when McCabe told them no.

At McCabe's final refusal, the cowboys trained the barrels of their guns at him and fired. The percussive sounds of shots signaled the cutting down of the dream of an all-Black state, a state admitted to the Union that would provide as much opportunity as a Black person could ever hope for.

The gunpowder smoke filled the air so thoroughly that the cowboys would have to literally wait until it cleared to see if McCabe had been killed. As the powder and dust began to dissipate, they could see that McCabe was no longer astride his horse.

Their deed, it seemed, was done.

Newspapers, both Black and white—sometimes laudingly and other times mockingly—had dubbed Edward P. McCabe as "Moses." This was because he was in Oklahoma Territory not as a land-grabber but rather as a solicitor, a booster, a promoter. In the early 1890s, Mc-Cabe and his allies had reportedly dispatched some two thousand agents throughout the South to recruit Black people, specifically those tired of being less-than in a country whose laws claimed that they should be equal to everyone else. He had already established three Black towns in Oklahoma Territory and had plans for many more in what he made out to be the Eden of the West. By September 22, the tale of his dream—a Black state in the Union colonized by Black people, one that, for the most part, excluded white people—was articulated simply: a call to begin again.

One year before, in 1890, the *Milwaukee Journal* had dispatched reporters to cover McCabe's ambition while he was still in Washington, D.C., pitching his idea—which seemed like a tall tale or maybe just a dream. Within three months, Oklahoma would have between fifty thousand and seventy-five thousand Black people. The reporters wrote, "If [the] plan [to make Oklahoma a state] carries a year hence there will be a negro state with two black senators and a representative in congress." The paper labeled McCabe as "the One Who Would Be the Moses."

It is easy to understand why the *Journal* gave McCabe that title and his plan an optimistic spotlight. In 1890, McCabe met with President Benjamin Harrison to lobby on behalf of an all-Black state. As he told the president, "Some of us have names borrowed from masters, some of us have the blood of those who owned us as cattle, but disowned us as sons and daughters"—an indictment of America's treatment of Black people. "But in a new country, on new lands, with a climate suited to our race . . . we desire to show you that we are men and women capable of self-government." And that was far from just talk. Report after report told of the trainloads of Black colonizers leaving neighboring states in segregated cars without amenities to accommodate them. They'd be demeaned on their ride to their promised land because "it is a penalty for a black person to ride in a 'white' compartment, and a like penalty for a white person to ride in a 'black' compartment," according to the *Atchison Globe*. For "educated colored people of the south," according to one "prominent local negro" quoted by the *Kansas City Times*, the entire ride was found to be "very much humiliated because of this caste law and it would be a class of sensitive people with money and brains who would go to the new country." But demeaning, humiliating, penalizing, and dehumanizing train cars did not stop them. They could not.

Still, the detractors of Black colonizers were many. They had found "an old negro," claimed the *Arkansas Democrat*, an unnamed one of three "prodigals" who came *back* to Arkansas, after realizing just how uncertain and dangerous the situation was in this supposed promised land. Moreover, the paper claimed he said that there were "hundreds of negroes" "who would willingly come home if they had enough money to buy tickets of transportation," although the newspaper presented no evidence of them.

The authors of articles in the *Democrat*, as well as leading papers across the South and even in Oklahoma Territory, denigrated the aspirations of McCabe and the many Black people who sought to make their home as settlers. To do so, they gave McCabe's dreams and the dreams of those he led—dreams of making Oklahoma an all-Black state—a two-word name: "nigger talk."

They couldn't understand the terms McCabe used, terms like "our own laws" and "govern ourselves unmolested by the selfish greed of the white man" and "A Negro, city, a Negro county, A Negro State."

But their incomprehension was not because the words were complex. They couldn't understand them when they were uttered by a Black man because this Black man, and the people he led, used these words to imagine something *beyond* the limited notion of freedom from slavery.

What McCabe wanted was not the lack of slavery or the absence of oppression, but citizenship in a state that he ran where he took his counsel from Black people. He wanted abundance. And the mere appearance that McCabe's ride to work might also be an attempt to claim land altogether made him a dangerous target. Sealing his fate just outside the Black utopia that he had been shaping would serve him right. After all, McCabe had been talking that "nigger talk" that Black people used to "soothe themselves" amid the horror that was sanctioned by the government overtly and subtly. They fired their shots to put an end to that talk.

They did not realize that "nigger talk" was not of a carnival-barking irritant so much as it was a creed—the framework for the creation of a new world. They did not realize that "nigger talk" was the speaking into existence of another life, one that felt just beyond the bounds of the believable, nonfiction, achievable to the cowboys and on the brink of being fully realized for the Black people who came to colonize the land.

This book is the story of that dream, which reaches far back, long before McCabe and his thousands of followers declared Oklahoma as theirs. It is the story of a people cast out of enslavement and into the wilderness, where they found creative ways to build lives of abundance for themselves—lives on their terms. That abundant living would not be relegated simply to the freedom granted by the letter of the law was of utmost importance. They cared not simply about being free— they cared about dictating the terms of expressing that freedom. That their world would be built by their volition, that no decision-making table would exclude them, but instead demand their presence. This is the story of those who dared to do more than dream about a promised land, but instead to build one. That it failed makes its brief existence no less real nor less valuable today.

—◄■►—

After the Civil War, even as Reconstruction was failing across the country, Black people in America faced a choice and found themselves asking the question: Should I leave, or should I stay? Large advertisements were taken out by the compatriots of McCabe that read, "HO! For Kansas," and reporters across the country weighed in on the issue by presenting the options of Black people in the South: "KU KLUX or KANSAS." All of this was attempting to answer an even bigger question: Is there a place for me here?

In past decades, some Black people had left—or been pushed—to leave the United States. They headed to Liberia, or Canada, or the Caribbean. Many of the pushes were supported by white leaders who are today sometimes rightfully valorized and memorialized: politicians like President Abraham Lincoln and others—ministers, philanthropists, and Brahmins whose names are still emblazoned on towns, schools, charitable foundations, and libraries. Even these white people had given up on the hope that Black people could find a home in America. President Lincoln insisted on adding an agenda item in his meeting with representatives from southern states: the fate of formerly enslaved people. Opposite Lincoln sat the vice president of the Confederacy, Alexander H. Stephens, who a month before Fort Sumter's bombardment that started the insurrection had proclaimed, "Our new government['s] . . . foundations are laid, its cornerstone rests upon the great truth, that the negro is not equal to the white man; that slavery—subordination to the superior race—is his natural and normal condition. This, our new government, is the first, in the history of the world, based upon this great physical, philosophical, and moral truth."

Rather than revulsion at this notion or at Stephens's proposals for comity between the North and the South, Lincoln, according to a hotly debated account from General Benjamin F. Butler, wondered aloud, "But what shall we do with the negroes after they are free? I can hardly believe that the South and North can live in peace, unless we can get rid of the negroes. Certainly, they cannot if we don't get rid of the negroes whom we have armed and disciplined and who have fought with us, to the amount, I believe, of some one hundred and fifty thousand men . . . what, then, are our difficulties in sending all the blacks away?"

Some Black people heard about Lincoln's unspoken question and left the United States for Canada, the Caribbean, and the relatively new West African nation of Liberia. Others answered with road-blocks. As the sun set on the Reconstruction era, casting shadows of despair across the South, what hope remained for Black citizens who were once again crushed with the weight of oppression on seemingly every measure? What hope that remained was met with violence and intimidation, and new laws were enacted which perpetuated that violence and intimidation while defending those who were violent and valorizing those who intimidated. And emerging amid this time was the unrelenting grip of Jim Crow on implementing policies to further install segregation practices.

A different answer to that question would come a half century later: Between 1910 and 1970, Black people would choose to leave the South in the greatest internal migration in American history, abandoning the violence of the region for the doubtful safety of the North. Most call this the Great Migration: a signal that there was a mass movement of Black people toward finding their own opportunity. But the term is a misnomer.

. . .

Because, for a brief moment, Black people went west.

This was a *previous* great migration, a movement from the 1870s to
the 1900s of freedpeople who pushed beyond the bounds of the old
North and the old South. Some called them Exodusters—people historian Nell Irvin Painter described as Black people who, like the Isra-
elites from the Bible, had urgently hatched less-than-deliberate plans
to pick up all they had and move west. First, these settlers populated
Kansas. Soon they fanned out across the Old West, into places we now
call Oklahoma, Nebraska, Colorado, and New Mexico.

What they sought was what most Americans had sought since the
nation was first settled and seek still: a place to call home. A stake. A
platform upon which to build a future. Not just freedom, but abundance: opportunity and the possibility for a future that's more hopeful than the past. Not just a life clinging to an elusive survival, but a
life of realized ambition.

They dreamed of a state that would be governed by Black people,
inhabited by Black people. For a brief moment, the state known today
as Oklahoma might have been such a place: thousands of Black people building all-Black towns and schools, seeking political office, and
even breaking ground on universities and hospitals. We still see remnants of these dreams in towns like Boley, Oklahoma, with its still
extant Boley Rodeo, the first Black rodeo in the country. Or in towns
like Tulsa, where we see in its northern neighborhoods the outlines
of what once was Tulsa's Black Wall Street, a hub of some 191 commercial establishments, along with churches, schools, and more, all
meant to serve Black people, circulating dollars within those communities without a touch of white approval. These self-sustaining communities have an intellectual antecedent, a seemingly once-immovable
mover.

They came because of the magnetism of one man's ambition that thousands shared.

Tales about McCabe—a never-enslaved Black man who had worked as a clerk on Wall Street, had been a former clerk to Chicago businessman Potter Palmer, and served as the Old West's first Black statewide-elected leader—had spread not just throughout the South in Black newspapers, but in white newspapers in the North as well. McCabe, the stories went, said that Black people could not only belong in Oklahoma, but be in charge.

This dream of turning Oklahoma into an American promised land for Black people was destined to collide with others' plans for the place—and in drastic fashion with their ambitions and futures. The white cowboys who took aim at McCabe were only one example of that collision.

At the time that McCabe was moving to occupy the Oklahoma Territory for Black people and volunteer himself as the territory's governor, the Cherokee, Choctaw, Chickasaw, Seminole, and Muscogee Creek Nations (once considered the "Five Civilized Tribes")—which had been banished to this part of the country under a law signed by Andrew Jackson decades before—were pitching separate Indian statehood for the same territory, calling it Sequoyah. While there were already Black people in Indian Territory, unlike McCabe, they already had claim over parts of this land as members of some of these nations. And Indian Territory became an attractive landing zone for white elites who saw the opportunity to make a buck, a buck that seemed endless as oil and gas were discovered there and literally sprang from the ground.

By the late nineteenth century, America was done reconstructing the states that were already part of the Union. But in Oklahoma and the Indian Territory, that was not the case. It was the area that

McCabe wanted, the place that white business interests and settlers wanted, and the region that the Native Americans already occupied and justifiably wanted to keep for themselves. Reconstruction was and is unfinished and enduring.

This, ultimately, is a story of ambition, the wherewithal to dream, to hope against hope. It's the story of the rise and fall of early Black settlers' ambition for the Old West and is a tale of the West, and of America, in microcosm. It's the story of being forced to leave in order to start again, only to lose it all, and a fight for a century to recover nuggets of truth among the wreckage. It's the story of hope and what comes after; of brief moments of racial equity, and what comes after; of dreams, big ones, and what comes after we wake up. It is the story of trying, why we cannot stop trying, and why being able to try is worth remembering at all. Most of all, this story shows that even the most American of promises was never available to all Americans. For centuries, America has inspired people to dream of the ideal lives they'd like to lead, yet it has offered staggeringly few a real chance to realize those lives on their terms. Because Edward McCabe's story shows that even striking out west—doing as Horace Greeley once instructed, "Go West, young man"—does not offer salvation.

PART I

ESCAPING BONDAGE

And it came to pass in those days, when Moses was grown up, that he went out unto his brethren, and looked on their burdens: and he saw an Egyptian smiting an Hebrew, one of his brethren.

—EXODUS 2:11

An eloquent fellow said that this was a movement of a race "irrespective of leaders," that it was an "irrepressible uprising that no man could put down," and the speaker added: "Every black man is his own Moses now, I tell you [. . .] every black man is his own Moses."

—*Chicago Tribune*, MAY 23, 1879

1

"Brethren, Arise, Arise!"

TROY, NEW YORK, 1843

If you must bleed, let it all come at once—rather die freemen, than live to be slaves. It is impossible like the children of Israel, to make a grand exodus from the land of bondage.

—HENRY HIGHLAND GARNET, "AN ADDRESS TO THE SLAVES OF THE UNITED STATES OF AMERICA," AUGUST 21, 1843

Over two decades before the country—at least the Union—declared the issue of slavery settled, two Black men, Frederick Douglass and Henry Highland Garnet, both formerly enslaved, had a vigorous debate in a northern church in 1843. The question before them: "How can we be truly free?"

That question animated the next sixty years of debates—what ought we to do with the Black people enslaved before Emancipation and, most important, after it? And it took nearly forty years for Edward McCabe to answer this question with his own innovation: escape the North as vigorously as a Black person would want to escape the South and begin again on the western frontier. Beginning again for McCabe would mean establishing a state run by Black people for Black people, with their white counterparts tolerated only at a minimum.

There are more elegant ways to describe this debate, but the gathering for it—a convention of colored people to discuss matters of economic and educational attainment among Black people as well as their political participation—represented an audacity and hope that deftly articulates the positions of marginalized people then and now. These Black people—as slavery was rapidly expanding, and the North was deflecting and abdicating moral responsibility—showed what a multiracial democracy could look like by deliberating over a present and future they *hoped* for but could not see. And yet they gathered, they talked, and they debated. And even if Garnet and Douglass sat on opposite sides of the debate, they both did as McCabe and his followers would do forty-six years later: They talked that *nigger talk*.

"While you have been oppressed, we have also been partakers with you; nor can we be free while you are enslaved," Henry Highland Garnet told his audience at the Convention of Colored Citizens in Buffalo, New York. The venue—Park Presbyterian Church—had the familiar trappings of a church congregation, which made Garnet's speech equal parts a political rally and a sermon.

In the audience, Douglass attentively listened to Garnet's every word. Douglass had already begun emerging as a leading voice of abolition. Just five years earlier, he had been an enslaved Black man in Maryland, until he escaped and was soon one of the most recognizable voices through his lectures and writing.

Abolition in any form for the two debaters—one from Maryland and one from Troy, New York—headlined the agenda of the convention, with the persistent question being: How to make freedom possible and permanent? The convention was situated as a platform to present survey data that could provide fifty-eight delegates, Garnet and Douglass included, and its raucous crowd insight into the state of

Black ownership, Black wealth, and Black employment, at any true scale. The stakes rose with every newspaper reporter in attendance, every political onlooker, and every tangible and quixotic aim articulated by the delegates, but all of it remained grounded in data. The survey data were by no means exhaustive and focused only on a handful of places in New York, Ohio, and one town in Massachusetts. Yet, the feat was impressive. Attendees learned that in Columbus, the average real estate wealth per Black person was only $35, compared to Albany, New York, where Blacks' average real estate wealth was $100 per household. The convention offered a snapshot of the state of Black America as convention participants understood and saw it. But Garnet saw the state of Black America differently. His view could be summed up by the persistence of the gulf between free Black people on one side and the rest of Black America on the other. While Douglass believed that there was still hope for a peaceful transition from enslaved to free and that America was uniquely able to develop into a democratic multiracial nation, Garnet could not bring himself to believe the same. He had been trained at the radical school, the Oneida Institute, and was taught that school's core tenet: "immediatism"—the immediate cessation of slavery without compensating the enslavers. Though formerly enslaved, Garnet hand made himself free, and his expectation for Black and white people alike was that everyone should fight for greater freedom. During the 1830s, he had been an itinerant minister while intermittently studying at both Oneida and Noyes Academy before it was destroyed by anti-abolitionists. Settling finally in Troy in 1839, he, with his friend William Allen, launched an abolitionist magazine and cultivated a crowd of people who could count on him for prophetic fire.

Still, as Douglass listened to Garnet's strategy, he couldn't help but conclude that it was no strategy at all—just an excess of moral outrage with unlimited potential harm.

"The gross inconsistency of a people holding slaves, who had themselves 'ferried o'er the wave' for freedom's sake, was too apparent to
be entirely overlooked," Garnet said. He castigated the people who
argued that the founding of the United States was based on a legacy
of freedom from their oppressor. Those who believed this were "oppressors themselves," Garnet argued, who "have become involved in
the ruin. They have become weak, sensual, and rapacious. They have
cursed you—they have cursed themselves—they have cursed the earth
which they have trod."

For Douglass, the stakes and potential peril increased once Garnet
said that the method for dealing with such moral bankruptcy was violence. "Brethren," Garnet urged, "it is as wrong for your lordly oppressors to keep you in slavery as it was for the man thief to steal our
ancestors from the coast of Africa. You should therefore now use the
same manner of resistance." As McCabe later amplified, Garnet urged
Black people to take and build what is theirs—don't ask simply for
permission. Don't wait, but embrace the ideals oppressors didn't in-
tend to be of use for Black people to create their own ideal. "As would
have been just in our ancestors when the bloody footprints of the first
remorseless soul thief was placed upon the shores of our fatherland."
To make his point clear, he told the audience, "If hereditary bondmen
would be free, they must themselves strike the blow."

The bloodshed would not be only of the enslaved trying to gain
freedom, but of the master who cannot see the beauty in their skin
and of those free Black people who might join in the cause of freedom
and abundance. "Tell them in language which they cannot misun-
derstand, of the exceeding sinfulness of slavery, and of a future judg-
ment, and of the righteous retributions of an indignant God. Inform
them that all you desire is FREEDOM, and that nothing else will suf-
fice. Do this, and for ever after cease to toil for the heartless tyrants
who give you no other reward but stripes and abuse. If they then com-

mence the work of death," he said, "they, and not you, will be responsible for the consequences."

Garnet was radically departing from the views that had captivated some of his fellow abolitionists. For decades, abolition had been grounded in notions of civil disobedience, which would implicate the evil wrongdoer (the white enslaver) and the good lawbreaker (the Black self-liberator). But the institution of slavery in the United States was still growing, and abolition took on forms of self-emancipation of people like Douglass (who escaped) or of these conventions and abolition-aligned newspapers that denounced the institution and demanded political leaders to change. Garnet's call was not for abandoning faith that people might change, but that that faith might need the help of people willing to take up arms to nudge faith along.

Like any Black preacher who knows when they've made their case, Garnet began his coda. As he did, whispers of concern shot across the convention. Yet these were drowned out by Garnet's thundering conclusion: "Fellow-men! patient sufferers! behold your dearest rights crushed to the earth! See your sons murdered, and your wives, mothers, and sisters doomed to prostitution! In the name of the merciful God! and by all that life is worth, let it no longer be a debatable question whether it is better to choose LIBERTY or DEATH." From Nat Turner, whose 1831 revolt sent shivers down the spines of enslavers who never anticipated the degree of success he'd inspire; to Joseph Cinqué, whom Garnet lauded for his rebellion as an enslaved man against the Spanish aboard the ship *La Amistad*; to Madison Washington, whose rebellion aboard the ship *Creole* just two years prior resulted in the liberation of 128 enslaved people and catalyzed heated debates between the United States and Great Britain over diplomacy and slavery; to Denmark Veazie (Vesey), whose execution was triggered by his decision to spark a rebellion in Charleston in 1822; to even McCabe's eventual nicknamesake, Moses—Garnet called upon these abolitionists from different eras and told the crowd, "Brethren, arise, arise! Strike for your lives and liberties. Now is the day and the hour . . . Rather die freemen than live to be slaves. Remember that you are FOUR MILLIONS! Your dead fathers speak to [you] from their graves. Heaven, as with a voice of thunder, calls on you to arise from the dust. Let your motto be resistance! RESISTANCE! No Oppressed people have ever secured their liberty without resistance."

As the applause roared in response to the homily turned political speech, Douglass lodged his dissent. "There was too much physical force, both in the address and the remarks of the speaker last up," he told the audience, according to notes of the convention. Douglass wanted to keep "trying," because "the moral means a little longer," implicitly calling the address by Garnet too radical to be moral. He feared that "the address, could it reach the slaves, and the advice, either of the address or the gentleman, be followed, while it might not lead the slaves to rise in insurrection for liberty, would, nevertheless, and necessarily be the occasion of an insurrection."

Not one to let a critique hang in the air, Garnet rose again. All he had done, he explained, was advise that the enslaved "go to their masters and tell them they wanted their liberty, and had come to ask for it; and if the master refused it, to tell them, then we shall take it, let the consequence be what it may."

Douglass thought this request was too likely to lead to an insurrection. By one vote, Garnet's resolution was voted down, and then twice more when the president of the convention, Amos Beman, lodged his strong dissent, citing "moral" reasons, just as Douglass had, for his opposition. But for McCabe, it was an invitation to find liberation and abundance for Black people in an innovative way—one not bestowed by his white peers, but one designed for and by Black people, even if it meant using the tools his white predecessors had used to colonize the country.

Garnet's "radical" resolution failed, just as McCabe's radical idea for colonizing a territory and turning it into a Black state was called a failure before it began. But Garnet sowed seeds of a different kind of liberation, the fruits of which were reaped by the likes of McCabe. And McCabe's plan for a Black state sowed new seeds for those who would come after, who aspired to a Black nationalism that persisted through representations throughout history—in Black political parties, Black cultural feats like the Black rodeo, Black towns, and more. McCabe's all-Black-state idea, innovative though it was, had its antecedent in a battle of ideas for how Black people might make their way in America.

Perhaps Douglass hadn't been aggrieved enough yet. Perhaps the country that once permitted his slavery hadn't let him down enough yet. Because twenty years from publicly opposing Garnet—even insinuating he was immoral—Douglass found himself where Garnet had been. In an editorial in his monthly circular, Douglass told his readers, "Men of Color! To Arms! To Arms!," detailing that "when the war is over, the country is saved, peace is established, and the black man's rights are secured, as they will be, history with an impartial hand will dispose of that and sundry other questions. Action! Action! not criticism is the plain duty of this hour. Words are now useful only as they stimulate to blows."

But that was decades in the future. For now, Garnet and his radical calls to "arise" were critiqued by Black people and maligned by many of his white counterparts. The Baltimore-based *Niles National Register* described Garnet's speech, and the speeches of others at this convention, not as "anti-slavery" but as for liberty. But the part that worried the writers of the article most was that Garnet's words were "recommending a servile insurrection, and declarations that if such insurrection should happen, the only part they would take would be to aid the slaves, and denials of the binding force of the constitution." The editors of the *Niles National Register* wanted to alarm their

readers that Garnet sought to disrupt the placid approach to liberation. "We would simply call the attention of all our readers to the fact
that the attempt is now being made to organize a political party
on these principles . . . It takes a shorter road to attain the end, by
raising the standard of servile war, and subverting the constitution
itself." The Constitution still deemed Douglass and Garnet as not
fully human, and both men's escapes were prosecutable by the Fugitive Slave Clause. And any uprising the likes of which Garnet was
pushing for violated the fourth article of the Constitution. He was
advocating they break enough laws to get them killed, and in so
doing, he was pushing for a reinvented and reconstituted America.

Such violence, according to the *Niles National Register*, was "the
very madness of fanaticism, and deeply injures the cause of the slave,
while it discredits the efforts, and abates the zeal, of those who abhor-
ring as much as the most ultra-abolitionist the institution of slavery,
and its inevitable abuses—are yet bound by their fealty to the constitution to fulfill its behests, however unpalatable, until they can, in a
constitutional mode, be altered."

Meanwhile, the local *Buffalo Advertiser* focused on Garnet's race.
Calling him a "Ci-Devant slave"—French for formerly enslaved—the
Advertiser noted, "His skin is jet black, indicating unmixed African
descent, but his head nearly approaches the Caucasian formation,
being one of the finest we ever saw on a negro." The paper asserted
that this formerly enslaved man was as white as they come not because of how he looked, but because his wit, his charm, his intellectual power made him of the "Caucasian formation." For his part,
Garnet had quoted a white man, Patrick Henry, for demanding, "Give
me liberty or give me death!" By doing that, Garnet knew that white
people would be addled by what they saw as unjustified speed and what
he knew to be a long time coming.

And it was true that Garnet had traveled some 260 miles to Buffalo
to call for a rebellion. But these were resounding themes emanating

from the Liberty Street Presbyterian Church, which Garnet pastored. In his time there, he loudly sounded the calls for freedom that shook the unsettled moral foundations of a country whose wealth was established by the free labor Garnet would attest was anything but free. McCabe would have undoubtedly grown up hearing these same calls. McCabe's beginning matters as much as his journey, as it contains the fragments of America's mangled tale of what drives people born without power, free or enslaved, who build dreams and hopes for better, to do.

———◁———▷———

Seven years after Garnet and Douglass's great debate, on October 10, 1850, Edward Preston McCabe was born in Troy. To this day, little is known about McCabe's parents. History has not recorded his father. But we know that his mother, Elizabeth McCabe, claimed to be free all her life. Garnet proclaimed that "slavery had fixed a deep gulf" between the lives of the people of Troy, New York, and all of the Black people still living in enslavement at the time of McCabe's birth. But because of his mother's claim and his fortune to be born in the North, McCabe came without the scourge of being born into slavery.

Troy was a place to prosper for both enslaver and the formerly enslaved. Its county, Rensselaer, was named after the Van Rensselaer family, the wealthy Dutch clan (at one point America's tenth-richest family) that owned the over one-million-acre estate they called the manor of Rensselaerswyck. Herman Melville pays indirect homage to his own Rensselaer family ties in *Moby Dick*: "It touches one's sense of honor, particularly if you come of an old established family in the land, the Van Rensselaers, or Randolphs, or Hardicanutes"— equating the Van Rensselaers to the families that led the colonization of Virginia, in the case of the Randolphs, and the family that ruled Scandinavia.

Stephen Van Rensselaer, the namesake of the region's university and the tenth-richest American in history (according to a 2009 study by *Forbes*), introduced enterprise and innovation where it was not necessary. His land sprawled from Albany east to Troy and to towns afar such as Saratoga and Schenectady. He provided leases at decent rates to local farmers, negating any need for workers to carve their own path to self-sustainability by buying their own land. Instead, he charged them rent, and in harsh times would accept grain and other crops they produced for their rent instead of cash. The goal was to make sure that the money they spent on a down payment for land would instead be allocated to improving the businesses they started, and Stephen was an equity partner in each of the businesses his tenants founded. Rensselaer and Albany Counties became a beacon of progress as eighty thousand tenants—white tenants—working the land tried to achieve greater and greater levels of productivity.

But not so for many of the Black residents.

Rensselaer's land, manor, and personal holdings were managed by slaves, fifteen of them. These he freed in 1799, when the Gradual Emancipation Act passed in New York—an incremental nod toward freedom by declaring children born to enslaved mothers after July 4, 1799, somewhat free (forced into indentured servitude).

Slavery was as much a hallmark of this area as its noted streak of abolitionism three decades later.

⊲━●━▶

McCabe's family moved from place to place, chasing opportunity. From Troy, they went to Fall River, Massachusetts, and from Fall River to Newport, Rhode Island, where his mother and father stayed, only to send McCabe to Bangor, Maine, to continue his studies. But when his father died, suddenly McCabe's life, at twenty-two years old, changed and his direction pivoted toward making a life of freedom, not just benefiting from it.

McCabe moved south to New York City and Wall Street, to answer what thousands of other men—white men—asked: "What are my prospects?"—only to ultimately adopt the quote attributed to Horace Greeley: "Go West, young man."

And West McCabe did go, because as a free man he could. But without realizing it, he had inherited the unresolved debate between Garnet and Douglass: Would there be a place for him in a changing country hurtling toward war not long after?

2

Nothing Was Promised, Paths Were Constructed, Everything Was Contested

BOSTON & KANSAS, 1855

> Far in the West rolls the thunder,
> The tumult of the battle is raging,
> Where bleeding Kansas is waging
> Warfare with Slavery!
> Struggling with foes who surround her,
> Lo! she implores you to stay her!
> Will you to Slavery betray her?
> Never—she shall be free?
> Hurrah!
> Swear that you'll never betray her
> Kansas shall yet be free!
>
> —"FREMONT & VICTORY" BY CHARLES S. WEYMAN,
> *New York Daily Tribune*, SEPTEMBER 13, 1856

The guns were drawn.

Alone, Charles Dow, a twenty-two-year-old free-stater, had tried to walk past the blacksmith shop where a group of white men had gathered, only to be met with taunts, insults, and jeers. Once his back was to them, Dow heard the unmistakable sound of a rifle being cocked. He might have even heard them call his name.

Here in Kansas Territory in 1855, far from the comforts and advances of eastern states, the little town of Hickory Point might have served as the backdrop for any spaghetti western a century later. The land was flat, the territory filled with gunfights, fistfights, and shouting matches, riven by the discord of militaries, militias, and cowboys. The standoff between Dow and his assailants was over the ownership of land. But unlike other firefights in the Old West, the events of that day would echo far beyond a small town in dusty Kansas Territory. The events of that day would make clear what was at stake for Black and white people everywhere: Would we continue to enslave or would Kansas be where the practice would stop?

Hearing the rifle click and the men shout, Charles Dow turned to face the men threatening him. He knew them. Like Dow, they were new to the territory; but unlike Dow, these men had come to Kansas to ensure that slavery would become the law of this land. The Civil War was still five years off, the emancipation of all slaves at least a decade in the future, and the question of which states would ban slavery and which would enshrine it into their constitutions was the greatest political question of the day.

Just a year before, Dow had come to Kansas to look for a place to call his own. This seemed a tall order. It was the land—that ownership, that abundance—that made him a target.

A small crowd that had gathered around this standoff watched in silence. Words, reportedly, were not exchanged—the actions and the sympathies of pro-slavery, newly arrived Kansans spoke louder than words. Dow turned to leave. A man who seemed to be in charge snapped his gun at Dow and the cap exploded. Perhaps it was the shock, maybe the horror, but Dow looked around to find the origin of the sound. Momentarily, he got a reprieve, because Frank Coleman— the man who had pulled out the rifle and threatened to shoot him— supposedly put down his weapon.

However, the men with Coleman cocked their rifles and reportedly fired eight shots toward Dow. Though his men fired, it was believed that Coleman's initial shot delivered the death wound through Dow's chest, while his men's slugs tore through Dow's body. Dow fell to the ground and the shooters left him where he fell. It took four to five hours for his friends to collect his bullet-shredded body.

This first shot was followed by countless others and plunged the territory into full-fledged battles and civilian massacres. Towns burned. And as Kansas bled, the bleeding left a bloodstained path to follow for McCabe.

—◄ ●► —

The trouble began just eighteen months before Dow's murder.

After decades of protest, Washington, D.C., finally banned in 1850 the buying and selling of human beings within its boundaries. One of the largest markets for the enslaved had been right behind the U.S. Capitol Building, on the south side of today's National Mall, along Independence Avenue. Although slavery itself was still allowed in the District of Columbia, the victory for northern states in banning selling was more than symbolic. Still, many in the South felt southerners in Washington had conceded too much. So in exchange for agreeing to end the slave trade in D.C., southern states had received the 1850 Fugitive Slave Act. Now, law enforcement, judges, and the like could override local state and city regulations where escaped slaves were offered sanctuary and slavery was banned. Suddenly, ordinary northerners were not just reading about slavery far away; they were seeing lawmen and federal marshals in their cities and towns dragging Black men, women, and children from their homes.

Just a few years later, another partisan Congress came to another toxic compromise. At that time, the states in the Union were almost equally balanced between slave states (fifteen of them) and free states (eighteen). Then, as now, political fights often came down to a handful of senators. Each state sent two senators to Congress, and the balance was already tilting toward free states. Now Kansas Territory sought to enter the Union. Should it enter as a slave state or a free one? Whatever Kansas entered as could well tip the balance—in the Senate, in population.

Months of debate over this momentous decision resulted in the 1854 Kansas-Nebraska Act. Congress decided to let the people living (and who would come to live) in Kansas decide their state's future on their own.

News of the upcoming vote to choose the first delegate in November 1854 was the starting gun for a race that would determine the future of the state and the country.

Slaveholders and their sympathizers, just like Frank Coleman, poured across the border from Missouri—a slave state—ready to cast their vote and committed violent acts to signal what would happen to others who opposed the spread of slavery. Outnumbered, free-staters began to organize militias and called on wealthy sympathizers in the North, especially in New England, to send money and guns . . . and, most critically, people.

—◄━▶—

"We went to bed one night old fashioned, conservative, Compromise Union Whigs," wrote Amos Lawrence of how much changed in the fateful year of 1854, and "waked up stark mad Abolitionists." As part of this transformation, Lawrence, a wealthy Boston-area textile magnate, became in 1854 the treasurer of the New England Emigrant Aid Company (NEEAC). Founded by Eli Thayer and incorporated by the Massachusetts legislature in the wake of the passage of the Kansas-Nebraska Act, NEEAC was constituted as a joint-stock company, one in which anyone could buy a share in support of the effort to send free-staters—people who stood in opposition to slavery being authorized as a practice in Kansas—to establish settlements, as many as possible. The settlements would soon be called Osawatomie, Shawnee, Topeka, even Lawrence—named after Amos Lawrence himself.

That Lawrence would become such a stalwart of national abolition that a town was named after him by some of the most radical activists of the day would have been a shock to him just a few years before. In his younger days, on a trip to the South, Lawrence wrote in his diary, "The negroes seem very happy here." He continued by referencing a conversation with "an old negro who was brought from Africa." He noted, "I think the Africans half monkeys; he cannot speak more like a man than a monkey could if he should speak."

As a young man, Lawrence thought there was no need for Black people to escape the South, where he and his family had made their vast wealth, often through the labor of Black people. But in less than twenty years, this child of northern privilege transformed from an old-fashioned bigot into an abolitionist—and a committed one. The same would be said of his friends.

How was this change accomplished so quickly? It was thanks to Anthony Burns, a Black man whose fate was as dark as Dow's. And this change in Lawrence's disposition created the mythic draw of Kansas—a place where McCabe could come to start his work of making a life for Black people, one unavailable elsewhere in America.

The Kansas-Nebraska Act was signed in May 1854 by President Franklin Pierce, but spring in New England was late that year, with frost lingering in Boston and the surrounding region. Even so, those cold shores and farmland must have provided collective warmth for Anthony Burns. It's easy to understand why. He had escaped the clutches of slavery in Virginia. To get to Massachusetts, he had hidden on board a ship for weeks, where his sustenance depended on his ability to wait for days for scraps and slop. He should have died as a stowaway. But Burns defied the odds and reached Boston, a free town, and he left behind his status as slave and stepped out of the ship—fugitive though his prospects would soon be.

He found work first trying and failing as a cook on a mud scow because he couldn't get his bread to rise properly, and then in a clothing store. But Burns sent a letter to his still enslaved brother back in Virginia. The letter was intercepted by Colonel Charles Suttle, Burns's former enslaver, whose subcontractors, as well as their wives and daughter, had taught Burns how to read and write. To Suttle, and by the letter of the law, Burns wasn't free. He was fugitive, a criminal—and property.

As the clothing store, operated by abolitionist Lewis Hayden, was closing one evening, the U.S. marshal's plan took shape. If Burns was arrested in the middle of the street where today's Financial District meets the opening to Little Italy, a commotion might erupt. But the marshal figured that if he could arrest Burns for a false charge of robbery, it would only confirm the suspicions of even the most progressive Bostonian. And yet when the marshal approached him, Burns did not so much as fuss.

Burns's eventual trial in Boston devolved into a sham almost as soon as it started. The government barred the public from seeing large portions of it; armed guards were posted supposedly to protect Burns; the attorney who volunteered to represent Burns was prohibited from any of the tasks one would associate with a typical attorney in a courtroom—no ability to strike anything from the record, no ability to speak on Burns's behalf. A member of the court even tricked Burns into dictating a letter attesting to his status as a slave to ensure that the law could charge him under the Fugitive Slave Act. The judge said that while he did feel sympathy for Burns, he was bound by federal law to rule that Anthony was guilty. Exodus for a better life was against the law.

When word spread in Boston that Anthony had been arrested, one of the city's oldest Black churches, Twelfth Baptist Church, quickly dispatched its pastor to the courthouse where Burns was being held and demanded that Burns receive "freedom from the United States Government in the hands of whose officers he is now held as a slave." Others convened secret groups across the city to determine how to reverse this travesty. They kept watch on his holding cell in the courthouse (Massachusetts law barred enslaved people from being held in jail), which his lawyer dubbed the "slave pen." All this was old hat to Black Bostonians, a confirmation of what they knew their government was. What was new about Burns's trial was that for perhaps the first time, the ugliness of racism was thrust onto the doorsteps of white Bostonians who otherwise claimed distance from the scourge of slavery.

Protests rang out. Newspapers rallied both support and condemnation. "It is with great satisfaction we announce to our readers the complete triumph of law in Boston over one of the most ferocious gangs of Abolitionists [. . .] that ever disgraced the country," the *New York Journal of Commerce* reported on its front page. Newspaper pages defended the man whose race was white and disparaged the man who was Black, saying of Burns's once-again owner, Colonel Charles Suttle, that he was "a worthy and estimable man"—alleging even further that Suttle had been deprived of his property and denying that Anthony was human. Protestors became rioters and rioters became insurrectionists. In the *Citizen*, writers satirically hypothesized how much better it would be if "the rebels had been shot down like dogs," adding that if any "white man of the Caucasian race" was slain during such riots, he would deserve the title of "Hero who accomplishes it to a higher seat in the seventh Heaven than St. Paul, the Twelve Apostles, or any of the noble Army of Martyrs who have died for the sublime doctrines, or for the freedom of man."

The riots continued, though they were quelled significantly after the first night, as federal marshals prepared to ferry Anthony back into captivity in Virginia. Suddenly, it seemed, the Brahmins—the elite who ruled Boston—came to realize that the protections and safeguards of their Boston bubble had burst. Some readied the arms "that God gave them"; others, like Lawrence, readied their pens to articulate what this incident had changed them into: abolitionists. But abolitionists on their terms, focusing their actions not on abolishing the practice of slavery everywhere, but on stopping the spread of enslavement anywhere.

Two months after Anthony Burns's trial, Henry David Thoreau called a meeting in Concord, Massachusetts, and implored his fellow Bay Staters to take action, delivering a speech that read, "Is it not possible that an individual may be right and a government wrong? Are laws to be enforced simply because they were made? Or declared by any number of men to be good, if they are not good?" He wanted the audience to step outside the veil of protection the law gave them—the law that doomed Burns. As Thoreau saw it, slavery had come to Massachusetts; bigotry and racism had found their way into New England life at the precise time that they, the landed elite of Beacon Hill and Brookline, thought they had ascended beyond such allegations. Burns became the rallying cry for Lawrence and others to engage in a version of abolitionism that did not force them to sacrifice the life they had built for themselves.

The Burns trial and Thoreau's speech had spurred Lawrence and many others to the realization that the institution of slavery and its extensions could spread in unexpected places. If it could show up in Massachusetts, it could show up in Kansas.

In the wake of the Kansas-Nebraska Act, the reenslavement of Anthony Burns, and the castigation from Thoreau, Lawrence became involved in the NEEAC. And it was that organization that hatched a plan, one familiar today in the wake of supposed reckonings over race and racism.

The plan was simple: transport as many people from New England to Kansas to set up settlements. Give them arms and tools and timber to build homes and schoolhouses.

For Lawrence, the West, starting first with Kansas, would be won by philanthropically and politically dedicated white men. They may not have had the courage to force slaveholding states to divest from slaveholding, but they could create a part of the country where slavery would not take root. White families would, in the estimation of the New England Emigrant Aid Company, kick-start exodus by achieving it themselves.

So Lawrence and the rest of the NEEAC solicited churches. Three thousand and fifty of them, to be exact, primarily throughout New England, with a specific ask of their congregations: "We beg your attention to the great work the New England Emigrant Aid Company has in hand. We ask your particular attention to the encouragement which divine providence has given to its efforts." The NEEAC circular told the recipients that Kansas would become a free state. But if freedom wasn't enough of a motivator, perhaps religion would do the trick. "For religion," they wrote, "needed, first of all, the Gospel." They reassured the faithful that church "service is regularly maintained" in those Kansas towns along with Sunday school (which they called Sabbath school). It wasn't just Sunday school, but schools the year round, as the circular pivoted, "For Education"—that their dollars would go to educating the children of the settlers. And because the trustees of the NEEAC knew many in their audience were Quakers and Congregationalists, the sort of Christians at the time who fancied the teetotaler lifestyle, they assured contributors that the money they'd send would be "For Temperance." The ask? Twenty dollars—nearly $710 in 2024 dollars. The money would fund new, righteous white towns throughout Kansas.

Soon, letters came in, enclosing contributions.

Reverend Horace James from Worcester sent $23.37, boasting of his congregation, "Never did fingers and thumbs move more nimbly in the performance of any good work." To him that meant that "Verily there is hope for Kansas." Others weren't so flush with cash. Reverend W. C. Jackson from Lincoln, Massachusetts, whose flock could only scrape together $15, reported, "Your circular for the Emigrant Aid Society came rather inopportunely for us farmers." Jonathan Lee, a pastor from Salisbury, Connecticut, had even less to give: "From my scanty purse a single dollar must be accepted in testimony of my interest in the cause of truth and freedom," because, he wrote, "I am without pastoral charge or salary."

The enterprise Lawrence and Thayer had envisioned leaned on rich and poor alike. And money simply wasn't easy to come by. Instead, it was the stumbling block.

"Send me $1,000," the NEEAC's founder, Eli Thayer, wrote to Lawrence in 1854, warning that "if we wait" any longer, "the question of slavery or freedom will be settled without us." The urgency was clear, and Lawrence scribbled his own letter to Dr. Charles Robinson and Samuel C. Pomeroy, both of whom were stationed out west. Lawrence and Thayer knew that together, the operation was building a narrative about freedom's song, one delivered by progressive men, white men.

"Money comes in very slowly," Pomeroy wrote to Thayer and Lawrence, but "you must not hurry here" to Kansas. He told them of a school he and his team had founded. To demonstrate the moxie of the anti-slavery settlers, he wrote, "Do not spare expense to make it comfortable." Money be damned, Kansas Territory was changing— schools, religion, the culture and the peaceful society they had aspired to were taking root. The plan was working. "Not a slave taken into the territory," Pomeroy wrote to Rhode Island NEEAC trustee John Carter Brown, who had begun to question whether the plan had already failed.

Lawrence tried to steady what he detected between the lines as forced confidence by Pomeroy. "It is worth a good deal to a man to have his pluck tried," he wrote. Lawrence told Pomeroy that he had the ear of the president of the United States, Franklin Pierce. His mother-in-law had made herself rather comfortable staying at the White House, Lawrence wrote, while boasting that his relationship with Pierce extended beyond strictly professional. They were friends, he thought, and not just friends: Lawrence and his wife were both first cousins of the president's wife, Jane Pierce. And that gave Lawrence the confidence to write a scolding letter to Pierce, alleging that the president remained "aloof" to the plight of Black people.

To Lawrence, the exodus of white men to Kansas had little to do with Black people and everything to do with this morality. Pierce was, however, aloof on slavery, not supporting politicians and activists who believed slavery to be an inherent evil. Like Pomeroy and Lawrence, Pierce perceived that the potential fracturing of the Union was far worse than slavery itself. Lawrence saw that slide coming and told the president that the foot soldiers of the NEEAC "must defend themselves" and admitted that he had been "furnishing them means of defense." In correspondence to various officials along the Kansas free-stater settlement landscape, Lawrence listed the number of guns, bullets, and powder he had already sent them and how much was on its way.

————◄●►————

November 29, 1854, was important in Kansas, as it was the date of the election to select a delegate to the U.S. House of Representatives to represent the inhabitants of the territory. Kansans—or rather the people who had recently moved to the territory, who nudged aside the Kaw, and the Osage, and the Wichita, and the Arapaho, and the Cheyenne, and the Comanche, the Pawnee and the Kiowa—were trying to figure out what living in their world would look like.

Where would they go for food? How would they educate their children? Who would build and maintain their roads? Who was going to dig the wells for fresh water? Was there sufficient timber? Could they survive the winters? Was the water potable? Was the soil tillable? All these questions superseded any measure of concern about an election for a delegate for the territory.

In contrast, Missourians to the east had been building their institutions, customs, and ways of life—lightposts, wells, schools, churches—since 1821. Not only had their customs and institutions taken root, but their factions and political machines had also sufficient time to evolve to cause trouble, especially when the topic had anything to do with slavery. So scores of them poured across the border the night before the election to cast ballots as Kansans because no one could tell the difference.

By nearly seventeen hundred votes, John Whitfield, a racist, pro-slavery candidate, won, and by a majority of total votes in some precincts outnumbering eligible voters.

The first cut. Blood was about to be shed.

The second cut came four months later, in the territorial election, when Kansans had to elect members to represent them in the territorial legislature. With the prospect of a constitutional convention to decide what the state would be and what it would allow, these elections put everyone on alert.

"The prosperity or the ruin of the whole South depends on the Kansas struggle," warned recently retired Missouri U.S. senator David Atchison. A southerner through and through, Senator Atchison marched some five thousand men into the Kansas Territory illegally to cast ballots for pro-slavery candidates. But these men didn't just show up with the intention to vote. They came to threaten and intimidate. One thousand Missourians even appeared in Amos Lawrence's namesake town of Lawrence, armed to the hilt with a fully loaded cannon.

At the time of the vote, there were 2,905 eligible voters in Kansas, according to the 1855 Territorial Census. Yet with the help of men like Atchison and his followers, pro-slavery candidates received more than 5,200 votes. Somehow, anti-slavery candidates received less than a thousand. Out of the thirty-nine seats open in territorial elections, the free-staters won only one contest.

The second cut. The blood began to pour.

Looking at these preposterous voter numbers and at the growing violence, even previously moderate heads began to swim. The governor of the territory, Andrew Reeder, was appointed only nine months earlier by President Pierce, who wanted to be sure that the new governor let the question of slavery or freedom rest with the voters. Reeder was happy to oblige: He respected electoral processes over moral impulse.

Yet by the time of the vote, even Reeder could see that the electoral processes were fraught with corruption, so much so that he voided the election. This would not do for Pierce, who was ever looking for what he thought would keep the Union together without pushing the southern states into seceding. So Pierce fired Reeder. This left Reeder with such a bad taste for the Democratic Party, to which he had been loyal, that he left the party altogether in 1860.

The third cut.

By now, there were two different realities across the land. With their territorial capital in Lecompton, east of Topeka, the pro-slavery Kansan legislature was filled mostly by voters from Missouri, and started replicating the South. Under this legislature, Anthony Burns would be slated for a fate worse than being forcibly returned to his enslaver. Black residents started to see whatever rights they had over their land disappearing seemingly overnight.

At the same time, the NEEAC flooded the state with as many free-staters as possible. By this point, the free-staters had stopped following the edicts of the Kansas territorial governor and legislature. They had moved their free-state capital to Topeka, propping themselves up with the money collected from the NEEAC. They started their own newspapers, elected their own governor, Charles Robinson, elevated to leadership their own representative, Samuel C. Pomeroy, and created their own constitution—all funded by the NEEAC.

Thus, two realities existed on the same land, which amplified a tension by the first act of open violence: the end of Charles Dow's exodus. He was shot less than three months after Reeder's replacement, the southern sympathizer Wilson Shannon, was appointed governor by Pierce. Now, in the wake of Dow's death, the pro-slavery forces hid Frank Coleman, Dow's killer, to make sure that no arrest could be made for more than two days.

"The War Begun!" the headline in the *Kansas Herald of Freedom* proclaimed on December 1, 1855, ten days after Dow's murder.

The aggressors may have been the pro-slavery forces, but pro-slavery forces led by Douglas County sheriff Samuel J. Jones arrested free-state legislators, even the free-state governor, Charles Robinson, one of Lawrence's closest colleagues at the NEEAC.

The free-staters anticipated these actions and quickly used the money Lawrence and others had sent to buy arms and organize a militia. The militia prepared for a standoff and made Amos Lawrence's namesake town, Lawrence, their base. Wilson Shannon, the newly minted territorial governor and former governor of Ohio, wrote

to Lawrence's colleagues that "Sheriff Jones, true to his threat, suc-
ceeded in obtaining his posse, variously estimated from 700 to 1000
men, mostly from Missouri," ratcheting up the tensions and whipping
up the fears in Lawrence.

Shannon wrote, "Proslavery men claimed that the object of calling
out this posse was for the purpose of enforcing the laws," while the
free-staters were considered rabble-rousers. Shannon believed that pro-
slavery men just wanted "to frighten and drive out the free state settlers
from the Territory, and deter others from coming here to settle, to the
end that Kansas might become a slave state."

Political killings, fifty-six of them, began, and some landed in
prison, including Charles Robinson, a doctor who had trained in
Massachusetts, and who took up arms against pro-slavery forces.
In May 1856, pro-slavery advocates took control of the city of Lawrence, even throwing the blocks used to put together the pages of the
paper into the river after they had destroyed the printers of both the
Kansas Free State and the *Kansas Herald of Freedom*. Weapons meant
for defending citizens were turned on citizens by pro-slavery militia
members who called themselves "rangers" and "border ruffians."

There seemed to be no boundary that the defenders of slavery
would not cross, and Kansas's conflict extended even into the halls
of Congress. Another ally of the NEEAC, Massachusetts senator
Charles Sumner, warned his Senate colleagues just two days before
the attack on the presses, "It is the rape of a virgin Territory compelling it to the hateful embrace of Slavery; and it may be clearly traced
to a depraved longing for a new slave State, the hideous offspring of
such a crime, in hope of adding to the power of Slavery in the National Government."

Finding Sumner's castigation of slavery repugnant, South Carolina
representative Preston Brooks entered the Senate chamber and, in a
memorable assault, swung his metal-capped cane at Sumner's head
numerous times for what onlookers considered a "long minute."

Brooks walked away quietly, a hero to some, while to others Sumner achieved near-martyr status.

Brooks's caning of Sumner was followed by the quasi-armistice in Lawrence being broken, as pro-slavery militia sacked the town. John Brown, a noted radical abolitionist, believed that violence would be quelled only by more violence. On the night of May 24, 1856, Brown, his sons, and other free-staters identified five pro-slavery settlers and returned brutality for the brutality of slavery, slicing a group of pro-slavery men with broadswords.

News of the savagery in the West spread back to the North and South, and it was becoming a microcosm of a war that would settle the question of what America's views on race and freedom would be. Kansans—pro-slavery and free-staters alike—took up arms in Osawatomie, another stronghold for free-staters. John Reid, a Missourian and eventual congressman, fought in the streets of the town. Combat followed as John Brown and most of his sons barely escaped as Osawatomie's buildings and homes were engulfed in flames, with one person killed.

It seemed that the violence of Kansas would not end. Perhaps the best outcome for the free-state cause and the end of violence was the election of Abraham Lincoln in November 1860, the secession of the South a month later, and the beginning of the Civil War in April 1861.

Simple math, really.

Kansas became a member of the Union in 1861 after the South seceded, and the states replaced the senators who had objected to Kansas becoming a free state and had supported laws that barred Black people from citizenship. Violence along the border between Missouri and Kansas continued throughout the Civil War, but Kansas became the bloodstained path for Black people looking for freedom.

But the history and mythology of Kansas became more important

both to Black people like McCabe, who was born free, and to those
who were born into captivity: Kansas, they believed, wasn't bloodied
in vain—it was bloodied to become a Promised Land of their own
making. Kansas was a proxy battle on behalf of abolitionists in New
England too nervous about the fragility of the Union to force abolition on the slave states. But it was also an invitation to McCabe and
those who came with him to know that fighting of all kinds could result in the creation of a part of America that would accommodate
them. The blood of the martyrs has been called the seeds of the
church. But the violence in Kansas led to an answer for the enduring
question: What do we do with the Black people that America won't
make adequate room for?

3

The Deal of a Lifetime

HAITI, 1863

Your race suffer very greatly, many of them by living among us, while ours suffer from your presence . . . It is better for us both, therefore, to be separated.

—ABRAHAM LINCOLN, ADDRESS TO THE DEPUTATION OF
FREE COLORED MEN, AUGUST 14, 1862

I cannot make it better known than it already is, that I strongly favor colonization.

—ANNUAL MESSAGE TO CONGRESS, DECEMBER 1, 1862

The road to a fuller answer of what to do with Black people in America would make a critical, underdiscussed stop outside the country—in Haiti, where Black people became colonizers, an identifier that McCabe would soon wear with pride. McCabe's decision to embark on the colonization of what would become Oklahoma Territory was marked by this antecedent—an effort to fix the "Negro problem" by dispensing with Black people.

. . .

It began with a letter sent in 1862 by a man named Bernard Kock.

—◄━►—

"I beg leave, Mr. President, to present my congratulations to Your Excellency for the promulgation of your late Emancipation Proclamation," Kock, a New Orleans import-export broker and trader, wrote to Lincoln, "and to offer my assistance in carrying out your philanthropic ideas of Colonization as connected therewith." It was October 1, 1862, about a year and a half after the shots into Fort Sumter began the Civil War. More important, the letter was written only days after Lincoln had signed the Emancipation Proclamation, promising that all enslaved people within the Confederacy—but *not* slaves in loyal states within the Union—would be declared free on January 1, 1863. It was a moment when the nation began to realize that soon millions of Black people would not have to stay put in the South.

In public, Lincoln favored what Kock diplomatically called his "philanthropic ideas of Colonization," encouraging (in some cases forcing) Black people to leave America for Liberia, Canada, and the Caribbean. In the discussion between Lincoln and Butler, though it is still hotly debated, it seems that in private, Lincoln framed his ideas as sending all the blacks away.

Long before McCabe pitched his idea for Black people to join a great exodus west, white people imagined a similar fate for them. Even Lincoln was fearful that Black and white people could not coexist equally and that racial strife would continue. His secretary of the navy, Gideon Welles, wrote that he believed Lincoln feared that "a war more terrible than that in which we were now engaged" would be brought on by the oppression of freed Black people *after* the Civil War concluded. Brought on, that is, *if* Black people and white people had to share citizenship. Welles was so convinced of Lincoln's views that he thought the idea had become "an essential part of [Lincoln's] emancipation policy."

The full experience of freedom, Lincoln and his acolytes believed, could not be guaranteed after the slaves were freed. At least it could not be guaranteed unless Black people, formerly enslaved or free, left the United States.

Conveniently for Lincoln and for Kock, white people already had been trying to achieve that enforced exodus for decades. They were concerned about the growing number of Black people in the United States experiencing some semblance of freedom, and with it the expectation that they could achieve self-determination.

Both Lincoln and Kock would have known of situations in which white men had tried to dispense with the supposed Negro problem. One surely was the American Colonization Society (ACS), the prewar effort to turn the enslaved into colonizers outside America.

◄━━►

Liberia, a country on the western coast of Africa, was seen as a suitable place for Black Americans to settle, as it had been colonized earlier in the nineteenth century by the ACS. John H. B. Latrobe, lawyer, inventor, and president of the ACS, stated in a speech with pride that Liberia had "good laws well administered, churches and schools, the mutual aid societies of more advanced communities, agricultural exhibitions even." He and others at the ACS were convinced that Liberia was the proper place for the United States' Black people.

But he warned that this dream scenario could be achieved only if the ACS ensured that the future government of Liberia was "modelled after our own." Latrobe believed that the government that could best serve Black people, in a country he had yet to visit (and reportedly never would), was like the one they were to be exiled from.

The United States proved to be a quick study on enforced exodus.

Americans were practiced at removing those they had marginalized while instructing them that the removal was their own idea.

Latrobe nonetheless had specific views of Black people. He referred to them only as slave and freedman, not people with potential as McCabe saw in them and in himself. Latrobe said that all Black people needed was to be "protected, provided with food, shelter and raiment." The life of the slave was relatively easy, in Latrobe's eyes, as the slave was "treated in the vast majority of cases kindly, affectionately often," and they lived "without care as regards his physical wants, and with constitutional good humor passes happily, in the main, through life." The freedman, he worried, didn't fully realize that he would be made to experience "social and political inferiority" and often "either frets away existence in aspirations, which [in America] can never be realized, or yielding hopelessly to circumstances falls with benumbed faculties into a condition that is little better than the slave's." These people, relegated either to being cared for by their "kindly" and "affectionate" masters or to receding back to a life as a slave, needed to leave for their own good.

Latrobe might have thought he was doing Black people a favor by advocating their deportation. In noting the enslaveds' weakness, Latrobe did not pin the fault on the white people who had reduced the humanity of Black people to nothing but property. Instead, he told them that in the view of the ACS, the only way that Black people could find strength and confidence was through "the transplantation of a people."

This wasn't charity, Latrobe boasted, this was a deal. Consider Robert Clive and Warren Hastings, Latrobe suggested, the men most credited with establishing the British Empire in India. Clive and Hastings "owe [to the colonization of India] their wealth and their renown. [Colonizing India] has built up for us, in ten years, an empire in resources and extent, on the Pacific." Latrobe dangled wealth and renown in front of the powerful: the landed, the educated, and the privileged, both within and beyond the borders of America.

⫷━►

Two decades later, the sunny optimism of Latrobe seemed misplaced. Even after nearly fifty years, the ACS had managed to send only a few thousand Black people to Liberia. By 1863, however, some four million Black people were about to be declared emancipated. Faced with such numbers and believing that Black people could not peacefully live with white people, Lincoln must have felt himself in a bind.

So Kock's letter to Lincoln was timely. After all, he had a plan for where the Black people could go. His plan was simply put: colonization in the Western Hemisphere. It was one that could be a money-making endeavor for the government—an opportunity Lincoln could not ignore.

In his appeal, Kock made special note of the thousands of Black people who had poured into Hampton Roads, Virginia, to get their freedom by fiat—dubbing the place, Fort Monroe, affectionately, "Freedom's Fort." Kock proposed sending the free Black people gathered at Freedom's Fort away, specifically to an island off Haiti called Île-à-Vache, or Cow Island. "A hundred square miles," Kock wrote to the president, known to be "free from reptiles" and to "have a healthy and agreeable temperature, the thermometer rising rarely above 80 degrees in the shade." The island had been nothing but a "solitary waste, awaiting the hand of industry to awaken its echoes." Kock was, he continued, "attracted by its beauty, the value of its timber, its extreme fertility, and its adaptation for the cultivation of cotton," and said that he had convinced Haiti's president, Fabre Geffrard, to lease him land first for ten years, with a condition of a ten-year extension. Kock planned to be the governor of this outpost, where he promised

that the "intelligent negro may enter upon a life of freedom and independence, conscious that he has earned the means of his livelihood,
and at the same time disciplined to the duties, the pleasures and the
wants of free labor."

Kock promised the Haitian government that the people who would
work the land would be Black or Indigenous, but he insisted that some
of the overseers be white. In addition, he proposed to actually indenture the newly free Black people who moved there. Each Black family
would get four-year contracts for hard labor—harvesting cotton,
sugar, indigo, and coffee—and they would be given a Christian education by New Englanders. In an echo of Thayer and Lawrence's
NEEAC, Kock promised to construct a "hospital and medical attendance, a church, and schoolhouse, with a New England Christian
minister, and New England schoolteachers." While being "educated,"
these indentured Black families would have to work their way to citizenship, until the lease Kock negotiated with the Haitian government
ended. Even then, they wouldn't become U.S. citizens but Haitian ones.
Only then would they be able to become landowners.

"As would be expected in a country like this, the soil and climate
are adapted for all tropical productions," Kock wrote, "particularly
sugar, coffee, indigo, and, more especially, cotton."

This was the kicker—the conclusion that the president wanted to
hear. After all, slave-grown cotton from the South had fueled the
North's mills and factories for decades. Before the Civil War, the
South produced the majority of the nation's cotton, which was a key
raw material for the textile manufacturing industry in the North.
Kock's plan for a government-sponsored and -compelled Black exodus to Cow Island was a bandage to the economic wounds torn open
by the ongoing war. Kock made clear that Lincoln's philanthropy
could have political and financial returns—a way to do well by doing
good. But the true purpose of this endeavor could be deduced from
the name of the colony: the American Industrial Agricultural Colony.

The name "Liberia" had promised a kind of liberty, but the settlement on Cow Island seemed fixated on agricultural rescue—and at a time when the Union needed it most.

In short order, Congress approved an earmark of $600,000 to defray Kock's expenses. It helped that Kock believed that the heavily timbered land on Cow Island—which he knew little about—would deliver much lumber and that he'd earmark a third of the profits for the Union. And after collecting $70,000 from financial titans of the time—Paul Siemen Forbes, Leonard W. Jerome (who also could count Winston Churchill as a relative), and Charles K. Tuckerman—Kock was well taken care of. According to the *Lexington Herald-Leader*, the investment was all but locked, because "the hearts of millionaires could not withstand the temptation of a project which promised a profit of more than 600 per cent in nine months, especially when it combined itself with great moral benefits," quoting John G. Nicolay and John Hay, Lincoln's secretaries.

Kock, his Black colonizers, and their supervisors—newly cast plantation foremen—set sail for Cow Island in the chartered British ship the *Ocean Ranger*. Accompanied by the first five hundred workers, Kock expected another forty-five hundred to follow. They left with the promise that more help was on its way, in the form of lumber, mills, steam equipment, people, money, and more. But before Kock and his boat even touched the shores of Cow Island, people got sick with smallpox. Kock holed up in his cabin, trying to keep away from the Black people who had contracted the disease. By the time they reached land, twenty to twenty-five of them—a likely underestimation—were reported sick, a harbinger of the devastation of the plan before it truly started. The land didn't yield plenteous harvests, and there were difficulties with the contracts that had been made with the Haitian government. Kock and his investors dispatched an investigator, A. A. Ripka, to determine just how bad events were progressing before the year was up, only to conclude that it was worse: The crops had been overrun by vermin, the Black families had moved off Cow Island and deeper into the mainland, and legal paperwork was being drawn up to recoup the investors' money if not their reputations for ever engaging in this scheme. All of this while people like Tuckerman blamed Kock and the Black people who had gone, stating that the Black people had "demanded luxuries to which they were unaccustomed in this country."

The colonization was an unmitigated disaster.

—◄—◆—►—

The forced exodus from Freedom's Fort to Cow Island was a black eye on the country. Even so, Lincoln did not learn the lessons of forcing exodus upon Black people. He continued to press for similar "solutions" to Black freedpeople in the final years of the war. Or perhaps the coming reality of Black freedom made Lincoln seek another solution to a problem that Americans had made themselves.

In 1864, Senator James H. Lane of Kansas pushed for a bill to colonize near the border at El Paso with formerly enslaved Black people. "I can tell the man of color that the hour of his deliverance from the bondage of Egypt has come," Lane declared, seemingly kindly, in the well of the Senate, "and that unless he removes, he is doomed to sink into a hopeless minority in the older States for all coming time." Like Lincoln, Lane had little faith that southerners would change: "It is not possible to re-educate a whole population like that of the South, or change their prejudices as to their former slaves," Lane said. "For generations the public mind had been taught to regard slavery as a thing sacred to the several States holding slaves; a thing too sacred to be criticized or touched by the stranger." Instead of compelling people in slaveholding states to abandon their ways, Lane thought it best to send Black people away and let white people live in peace.

Lane's bill asked for no money, just a request that a portion of what wasn't spent in the catastrophe of Kock's Cow Island scheme be used to pay administrators in Texas—white ones—to oversee Black people moving to Texas at their expense. Lane's bill died in committee; and Lane himself died by suicide not long after, maligned by accusations of corruption and graft. But it was clear that the federal government was looking for a Black exodus: a forced one, a cheap one, a profitable one.

It was not Edward McCabe's idea to flee. It wasn't even his original idea to colonize. It was his innovation to begin on his own terms, devised from strategies that benefited first and in many cases only Black people, on land that was part of the continent but not yet admitted to the Union.

He wanted to begin, not simply to exit.

"Take Care of Yourselves"

THE FORMER CONFEDERACY, 1876

The slave went free; stood a brief moment in the sun; then moved back again toward slavery.

—w. e. b. dubois, *Black Reconstruction in America*

Since at least 1865," W. E. B. DuBois wrote in 1934, "we have been holding back the Negro to keep him from getting beyond the white man. Our idea has been that the Negro should be kept poor." The reasons could be pinned on numerous actions and policies, but also sentiments clearly articulated by leaders in the years following the Civil War. As General Ulysses S. Grant wrote to a congressman in 1863, "I was never an Abolitionist, not even what could be called anti-slavery," he admitted. "But I try to judge fairly and honestly and it became patent to my mind early in the rebellion that the North and South could never live at peace with each other except as one nation, and that without slavery." Slavery wasn't the evil about which Grant was most concerned. Rather it was an impediment to unity between the North and South; it had to be removed so as to preserve the nation. It should come as no surprise that when Grant became president in 1869, he was more concerned with protecting the reunified government than protecting Black people.

Many agreed with him. Take Carl Schurz. On his own exodus from political repression in his native Prussia, Schurz emigrated to the United States in 1852. During the Civil War, he served as a major general in the Union army, fighting at Chancellorsville and Gettysburg. But after the Civil War, he worked with the Freedmen's Bureau to investigate the liberated slaves in newly conquered southern lands. "Some planters held back their former slaves on their plantations by brute force," he wrote. "Armed bands of white men patrolled the country roads to drive back the Negroes wandering about . . . A veritable reign of terror prevailed in many parts of the South."

Yet by the time Grant became president, Schurz believed that white people had helped Blacks enough. For years after the Civil War, federal troops had been stationed in former Confederate states to protect Black people and Black voting rights, as well as those who had defied their white neighbors in working to build a multiracial democracy. Those same troops even hunted down the first iteration of the Ku Klux Klan, a cabal of ex–Confederate soldiers that took to killing anyone—Black *or* white—who supported the new "Reconstruction" governments. But with southerners complaining about what they saw as overreach by the federal government, and centrists moaning over the costs of maintaining a standing army, many felt by the late 1860s that Reconstruction had gone far enough—even once-radical supporters of Black freedom like Schurz.

Black people had become what some white political leaders believed Black people always had been: an impediment toward the goal of building a coalition of white people committed to creating a powerful country. Consider Grant's opinion of the Fifteenth Amendment, which gave formerly enslaved people the right to vote. "It had done the Negro no good," Grant told Hamilton Fish, his secretary of state, in private, "and had been a hindrance to the South, and by no means a political advantage to the North." But the implications were worth accepting if it meant accumulating political power by making a hospitable world for white men. Bent on enlarging the tent, the white politicians in control made it larger for the white voters who were already there while turning blind eyes to those who could not fit in that tent.

Eventually a deal was struck to let the South be free of outside interference, and the federal army pulled back and put the reins of government back in the hands of the southern states. By then, everyone knew what that meant for the South's Black residents. As John Martin, a Republican Party chair in Atchison County, Kansas, and a longtime member of the Republican National Committee, put it, "I think the policy of the new administration [that of incoming president Rutherford B. Hayes in 1877] will be to conciliate the white men of the South. Carpetbaggers to their rear, and niggers take care of yourselves."

What Martin feared in 1877 was a reversal of the transformative reforms that had followed the Civil War and a conservative reaction to the real victories of multiracial democracy that had been made over the last decade. The federal government began to rapidly reconstruct what the ruling class of white political leaders thought America could become only a decade before.

Radical Republicans began to bookend their military victories with legislative strategies. First, the Thirteenth Amendment abolished slavery as the Civil War ended (though leaving a carveout for Black people in prison). Next, the Fourteenth Amendment secured citizenship rights and the equal protection of laws for all people. It took another two years for enough states to ratify the amendment. Before a full year had passed, the complicating circumstances and deteriorating opportunities in the former Confederacy for freedpeople compelled Republicans in Congress to propose the Fifteenth Amendment to prohibit voting rights discrimination.

Underlying each amendment were painful battles—political, legal, and physical—leaving in limbo Black people who had become targets of growing postwar antipathy and racism.

———◄═► ———

"The wage of the Negro worker, despite the war amendments," DuBois warned, "was to be reduced to the level of bare subsistence by taxation, peonage, caste, and every method of discrimination." In some important sense, the socioeconomic straits of the never-enslaved, like McCabe, and the formerly enslaved seemed to be converging. And in so doing, DuBois lamented, "the white laborer joined the white landholder and capitalist and beat the black laborer into subjection through secret organizations and the rise of a new doctrine of race hatred."

During 1866 and the first six months of 1867—when McCabe was seventeen years old and left the comforts of New England for New York—there were 197 murders and 548 cases of aggravated assault of Black people in North and South Carolina alone. In one South Carolina community, nearly 80 percent of Black people had fled to the woods to escape danger. Even when sympathetic white people, few though they were, attempted to protect Black people, they continued to be assaulted in those states. In 1871 alone, the KKK in South Carolina reported to having whipped 262 Black people, killed 101, and raped two Black women. By 1869, according to DuBois, in much of Texas "there was no civil government."

DuBois wrote, "The civil war in the South which overthrew Reconstruction was a determined effort to reduce black labor as nearly as possible to a condition of unlimited exploitation and build a new class of capitalists on this foundation." McCabe and his counterparts in the South were legally free, but the experience diverged in an important way: McCabe was exploring what abundance could look like while his counterparts in the South wondered if they'd ever be given the chance to do the same, let alone survive.

"Take care of yourselves" became government policy and practice at every level, leaving Black people, especially in the South, to construct their own economic survival on the margins where they had been pushed. Of preeminent importance for the federal government was not Black people but unity over repairing the damage done intentionally or allowed passively to happen to Black citizens. In the wake of the 1876 presidential election, the reimagining of where and how Black life might survive accelerated the exodus. The sentiment was that if there was a Democrat in the White House, the fate of Black people would be sealed. "Blacks were said to be especially agitated convinced that in the event of a Democratic victory, 'slavery is to be reestablished,'" Eric Foner wrote. "The [Republican] party's Southern wing must be recast so as to reduce the influence of carpetbaggers and blacks and attract the 'better class of local whites.'"

It wasn't a new sentiment that "niggers take care of yourselves"—it was old. As Foner reminds us in *Reconstruction: America's Unfinished Revolution*, "Nor did Reconstruction create new bureaucratic agencies institutionally committed to protecting black rights. The Freedmen's Bureau had always been conceived as temporary, and the long-term burden of overseeing the local administration of justice would fall to the overworked, understaffed Justice Department and to the federal judiciary with its newly expanded jurisdiction." McCabe's vision would endow Black America with a permanence of stakes, rights, and a seat at the decision-making table. And the emerging vision for the South and the northern Republicans sidestepped a fully reconstructed South, but a negotiated one—setting the table of frustrations that doled out crumbs of satisfaction to Black people sparingly. The negotiated and retreating Reconstruction made McCabe's argument for a Black state for him.

This is why soon many Black people began giving up the notion of a life of comity in the South for Black and white people. It is why they began to be excited by the thought that autonomy and political power could be gained by settling in the West, because the world as they knew it was ending.

Around the same time, a Black man named Henry Adams warned in 1877, "The whole South, every state in the South, had got into the hands of the very men that held us as slaves." Adams had been actively working for the safety of Black people in his home state of Louisiana. But with the Compromise of 1877 and the pullback of federal troops, with the restoration of southern control over its own policing, laws, voting, finances, Adams knew that Reconstruction was over. He urged his fellow emancipated to leave. In testimony before Congress, Adams, reflecting on the words of his former enslaver, testified, "The colored people could never protect themselves among the white people." They deserved a life under their own banner.

But to where? To Liberia, where some eleven thousand people had made that trek with limited success? Adams looked elsewhere, and he began to believe what thousands of Black people had become captured by: Kansas.

Thus began the Exodus(t), the movement of thousands of Black people from the lands of the former Confederacy into "new" lands out west. Their former enslavers in the South saw them as emancipated slaves at best. For the thousands of Black people seeking their own exodus from the rest of the country, many were left to rely not on a government, but rather a collection of philanthropic interests meagerly dispensing goodwill.

They became refugees.

Black people began to leave Mississippi and Alabama, and in even greater numbers Tennessee and Kentucky, to seek a new beginning. At first, they headed to Kansas. They abandoned their homes and all they knew for the hope of land beyond dangers for a state that had set the stage for the Civil War, for a state that had stopped bleeding long enough to let them reimagine what their world could be like.

For McCabe, these Black people, people like him, had grown tired of the limited expectations they had for life in America. The end of Reconstruction had signaled to them that they'd be on their own. McCabe knew that this was their chance to begin again because the message was clear: "Niggers, take care of yourselves."

PART II

SURVIVING THE WILDERNESS

————◄ ■ ►————

After the reconstruction period the Negro of the South became tied to the soil by the cropper method of farming. When he rented, he had no money, tools or supplies with which to carry on his work. The land owner would advance to him credit necessary for a year's support, while he made a crop. The Negro could not keep books. He never knew how his account stood, and he was in arrears each time when the account was totaled and balanced. He could not leave until the alleged balance against him was paid off. Year after year he continued to work without progress . . .

[But] among the results of that migration were the founding of race communities still extant . . . in the Solomon Valley region, amid much travail and sacrifice, a complete answer to their hopes and prayers.

—LULU SADLER CRAIG, *Manuscript on the History of Nicodemus Colony*

5

"Ku Klux or Kansas?"

ST. LOUIS, MISSOURI, 1879

With sad hearts and weeping eyes, [the refugees] tell of their sufferings on the roads, and of five of their company who were left in the wilderness, frozen to death! And yet they do not repent leaving the South . . . Exposure by the way, trouble and sorrow, produced sickness, which was augmented by the want of fresh air and comfort in our crowded barrack, and he died there a few days ago. His poor wife and daughter, forlorn, ill, penniless, and among strangers, are greatly to be pitied.

—LETTER FROM ELIZABETH L. ROUS COMSTOCK
TO CATHERINE HALE, FEBRUARY 9, 1880

During Reconstruction, Curtis Pollard was a Republican state senator in Louisiana, one of the state's first Black legislators. At first, Pollard had no desire to leave the South. But then he was told by a white seed broker that his "neck would be broken; he told me on the streets before a large crowd." Armed men roughed him up, laid blows on his body, and he was convinced to flee immediately on a steamboat, leaving behind his wife and children. Unlike

McCabe, he had no plans to build or found a state. His aim was seeing the next day. So he was unequivocal in explaining his exodus: "My object in leaving the South was on account of threats of my life."

Pollard was not alone. As renewed racism emerged, a sense of urgency came over many Black people to leave. "They were forced to leave the South," reporters wrote in the *St. Louis Globe-Democrat* in 1879, "where they were living a life in death, wavering between the terrors of starvation and the muzzle of bull-dozers' muskets."

Thousands picked up their lives and fled west. One of these Exodusters was Frederick Marshall, who, as he sat cold and hungry and unhoused in St. Louis while he waited for a way to get to Kansas, explained to reporters, "I want to go some place where I can work without being afraid of my life . . . I wouldn't go back South again." Another was Claurence Winn, who told reporters that as a Black person in the South, he had been forced to vote for Democrats or die. If he dared to vote in his interest for Republicans, he explained, "the Democrats would get up in a mob and kill us off."

Perhaps this is why the *St. Louis Globe-Democrat* headline read "KU KLUX OR KANSAS?," opining that there were "Terrible Sufferings of the Darkies Under the Reign of the Shot-gun."

Just as the tribes of Israel were forced from Egypt into decades of danger and wilderness, these Exodusters knew they had to leave. And they were animated by more than just a political or economic plan. It wasn't that they heard that Kansas might be something better than a "life in death." It was that they believed it could really be a promised land.

The Exodusters' "salvation," wrote historian and Princeton professor Nell Irvin Painter, was "to be accomplished by a supernatural agency."

In this case, the agency was "the Federal government, which in their eyes, exercised extraordinary, marvelous powers. It had given them their first nominal freedom, delivering them from the everlasting fire of slavery."

For the Exodusters, salvation couldn't be a matter solely of spiritual import. It had to be "collective, terrestrial, imminent, and total," four characteristics that comprise the idea of millenarism, characteristics Painter argues Exodusters exhibited. Salvation was collective, because it was for a coherent group: Black people in the South. It was terrestrial because they planned to find salvation in the real land of Kansas. Imminence was never in question: As Reconstruction collapsed, Black people had to act—and quickly. Exodus represented what they saw as their *only* way to freedom and liberty. This salvation that they'd gain in Kansas, according to Painter, really was "total," as "millenarians made no future plans," because millenarians believe that all things will fundamentally change after a coming fundamental transformation of society. Listen to James Brown, a thirty-year-old from Madison Parish, Louisiana, who fled the South hoping that "the Government had furnished land for us [him and his wife and his many children, as well as his mother-in-law] in Kansas, and was giving free transportation from St. Louis." But he admitted, "I have no money." Getting to Kansas was the totality of his and his family's plan for salvation.

It wasn't just those who had little education or money. All it took for exodus was desperation, which drove them to leave without a plan, just hope in salvation. In the *Chicago Tribune*, another Exoduster found that there was no single anointed leader deputized to take God's people to the promised land. "Every black man is his own Moses now, I tell you; we tried Andrew Jackson, and he deceived us; we tried [Henry C.] Warmoth, and he betrayed us; we tried [William P.] Kellogg, and he deserted us; we tried Hayes, and he sold us out— and now, I tell you, every black man is his own Moses." When every

Black person became Moses, all they needed was to act together. They didn't need anything else.

They just went.

—◄——►—

Many of them stopped first in St. Louis. That's where Pollard stopped first, picking up a seat on a mail steamer that dropped him off as it moved up the Mississippi. He was lucky to get even there. According to Painter, hundreds of families lined the shores of the Mississippi River during the spring of 1879, trying to hail passage on packets— small ships meant to carry mail more than people, and especially not that volume of people. Often, these vessels would not take them directly to Kansas, or even to St. Louis. Instead, they would have to go where the vessels were willing to take them. Sometimes that meant Arkansas or northern Texas, where they'd then hope that the little money in their pockets could get them additional transport to Kansas. Waiting brought more families waiting for their chance to leave.

—◄——►—

Even in the North, Black people began to think that the West was their chance for something better.

Edward Preston McCabe was not necessarily one of them. While he was stricken by the same limits of Black ambition that families fleeing the South knew all too well, he was not constrained by violence, but by economics, indifference, and unflinching racism in high places.

McCabe had never been enslaved and was born of parents who also had never been. During the Civil War—as men Black, white, Indigenous, and Black-Indigenous served in both the Union and Confederate armies—McCabe was attending boarding school in New England and the Northeast.

It was only after the Civil War that McCabe's life really changed. His father died unexpectedly, and suddenly it was his duty to support his family. But rather than staying in Newport, Rhode Island, where his family lived, or Bangor, Maine, where he was attending school, McCabe went to New York. It was clear that he was looking for more than money (if money was all he needed, he might have stayed closer to home). He went to New York to clerk, an end-around the apprentice model to success, and found a job at Shreve and Kendrick & Co., first on 35 Wall Street and then at 45 Wall Street.

It was the Gilded Age of big aspirations, and ambitious men—almost all of them white—were flooding into New York attempting to prove, as historian Brian Luskey wrote, that "ambitious strivers made their own success." Some three hundred or more stocks and bonds were being traded on the New York Stock Exchange, and a clerk could count on this new role as a way up the ladder through hours spent serving as a notetaker, taking dictation from his bosses, time-tabulating in countinghouses, or even servicing customers (called "counter jumpers" for their willingness to literally jump over counters and push each other out of the way to see to a job). These clerks would offer to answer any question, accomplish any task, and fulfill any request by any patron, reasonable or not. Clerkships gave those who had them the ability to "accumulate the economic and cultural capital that would enable them to become self-made men." That was the aim: not just money, the ability to say that they were self-made, a brand that conveyed a newer version of power and prestige.

But for a Black clerk, the experience could be anything. Reportedly McCabe and many other Black clerks would be remanded to porter tasks such as lugging up the paper that the clerks used to write their bosses' notes and dictation on and holding doors open, hoping for a tip. They cleaned up waste, served drinks and food, and did whatever other custodial duties often awaited, rather than the vaunted path to the advisory work that white clerks aspired to. Even in New York, with all the ambition in the world, McCabe found his prospects constrained.

So in 1872, he left to try his luck in Chicago. Chicago had become a central hub for speculating about the future of the West, and that meant opportunity. There, McCabe quickly found work performing clerical duties like countinghouse management, sales and promotion, and the like—skills he'd take with him to Kansas and Oklahoma. He started work with not just anyone, but with Potter Palmer, the King of State Street. Palmer had once been a clerk, armed with untamed ambition, who turned a $5,000 gift from his family into a dry goods store that eventually grew into a retail empire. McCabe learned that Palmer would take out "foot long advertisements in Chicago newspapers," which had large readerships outside Chicago, about the fiefdom he had built that took up much of the block between State and Wabash Streets. In those advertisements, he'd tell his customers what they weren't hearing in New York—about his innovative way of selling with money-back guarantees, frictionless shipping and purchasing experiences. At a small cost, a one-way ticket to Chicago, customers would have "an OPPORTUNITY, AT A TRIFLING EXPENSE, of seeing a choice selection from the largest stock of Goods west of New York."

Working for Palmer, McCabe learned how to sell a dream. Palmer imbued his clerks with great responsibility and opportunity, dispatching them beyond Chicago to use sophisticated techniques to sell those dreams face-to-face. "If I learned of a man two hundred miles away, buried in a clearing in the forest, who might buy, I got the name of my establishment to him and invited him in. After he once got acquainted with the store," dubbed eponymously Potter Palmer & Co., "we rarely lost him." Palmer's orientation toward customer and client engagement lit a path toward McCabe's eventual promotion of the land that he felt must be won for Black people.

But the realization had also occurred to a newfound friend of McCabe's in Chicago, Abram T. Hall, Jr., a newspaperman and son of one of the co-founders of one of Chicago's oldest Black churches, Quinn Chapel African Methodist Episcopal, that despite what he could learn from Palmer, they could never realize their ambitions as Black people unless they built their own world. Hall hadn't grown up with the humiliation of enslavement. Rather, he spent a year at medical school in Indiana, served as a boatman on the Great Lakes, and then embarked on a career as a journalist.

It was perhaps the combination of McCabe's impatience and Hall's skills as a journalist that enabled Hall to connect to McCabe—in his words, a "political chum"—and the two set their eyes on Kansas. Hall, an editor at the *Chicago Conservator*, had been reading and editing stories that told of the opportunity of Kansas.

These tales and their ambition made clear that the world Hall and McCabe wanted couldn't be built in New York or Chicago, no matter how unbound the opportunities seemed. So these two highly educated Black bachelors began to read the newspapers for which Hall reported, to learn of Kansas, which seemed a magnet for Black people wanting, like them, to escape lands of limited ambition and basic emancipation for a world of abundant living built by and for Black people.

◄—◄—►—

The plan was simple, though the train routes could be generously considered circuitous. They would take the rail, perhaps the Illinois Central or the Chicago & Alton, to get from Chicago to Leavenworth, Kansas, bustling and near the border of Missouri, with Kansas City just slightly to the south. From there, they would hitch a ride on a train toward Colorado. Unlike Exodusters, they weren't dependent on a charitable individual or meager earnings from their jobs in the South to purchase a ride. Their plan was to get off before the train reached Colorado, in Dodge City or Jetmore, and walk and ride to Hodgeman County, quiet, but nearer to some rail and with tales of some Black colonization and settlement there.

In Hodgeman, they'd build nice lives for themselves. Maybe one or both of them would find their way into politics while Hall continued writing. But chief among their interests, according to Hall, were the business opportunities that would come with the "boundless acreage, fertility of soil[,] equable climate and golden opportunity to acquire and own a home on lands west of the Missouri river, in the State of Kansas." Out there, they felt sure they could make a place for themselves. They couldn't yet know just how much wilderness that frontier would contain.

"Where Is Nicodemus?"

KANSAS, 1877

That was the crux of why they wanted to come and homestead in northwestern Kansas, where they could govern themselves, have their own educational systems, their own government and also have their own source of income . . . That's one of the reasons that Nicodemus even came to be, was to help them have their own freedom.

—DR. JOHNELLA HOLMES, FIFTH-GENERATION
DESCENDANT OF NICODEMUS SETTLERS AND PRESIDENT
OF THE KANSAS BLACK FARMERS ASSOCIATION

After traveling more than nine hundred miles, Willina Hickman was eager to find her new home. Hailing from Kentucky, the formerly enslaved woman had traveled by train from her home state to St. Louis, and from St. Louis to Ellis County, which is nowhere now and was less than nowhere then. Now, in Ellis, she realized, she would need to walk. Her new home was still some forty miles away.

She was not alone. Another formerly enslaved woman, Emma Williams, was one of the first people to make their way to these lands from Kentucky. Except Williams was eight months pregnant by the time she reached Kansas. She had come without her husband; he, her descendants believed, was still indentured to a white man in Kentucky. Williams, too, had to walk.

The new town, only recently dubbed Nicodemus, was to be populated by Black people like Williams and Hickman: to live in, to raise children in, and even to run. Clearly, that was worth crossing a thousand miles.

But when Hickman finally arrived, Nicodemus was not what she envisioned. Instead of a built-up town—a promised land—she saw buffalo grass browned by relentless sun, not green fields watered by a nearby river. She saw very few trees, outlining even fewer houses built of wood, stone, or brick. She didn't even see tents, because the plains had such strong winds that they would have quickly blown over.

"Where is Nicodemus?" she asked her husband, "I don't see it."

Her husband answered, "That is Nicodemus."

The dirt mounds that looked like "ant hills," Willina realized, were actually human-built dugouts: holes dug under hills, supported by wood and filled with dirt and mud. Indeed, these dugouts were the only shelter that the colonizers of Nicodemus could construct when they arrived. Wood was in short supply—at least the kind of lumber and timber that could build homes. And the nearest train depot to receive a shipment of timber was forty miles away. Yet Willina and her husband did not even have a dugout. So while she waited for her own dugout to be built, she and her husband pitched tents, hoping they'd stay upright.

"The scenery was not at all inviting," Hickman remembered, "and I began to cry."

Hickman and her husband stayed, but it is no wonder that sixty other settlers, seeing what Hickman did, turned around immediately. Having survived the South, they were not ready to brave what nineteenth-century novelist Albion Tourgée called the "untried horrors of a life upon the plains of Kansas."

The town had been founded by a white employee of rail companies and five Black men. Two of the town's founders, W. R. Hill and W. H. Smith, hadn't realized how limited the financial capacities of the newly relocated Black people were. For many of the settlers, the five dollars to claim their land in Nicodemus could well have been the largest single expenditure they had ever made.

And after Nicodemus's first several hundred people—like Hickman and Williams and their families—spent what little money they had buying the land before they left, they still had to pay for train tickets to get from Kansas City to Ellis and then travel by wagon, as well as pay hired hands to help with transport of the wagons from Ellis to the Rooks County line, and then more to guide them across the Solomon River valley into Nicodemus. By the time they reached the town, most families were nearly destitute. They needed to start making money immediately or plant crops to sustain themselves.

Because the town's founders did not think carefully about the climate—how this arid place demanded that they plant and seed the ground earlier than towns in eastern Kansas, where the fields were lush and fertile—the eventual crops didn't amount to much. And because the residents of Nicodemus lived so far from towns with existing economies to support jobs during the winter, they suffered desperation and, for some, literal starvation. Wild game was hard to find, hunting was a challenge, and most of their horses died from the limited food and vegetation and the cold. Their situation was only alleviated by the native Potawatomi, who in the dead of their first winter brought the townspeople buffalo meat to eat.

Still, these "houses"—the ones Hickman bemoaned—with roofs made of poles covered with a layer of willows, sunflowers, or stalks, and accompanied by "a layer of sod and another coat of magnesium lime," became welcome abodes for the formerly unwanted. "Fleas,"

Craig wrote, "were the most tormenting of insect pests that the early settlers were bothered with."

The Wimms family, one of the earliest to settle in Nicodemus, figured out with the others how to deal with these unwanted pests. According to Lulu Sadler Craig, "When preparing for bed stand on a chair while removing the clothing; slip quickly into the night robe, and hop from the chair into the bed, thus leaving the fleas on the floor." Finally they lived without the oversight of someone dictating what they were to do, and they found ways to make life work.

Little is known about John Wayne Niles, one of the earliest leaders of Nicodemus. His entry into the lives of McCabe and Hall and to the whole of Nicodemus was not immaculate like the savior Niles thought he was. His birth was a scandal—his mom an enslaved Black woman, his father a white man from Mississippi. The child they produced was known for his light skin and his burly voice with convincing oratory.

After being pardoned for murder in Tennessee in 1869, Niles made his way to Nicodemus after having helped organize Exodusters in Kentucky. His voice made him an attractive storyteller and a convincing hustler and earned him the title "Shrewd Scoundrel."

He landed in hot water with Nicodemus's residents not long after he arrived. Elected the town's president, he had one job: to draw as many resources into the coffers of the struggling town as possible. In the estimation of the town's founders and as history has recorded, Niles's "efforts to obtain support and resources for the settlement [were seen] as unauthorized, dishonest, and self-serving." County attorney C. W. Smith alleged that Niles had "converted to his private use and comfort the funds entrusted to him by devoted followers and because of his loose ways of living." Smith pointed to Niles's "sporting a fine white team of ponies and a shining buggy" while residents were living off rations he supposedly had won after begging around town for them.

In his defense, Niles spent most of his days crisscrossing Kansas and bordering states selling pity to whites, the aspirational opportunity to help establish Nicodemus for Black people. And according to the *Atchison Weekly Champion*, he had become synonymous with Nicodemus: "You can hardly be said to have seen Nicodemus if you have not seen Niles."

McCabe and Hall had no plan to land in Nicodemus, yet Niles's deceitfulness was sinking the viability of the town he was appointed to lead. And that presented opportunities for both men.

The Arrival of McCabe and Hall

NICODEMUS, KANSAS, 1878

I am the leader of the flock and it all would have come into my hands. I was sure broke, and to keep up my station I was forced to borrow . . . But when you come back to the first principles, wasn't the money mine, or rather the colored folks? . . . I am pleading not only for myself, but for the colored people whom I represent. Now because I got a little money from a white man's bank and had no corn for security, I am to be punished.

—JOHN W. NILES, REPRESENTING HIMSELF ON TRIAL
FOR SEVERAL CIVIL AND CRIMINAL OFFENSES

John Niles's voice interrupted what would have otherwise been a shared meal between McCabe and Hall. They had just finished their days-long trip from Chicago to Kansas and had decided to take the train from Leavenworth, in the northeastern part of the state, to Hodgeman County in central Kansas and settle there. But Niles, unwittingly, diverted their plans.

As McCabe and Hall made their way to Leavenworth from Chicago, they had heard Niles soliciting for assistance for the plight of people in Nicodemus. Historian and early Nicodemus resident Lulu

Sadler Craig said the two also heard of women at their boardinghouse talking about the boisterousness of Niles's advocacy. This wasn't unusual for Leavenworth. In the frenzy of Black people arriving from all points, this was often the first stop for them in Kansas Territory and many of them needed assistance. The town's kingmaker of Black politics was a formerly enslaved man from Alabama, W. B. Townsend. His colleague, William D. Matthews, had already distinguished himself as a leading abolitionist before the Civil War and had been making good trouble throughout the eastern part of the state since 1860. Neither was especially keen on Niles, the man bellowing to whoever would listen as he asked for help.

The residents of Nicodemus were in trouble, Niles said: The town had less food, less timber, and the lands had been far less fruitful than they needed to survive. But the townspeople were also enterprising, and they had taken to heart the call to come west.

Hall's initial thought was similar to what most journalists would think: *There's a story here.* Or as he put it later, "Here was a human interest story fairly crying out loud for investigation and publication."

Niles was effective at holding court and convincing outsiders that the people of Nicodemus might be worth caring about. But the power brokers of Leavenworth worried he might be *too* convincing. Townsend and Williams took umbrage as Niles solicited funds in their town for a place so isolated most thought it best not even to visit. Yet both watched as donations for supplies were stacked high in the Leavenworth train yards.

Their suspicion was bubbling over into disdain when people who knew more of Niles's murky reputation back in Nicodemus alerted Townsend and Matthews, who eventually refused to release the donations that Niles had collected. The heated conversation spilled over into a meeting that night at the local Black church. Hall and McCabe followed Niles to the church and conferred with him. After they spoke to him they found merit in his claims, so the two launched into a full-throated defense of releasing the supplies to Niles. If the two hadn't come to his aid, Niles would likely have lost those supplies— supplies the people of Nicodemus needed. With McCabe and Hall's help, the donations for Nicodemus were finally released—but *only* under the stewardship of Niles, McCabe, and Hall jointly. They had already made their mark on the West.

How could Niles not invite these two new men from Chicago to abandon their plans and come to Nicodemus? And how could McCabe and Hall not oblige?

◄—►

The trip to Nicodemus for McCabe and Hall was harrowing, especially for McCabe. Crossing rivers, scaling hills, and swatting insects were not activities he had learned in the countinghouses of Chicago or New York. It also must have been overwhelming: McCabe was unaccustomed to a life in which he'd have to stoke his fire with cow pies, which Hall would say later that McCabe's constitution could not tolerate.

Finally, the outline of Nicodemus came into view. A silhouette of what initially they took to be anthills struck the two men deeply. From miles away, McCabe and Hall were so moved by the sight that the friends marked the moment by slicing their palms and clasping hands—a blood oath between brothers bonded by ambition.

To the two friends, arriving in that town at that moment must have seemed like fate. The town was in crisis. Niles had no education and no interest in cultivating the skills necessary to lead a town. McCabe and Hall were the exact opposite. McCabe, who understood finance, was a trained clerk and had some legal training; Hall, a seasoned reporter, came to town with a desire to turn what they both saw as possible: a promised land for a new world.

Within a day, the two took control of town government, effectively sidelining Niles to a subordinated agent. McCabe immediately became the town's disbursing clerk, removing Niles from the job of determining how ration day would work—determining which of the solicited materials would be doled out to each household. It was a job—a thankless one—in which solving the immediate needs for food and building materials would have to contend with short-, medium-, and long-term planning. Hall became the clerk of Nicodemus, keeping tabs on all functions of town management, such as recording the town's addresses, keeping tally of who lived in town, who was moving, who was leaving. In the language of the twenty-first century, they ascended to managing the business of this burgeoning colony and turning it into a managed town.

A conference of the town's leaders convened the night of their arrival to ratify these new appointments. It placed McCabe at the very center of Nicodemus's decision making, putting him in charge of asking and answering crucial questions of survival: How much should each household get to eat? How many building resources would each person be allotted as they sought to put a roof over their heads?

Together McCabe and Hill framed ways for the town to handle its own affairs without making daily journeys to predominantly white towns dozens of miles away. According to Craig, "The colonists were loath to quit their camp on the townsite and continued to occupy the temporary dwellings, regardless of the fact that all of them had been shown and allotted preemption, homestead or soldiers claims, all of which required whole or partial residence and a certain amount of cultivation of them. A. T. Hall, Jr., ever vigilant, notic[ed] their reluctance to go," while McCabe, using his communication skills, "collated their applications and made a journey to the District Land Office then located at Kirwin in Phillips County, forty-five miles northeast and had them duly recorded on the official plats."

Such jobs weren't one-time endeavors. According to Hall, "It required several trips to be made before all were on record. On one of these trips the land officers who appeared deeply interested in the success of the colony informed him that there would be a big rush of home-seekers to Graham County [home of Nicodemus] after June first of that year. They cautioned him to advise the colonists to move in on their claims without delay, else the first persons to do so would—under the law—have priority of right to the lands. When this information was given to the colonists, within a few weeks, the townsite was virtually without inhabitants, the people having in alarm be taken themselves to the lands for them obtaining of which they had left all behind, come to a strange land and endured so much privation."

In short order, these two men transformed themselves into local men of government. Not long after, Hall became the deputy district clerk of Rooks County, the county that became the jurisdictional seat for Graham County to the west and the over one hundred miles that surrounded it. McCabe, meanwhile, became the county's notary public. Notaries were crucial stakeholders in the commerce process, "as parties on both sides depended on them to be honest third parties in reporting damage or loss to a ship's cargo," according to the National Notary Association. As rations came into Nicodemus from different sources—government, businesses, charities—it was the notary who would count and verify that the goods were received properly and arrived in good order. It made McCabe a man crucial to the well-being of the townspeople.

Now all residents of the county, but especially the Black ones, the immigrant ones, the poor white ones, and the Indigenous ones desperate to homestead, could execute contracts, sales, and bargains, make affidavits, and so on without having to hit the trail for the county seat. The collective talents of McCabe and Hall lay not in just their enterprise but in their willingness to help people with the mundane, bureaucratic parts of life that often were stumbling blocks for the poor and marginalized.

Just a few months after arriving in Nicodemus, McCabe and Hall launched their own firm, Hall and McCabe, Locators and Surveyors. "The summers of 1878 and 1879 witness[ed] the arrival of hundreds of home seekers from all parts of the country into Graham County," remembered Nicodemus resident Lulu Sadler Craig. "They came in all sorts of conveyances with and without adequate means; but all of them hungry and eager to get located." In that short time, McCabe and Hall—who had been allowed to join the practice of law, because they were deemed men of impeccable record and repute—processed more than fifteen hundred land claims in Graham County and the adjoining counties in the first couple years of their time there.

And yet many of the people they had helped to settle had been white. "Most of the newcomers were white persons hailing from various states east, South and North and representing almost all strata of human society. They appeared to be actuated by the notion that, if the land was good enough for the Negro, it was good enough for them," according to Craig.

Life in Nicodemus improved when hearty rains fell toward the end of 1879 and into early 1880. One observer noticed that "the spirits of people rose in corresponding ratio" to the growth of the crops. And with that rise came the building of actual houses. The silhouette of anthills that had greeted McCabe and Hall when they arrived was now broken by new houses, many of which they had organized as land lease agreements. Hall and McCabe requested that the territory's governor, John Pierce St. John, dispatch state leaders to the county, specifically to Nicodemus, to incorporate the town officially—or, as they put it back then, "maintain organization" of the town and the county.

The governor obliged, and as part of that incorporation, the report of the county census, presided over by Hall, counted 5,017 residents that sat under the leadership of the two. And without delay the governor directed that Nicodemus would become the county seat of Graham County.

McCabe was then elected county clerk, which, unlike the clerk-ships of the past, made him the person where the buck stopped, where decisions were made, where county government power sat, and the person who could help politicians for statewide office who needed Black votes and west-Kansan white votes.

◄ ◆ ►

This may feel perfunctory, but when building their world by their rules, they had to decide which elements of this lived reality they wanted to bring in to create the conditions under which they would deem this new world successful. By formally establishing a town, they were setting up the town to have political power, to make a Black town the power base through which politicians would visit to cam-paign for their votes. They were flipping the paradigm of Black par-ticipation in politics. By shaping their own Black nationalism that trafficked in the realpolitik of the yet-to-be-invented Old West, they were determining what a Black frontier world would look like and what powers their world would have. They were becoming the arbi-ters of their own fate—a notion that felt, for most Black people, like fiction, not fact.

Put more simply, they were world-building—a far Blacker world than the United States had known. And this Black world-building led to opportunities for the very people white America would rather for-get, that the country's leading white citizens and politicians had called a "Negro problem" and tried to "fix" by shipping them away from America. McCabe's and Hall's work as land locators, agents, and town leaders especially helped Black women achieve success and fi-nancial independence.

The deal was simple in theory, and its simplicity and the homestead-ing claims gave McCabe and Hall more business and cash than they ever reasonably expected. Either as a declared head of household—

technically regardless of race—or as a twenty-one-year-old, a person could, according to the 1862 Homestead Act, become a landowner.

According to historian Tonia Compton, during this period the United States wanted to solidify its imperial footprint in the western part of the continent at the same time that McCabe and the people of Nicodemus had their own ideas for making this town in their own image. For them, homesteading had less to do with expanding the American Dream than it did with using the myth of it to help people who had nothing—Black people, immigrants, and poor whites, even citizens of Indigenous nations who had already been displaced—to become settlers, colonizers empowered by the law.

What federal and eastern politicians never expected was what could happen when the rules and conditions were implemented by the disinherited. "Charitable" white political and social leaders believed that Black people came from the South with nothing—including no moral acuity or capability—and languished without the guidance of thoughtful white leaders.

One of those disinherited was Mary Hayden. As a forty-three-year-old unmarried Black woman, Hayden was an unlikely "colonizer." She came to Nicodemus as an Exoduster, and like the men, she had to find work outside of Nicodemus. But the deal was that Mary Hayden's homestead could permanently become hers only if she remained on the land. So no matter how far or how arduous the commute from "home" to work might have been, Hayden did it. Within short order, she used her earnings as a housekeeper to commute the land and acquire her own 160 acres; by April 3, 1885, she made that land her land.

Against all expectations, she then doubled her land claim. While the 1862 Homestead Act accounted for some of the quick ascent of Black women in places like Nicodemus, Compton's analysis of thousands of homesteading records and of Graham County's land holdings tells a different story. According to Compton, women stuck out their claims at a higher rate than men. Fifty-five percent of women who claimed land assumed ownership in Graham County, whereas men only got to 48 percent.

Black women in Nicodemus, unlike in other towns, had the legal and infrastructure support built by McCabe and Hall to make business decisions that redounded to their economic benefit.

What the people of Nicodemus were building wasn't just their own world. They were building their own brand of Black nationalism, one that created a world of promise separate from the world they left behind. And if it could work on the edges of what many might consider civilization in dry, destitute Kansas, perhaps it could work elsewhere.

For better and for worse, others, Black and white, were taking notice. And both supporters as well as detractors were taking action. Word had gotten out about what McCabe and Hall and a collection of others were building: a new Black world in the Old West.

Not Homeowners or
Humans—Only Refugees

TOPEKA, KANSAS, 1879–1881

We can see why the colored man is dissatisfied with this
state . . . his idea of freedom was too high, he expected too
much and as a matter of course has never been obliged.

—JAMES M. LEWIS, A DOCTOR FROM MISSISSIPPI, IN A
LETTER TO GOVERNOR ST. JOHN OF KANSAS

By 1880, McCabe, Hall, and thousands of other Black people
had taken up residence in new Black towns across Kansas. The
census showed over forty-three thousand Black people. But
many white people overlooked this success as they began to worry
that the fate of Kansas would determine the nation's.

This, Stephen A. Hackworth of Texas feared, was a latent problem
with the influx of Black people into the state. But a problem on which
this man thought he was uniquely qualified to advise because, he
wrote, he was intimately knowledgeable about "the general condition
of the colored people of the South." And that if dealt with properly,
the people whom the country saw collectively as a "Negro problem"
could become Kansas's negro opportunity.

"I am a native of [Texas], am 39 years of age, and served one year in the Confederate Army, but I do not claim any honor or glory upon that score," wrote Hackworth to Kansas governor John Pierce St. John. Now that Black people fleeing the South—whom he called "refugees"—were pouring into Kansas, St. John worried that Kansas was now *too full* of Black people. And Hackworth, not even a resident of the state, was putting himself forward as an agent, of sorts, overseeing the Exodusters, writing, "My father was a Slave owner, and from my earliest recollection I have lived in a portion of the South where the Blacks, both as Slaves and Freedmen, largely outnumber the whites." This was his attempt to signal to the governor that he knew Black people better than most—at least more than the governor.

"My father was an old Whig, and a Union man, and of course my devotion and fidelity has never run very deep for the Secession and Bourbon Democracy. In 1866 I became a Republican, and since that time I have continued to be an active supporter of Republican principles"—trying to prove that the governor could trust him as a political ally and as someone well-versed in the ways of Black people.

"I believe that I understand the character and know the general condition of the colored people of the South, and in order to fully explain this well it will be necessary for me to classify the Blacks and to give the general causes and reasons that has crested the different conditions and classes to wit."

What Hackworth's letter articulates is a sudden frenzy about the Exodusters. From across the country and even the world, white people began to write to St. John, insisting that they knew best what to do with the Black people who were arriving.

◄—◆—►

Hackworth's observations, as well as those of the hundreds of others who wrote unsolicited letters to the governor telling him what he ought to do with Black people, were just that: observations, not informed by the consent or interests of the Black people of whom he called himself *a friend*. Kansas's charity to Black people had little to do with giving them a hand up. It had much more to do with moralizing.

Thousands had poured into Kansas when Governor St. John received the first of many letters from the British-American Quaker activist Elizabeth Rous Comstock. "I have read with lively and painful interest the statements in some of the papers of the Exodus of the colored people from the South, and of the destitute and sufferings conditions of many of them in your State," she wrote in 1879. She had heard tales that she interpreted as despair, not as the treasured beauty of escaping and beginning again. "I am endeavoring to awaken the feelings of interest and sympathy of our 'Society of Friends' in these parts and elsewhere on their behalf." She was well networked in the Quaker community, in the United States, Canada, and England, and she organized with her close friend Laura Haviland.

During the height of Reconstruction's fall, Comstock traveled throughout England, where she raised $60,000 (approximately $1.8 million in 2024). "I propose to gather up bedding and clothes and what I can in the way of more substantial Metallic Sympathy"—donations. She knew that while clothes, pillows, and blankets might help these "refugees," money would better sustain the people who came and were coming still.

Within a year of her arrival in Kansas, Comstock opened the Agricultural and Industrial Institute for Refugees, which sat on four hundred acres not as far from the state's capital as Nicodemus. She saw herself as heir to the work of Lincoln himself, a man she admired. "[Lincoln] crowned the labors of Abolitionists," she said, a category she included herself in. Now, she continued, "It is left to the Christian Philanthropists of our age to crown his great work."

Like so many other Quakers and those with charitable inclinations, she believed that these Exodusters needed Christian education and, as she routinely put it, "Metallic Sympathy." And she seemed keen to inform St. John's understanding of Black people, and how best to deal with another alleged "Negro problem."

In this, Comstock and Haviland shared more than they might have guessed with Hackworth. In a letter to St. John, Hackworth instructed the governor that all Black people were divided into three classes:

1. 1st Class, as he put it, Blacks "comprise about one tenth of the freedmen, who as slaves, were owned by masters who made mechanics, overseers, trusted body servants and confidential agents of them. In these several capacities this class had opportunities and practicable experience by which they were enabled to learn something about the ordinary business affairs of everyday life, and how to be industrious frugal and thrifty. This class are today the trusted leaders of their Race, and they generally own small farms or else homestead in the towns and cities of the South."

   This first class of Black people, Hackworth believed, was one that St. John could entrust to run the small towns and cities. These were the ones who likely had the most favorable views of white people and the United States. They were the ones who had what he called "practicable skills." The kind that would convert the charity of those like Comstock and Haviland into investments that would pay large returns. Such a discrete group of people, Hackworth argued, could be the hope of Kansas, insofar as Kansas had a problem with an influx of Black people.

2. The 2nd Class Blacks, however, comprised about 40 percent of Black people. There was hope for the governor, because in Hackworth's estimation, they had been "formerly owned by masters who fed and clothed them well, never punishing them severely, except

for very grave offences, and they were taught to be honest and industrious and were encouraged to attend their churches on Sundays."

This class of Black people were the "best laborers and tenants of the South, and Southern planters prefer them to any other class of tenants, because they are generally industrious and honest, and will live contented in small cheap cabins, which good white tenants would not do." To Hackworth, this distinction mattered. It's why Hackworth assured the governor that the 40 percent of Black people generally were known to "own farm stock and farming implements and are able to furnish their own supplies with but little assistance from their landlords." The old South's productivity could be exported to Kansas, Hackworth believed, while leaving behind only the old titles: exchanging "slave" and "slaveowner" for "laborer" and "tenant."

"But they are extravagant," Hackworth warned. He might try to help these people but he had no respect for them. "They spend their money freely for gaudy clothing, shoddy jewelry, attending shows and circuses, whiskey, tobacco, building churches and in supporting an army of ignorant fanatical, and often immoral preachers, and but for these extravagant habits, they would soon become the absolute owners of the most fertile portions of the South."

The goal of the charitable white people in Kansas who made the state's more recent Black residents their focus was to change the assumed behavior of Black people. It wasn't to change them personally, but to make them good Christian folks who would vote like "good Republicans" and extract from their labor a slightly better wage with lower rents than what they had seen in the South. As much good as these people hoped to do for Black people, their work had little to do with structurally reorganizing the circumstances under which all people in the United States lived. It was only about ensuring "their devotion and fidelity to the Republican Party."

There was one last class of Black people:

3. The 3rd Class "compose about one half of the Black population, and as slaves were owned by masters, who half-fed, half-clothed and punished them severely for the least disobedience or breach of discipline. Worked incessantly from early [dawn until] dark, day after day—Sundays often included—often forced by hunger to steal, wives and husbands often sold and thus separated from each other, or perhaps compelled by overseers to exchange wives and husbands with each other."

This description did not make Hackworth sympathize with these people, but rather to pathologize, judge, and critique them mercilessly: "Is it a matter of surprise to anyone," he wrote, "that this class are today thriftless, often dishonest, and entertain small respect for morality and marriage obligations?"

Such sweeping bigotry would only have endeared Hackworth to the likes of the governor. This is because such racism freed someone from doing more to improve such people's lives. Money, jobs, and education wouldn't change them, Hackworth was saying, so there was no need to fight to provide them. There was a moral unlearning and relearning that Black people needed to do, in Hackworth's estimation, to lighten the otherwise unbearable burden on the white people of Kansas. Put another way, Black people needed to be trained to become productive members of society in order for their presence and acceptance into the young state of Kansas to be worthwhile.

Hackworth sent the governor sixteen letters, seven of which focused exclusively on how to deal with "the blacks" he claimed to know so well—a relentless promotion of his ideas if given the job of managing the Exodusters. Should the governor follow them, Hackworth believed, the political and economic prospects of the state's white political leaders would improve. Below are Hackworth's rules, annotated for clarity.

1. "None except the 1st or 2nd classes [of Black people] to be colonized together for the present." *That is, refuse entry to 50 percent of the Black people.*

2. "No freedmen belonging to either of these [1st and 2nd] classes, who is known to be quarrelsome, or of bad character permitted to settle in any of the colonies formed." *Impose a moral standard on Black people.*

3. "To not sell less than 40 nor more than 100 acres to any one family, and to charge a reasonable price for all lands, giving from five to 10 years to pay or annual instalments in which to pay for lands so sold." *Black people would not be able to manage farmlands at the same scale as whites. Yet McCabe and Hall, who were coordinating land deals incessantly, both had land holdings more than this.*

4. "Laws should be enacted and faithfully enforced, enforced, prohibiting the selling or giving away of spirituous liquors within any colony so established." *Black people would not be able to maintain their sobriety with the free sale of liquor. While St. John was a temperance abider, a teetotaler, clearly they believed that Black people were more likely to drink wildly than whites.*

5. "No preacher, who is not known to be an educated and moral and a worthy man to be permitted to preach to them." *Black people can't discern for themselves whom they should listen to.*

6. "To license only such merchants to establish stores among them, who are known to be honest and fair in their dealings, and

prevent peddlers, showmen and gamblers from practicing their avocations within the colonies." *The assumption is that Black people were more attracted to crime, vice, and immorality than whites. Hackworth was advocating for laws to keep Black people on a tighter leash—Jim Crow, to some extent—but with a veneer of moral concern.*

7. "To establish a thorough system of compulsory education, and to employ good moral teachers to teach colony schools." *A reminder that Black people needed special education to learn good morals.*

Hackworth's intention was clear: prioritize finances over people. The goal, even with charity, was to clarify just who it was that the government needed to serve, for the least amount of time, to ensure they didn't create a drag on the state's finances. And the consensus was emerging that beyond the labor and economic productivity of the Black people who had made Kansas their home before Kansas could ask them to, these were impressionable people. People who without proper guidance could give in to what Hackworth called "gaudy" activities.

What motivated the actions of such men and women was, in some important sense, charity. But this charity was not born of altruism, but of a fear that white people would be on the hook for taking care of people they didn't want beyond the economic and political benefits.

—◄●►—

McCabe's aspirations for higher political office and greater Black self-determination weren't just stymied by misconstrued charity or Hackworth's perspectives. He also had to contend with the desire to further indenture Black people as a compromise between business leaders and the governor.

James H. McKay and his colleagues at the short-lived Pacific Coast Immigration Bureau were responsible for locating laborers to bring to California and Hawaii, then known as the Sandwich Islands. In 1879, he wrote St. John, convinced that the forced immigrant laborers in his state—most of them Chinese—"must go." He offered St. John a political solution to the overwhelming number of Black people arriving in Kansas. McKay wrote that "we want reliable labor and invite it here, the Immigrants want a home, and certainly will give that state the preference that compares favorably with the one he has been accustomed to all his life. The Colored Immigrant is such calculated to stand the rigors of the climate of the western states neither has he been educated to provide subsistence for himself and family, as well as his stock to carry him through a long winter."

As winter was coming and the Black people Kansan landlords saw as potential laborers would not be able to work as much, why not send them away, this time to California or out into the distant Pacific?

McKay sweetened the offer with what seemed like an accommodation: "We purpose to provide every man of [a] family or single person with a home either for a portion of the crops he makes, being provided with everything necessary to raise such crops, and he either pay in money or otherwise as agreed upon for such advances as have been made, or we will ensure him a certain amount of wages per month under a contract for one year, or we will provide them who are calculated for it, situations in Families as servants, so that they will know they have some employment at fair wages before they leave."

—◂▸—

What did Governor St. John do with this outpouring of interest in the recent Black migrants? He abdicated his role as governor, as so many do when a crisis affects Black people, and became a philanthropist. Instead of proposing new ways to more easily facilitate Black immigration into the state, he promised not to use government resources to support Exodusters, and instead created the Kansas Freedmen's Relief Association (KFRA). The point of the KFRA was "to relieve, as far as possible, the wants and necessities of destitute freedmen, refugees, and immigrants coming into this State to provide necessary food, shelter, and clothing for them when unable to provide for themselves." And the group's president made clear at the start of their report, "Our enterprise is not political." Because undoing nearly two centuries of oppression could be accomplished in a tenth of the time as the slave trade lasted without political costs. As a result, they capped the life span of the KFRA's incorporation at twenty-one years.

These efforts did make a difference to some people. Within less than a year, white philanthropists had built a storehouse in Kansas and had received "1380 packages comprising barrels, hogsheads, boxes, bales, and crates, many of them of large size." They imported "second-hand clothing of every kind and description, bedding, old boots, and shoes, hats, caps." To make sure these goods reached the people in need, they even fought the former mayor of New York City, Fernando Wood, a sympathizer to the southern cause who tried to obstruct the importation of these goods by imposing higher duties and taxes in his role as chair of Congress's Ways and Means Committee. England reported sending fifty thousand pounds of material and more than $4,000 in donations.

But charity alone could not solve the plight of the Exodusters. Charity not informed by justice obstructed the progress McCabe and other Black Exodusters demanded: It had the effect of amplifying the narrative of Black people being feeble and useful primarily, if not exclusively, as labor.

Even though the KFRA emphasized in its report that these "refugees" were also "American citizens," the organization took no responsibility that it was part of the problem. "Should [the KFRA's] results develop such a [political] bearing, not we but those who drove those colored people from the South are responsible for it. Our cause is . . . the cause of Christian humanity." As Nell Irvin Painter has noted, the KFRA "did not actively encourage black migrants to become homesteaders." In fact, they didn't even "envision Blacks as landowners." They were only refugees, not yet fully liberated Americans deserving of equal protection and opportunity.

Their charity stood in direct contrast to the life McCabe and others were trying to build—one of opportunity and abundance; of self-determination and not of dependence; one that accepted that there was nothing wrong with Black people.

—◄═►—

Justice isn't simply an outlay of capital that demands pats on the backs of those who do the doling. It is an ongoing account of who failed whom and an understanding that the goal should be equity. The state of Kansas and those who made its decisions did not prefer justice. They preferred charity—a preference that echoed and still echoes beyond Kansas and beyond that historical moment. And charity can be just as damaging to the hopes of Black people in America.

Weigh all that against the establishment of Nicodemus: a largely self-governing town that was fully engaged in reinventing the future by building inheritance and opportunity on the frontier. Nicodemus represented the enduring quality of Black life in America: to determine who it is we are without the conventions of charity dictating how we should build our future.

In Search of a Quotidian
Life of Consequence

NICODEMUS, KANSAS, 1881

The colony, or settlement, consists of about 125 families, comprising a population of about 700 souls, scattered over an
area of twelve miles in length by six in breadth. Nicodemus
is the town-site; has its post-office, store, hotel, land-office,
etc.; and, like nearly all new towns aspires to the possession
of the county seat.

—"THE NEGRO EXODUS: A VISIT TO THE NICODEMUS COLONY,"
   Chicago Tribune, APRIL 25, 1879

Sometime in August 1881, as enough prosperity overcame Nicodemus's agricultural woes, McCabe reached out to a local minister who called himself Reverend Samuels. He told him, "Rev. I
am going to Kirwin Sunday, returning Tuesday evening bringing the
girl I am to marry, please come over to my cabin and say the word for
me." Reverend Samuels returned McCabe's request: "Certainly," he
said, "I will be there."

As Lulu Sadler Craig remembered it, Samuels rode off on Tuesday
evening to what she called "Mac's place." The minister who brought

with him the food his wife had cooked for them waited for a storm to subside and for the sun to set before he lit a fire.

In these Black towns of the West, churches were far from formal and were often made from the same building materials that stitched together their flimsy homes. As such, homes often had just enough holiness to consecrate a marriage.

There was no need for fancy food or drink. Instead, Samuels made himself a pot of coffee and waited for Mac to arrive with his bride.

Near eleven at night, the minister heard McCabe in the yard. His fiancée—a young woman named Sarah Bryant—was led to the door as the minister rustled up his book to say the words, perhaps not many, as McCabe wanted to quickly solemnize his marriage to the woman he had admired for some time.

"Stop right there, son," the minister told McCabe before he could cross the threshold. The light from the house was dim and rain was pouring. The pastor blessed the marriage and led them through the vows, with McCabe saying his vows loudly, while his wife whispered hers.

After the vows were spoken and the minister yelled, "Now bring her in," McCabe hoisted his wife, both of them drenched by rain, and carried her over the threshold. Their reception included only the newlyweds and Samuels, the minister, not even his wife, who had prepared the basket of lunch with a baked chicken and some cake. McCabe helped his bride by unwrapping her from her wet coverings as "her teeth were chattering" from the chilling rain. So instead of chicken and cake for the reception, McCabe grabbed the same coffee and offered it to the new Mrs. McCabe, who quickly succumbed to sleep.

—◄◆►—

Most classic American westerns are remembered mostly for their gunfights, bank robberies, and the taming of a wild that isn't nearly as wild as the fiction that writers have wrapped around the truth. The truth is that for Black people, winning the American West had far more to do with wanting to live a peaceful life, and for many that peaceful life required the violence our westerns have catalogued.

But tucked within these outbursts of violence were moments in which the sweet stillness of the love that this ambitious town leader had found in Sarah Bryant could be found. Passed over are the moments when people like McCabe would go into their houses at night and greet their wives and tell each other that they loved one another, shared their troubles of the day, their fears, and their ambitions. It was this quotidian life that white southerners had wanted to block.

McCabe's success meant that he spent most of his early days not just digging his own dugout, but also notarizing documents and settling disagreements. Hall, meanwhile, busied himself trading his reporting and editing skills for a job as clerk and a lawyer, teaching himself the law while administrating and executing contracts and deeds, all while moonlighting as a writer highlighting the opportunities of the town.

By 1881, McCabe was no longer just a notary. He had become both the town and county clerk. His involvement in Republican Party politics had become pronounced. The governor had appointed his friend A. T. Hall to head the census for the county. No longer were Nicodemus residents faced with six to seven hours of walking to conduct business in the town of Stockton. People came to them.

Nicodemus's downtown had begun to assume, according to reports of the time, "a uniform appearance," and it attracted people like Z. T. Fletcher, another Black man, who opened a general store that was soon overrun with customers to whom, as the town's postmaster, he could cross-sell postal goods and services. White men, too—S. G. Wilson, C. H. Newth, William Green among them—had found success in this town building their own stores, outlining the downtown landscape with two-story buildings to accommodate the growth. As a store owner, Newth dabbled in pharmacology and offered residents quick access to needed drugs. He even added butchery.

The colony was becoming a town.

———◀━▶———

However contented McCabe might have been, there remained an urge for more. That hope had been on display with McCabe's every move from the time he left boarding school. This wasn't the promised land that it seemed. The growth that Nicodemus had experienced would be capped without an influx of new people with money-stuffed purses, or a railroad depot, or a state government willing to subsidize the growth of the town as they had done for other towns.

"We are creating no new debts, but pay as we go," Governor St. John declared at his 1881 Biennial Message to the Kansas House of Representatives.

This became the resounding theme of the state, that a fiscal conservatism was to be followed, which limited the state from helping its citizens when they needed it most, even the Black citizens the state recruited and received with its own Freedmen's Relief Association. The state wouldn't overspend for moral causes but would encourage those advocating for them to be industrious on their own.

Because of that fiscal policy and because the Kansas government froze the state debt at $1 million, state lawmakers allowed municipal governments to operate fiscally as they pleased. So much so that debt taken on by local towns soon outpaced state debt by some forty-seven to one. The goal was for communities to do all they could to attract business investment. Securing a quotidian life—one elusive to most Black people—had consequences. It meant taxing residents, mortgaging farms, and trying to raise cash crops in dry lands, and it caused a boom in the Kansas economy the likes of which nobody expected. While farmers around the state actively mortgaged over two hundred thousand acres and had incurred debts of $175 million—twice the level of their Nebraska neighbors—according to one account the people of Nicodemus pursued more cautious strategies, both because farming wasn't as prosperous an endeavor there as in other parts of the state and because risky behavior could sink the town.

As Scott G. McNall put it, "Kansas was becoming a state of small businessmen." Surviving the harsh life in Kansas was nothing if not an investment in the crafting of what for some became a "promised land." But for McCabe—a burgeoning political entrepreneur—it became a testing ground for what it would take to build a life. Because when Black people get to live lives organized by Black people, they demonstrate new ways of being American. McNall believed that in Kansas "the politics of the community revolved almost exclusively around the issue of how to boost business . . . [People] arrived in town with capital, or a skill, or just an idea for making money, and stayed to do so . . . Most people took their business to be business: they wanted to participate in the growth and expansion of the town."

And while this might have been the case for many people coming to the Old West, for McCabe and the Black people who came to Nicodemus, the politics of their community were not rooted strictly in making money—that was not the end. The end was to create a nation within a nation, to construct a seat at the table called the American West. And at this table, Black people would have power—more than they'd ever have in most other states—to dictate their own existence.

Perhaps the promised land wasn't everyone's vision of excellence. Maybe the promised land for the residents of Nicodemus included the opportunity to send children to school, to vote their conscience in elections without fear; to struggle, to succeed, or even to fail on terms they created.

10

Exodus on Trial

WASHINGTON, D.C., 1880

If the Southern whites are to teach the colored people their true interest, no one will complain; but it is perfectly optional with the colored people whether they will accept their teachings or not . . .

. . . If the Southern employer can not ascertain how to keep [Black people in the South], or in other words does not know how to look out for his own interest, he can get no help from Congress. He better devote his chief study to his own interest, and leave the colored man to discover his.

—*St. Louis Globe-Democrat*, JUNE 3, 1880

What McCabe created had attracted thousands of Black people. But many white leaders, both from the South and the North, remained unhappy about the exodus of the South's former Black residents. And those who also heard McCabe's promises were concerned for two reasons.

First, if Black people were leaving the South en masse, it would indicate to the country as a whole that whatever abolition they witnessed had been nothing more than a ruse—a ghost of progress that never existed. Second, Black people leaving the South would hollow

out the inexpensive labor force that white leaders in the region re-
lied on.

How could opponents end this exodus? It began, as so many iniq-
uities have, in the U.S. Congress.

—◄●►—

On January 19, 1880, Senator Daniel Voorhees of Indiana convened
the Select Committee of the United States Senate to Investigate the
Causes of the Removal of the Negroes from the Southern States to
the Northern States. And since Voorhees, though a northerner, had
once opposed the Civil War, the notion that the senator was now earnestly concerned about the fate of "the Negroes" surprised many.

Before the committee meetings began the *New York Times* mocked
the motivation for the investigation, calling Voorhees "The Aston-
ished Voorhees" precisely because they believed that he should've
known better. After detailing how difficult life in North Carolina
specifically, and the rest of the South in general, had become for Black
people in the wake of Reconstruction's fall, the *Times* synthesized
Voorhees's delayed reaction: "[Black people in the South] ought to be
satisfied. They are allowed to live. There is no law prohibiting their
existence." The paper suggested sarcastically that it was this assumption held by Voorhees that animated his astonishment when he finally
realized that Black people were mid-exodus. The *Times* noted, "The
benevolent Mr. Voorhees, like the work-house beadle, is horrified to
think that his colored *Oliver* is 'asking for more.'"

The committee's witness list grew to some 153 witnesses from North
Carolina, Georgia, Alabama, Mississippi, Louisiana, Texas, Missouri,
Kansas, and Indiana (with the least number of witnesses from the state
with some of the highest levels of Black immigration—Kansas). The
senator's state newspaper, the *Indianapolis Journal*, added up the
daily costs of the select committee investigation and speculated that it

hovered near five times the salary of each senator. The newspaper estimated that each witness from Indiana would cost Indianans some $100—the whole affair costing $15,000 (approximately $480,000 in 2025 dollars).

Kansas was an indictment of the narrative about Black life in America that antagonists to the Exoduster cause wanted to craft, explained the *St. Louis Globe-Democrat* as it critiqued the Voorhees Committee. Kansas was by no means perfect, but from it emanated enough success that investigating its value might indicate what Voorhees and his colleagues in the South could ill afford: that in the halls of Congress, people might come to learn that life could be better for Black people outside the South.

During his first term in the Senate, Voorhees did his best to ensure that the South appeared far better than it was—as well as show how unfit the North was to accommodate Black people from the South. To accomplish this, he picked a state to which few (relative to Kansas) Black people would head, where no metaphorical Black beachhead had been established. Indiana, his home state, became one of the states of focus for his congressional inquiry. And in so doing he sent a message to whoever would listen: Black people ought to stay in the South because there was no room for them in the North.

◄——►

To Voorhees, McCabe might have been part of a conspiracy to entice Black people to leave the South, to depress its economy and dupe Black people out of the consistent work to be found there. He even said that theoretically he'd be happy to have Black people come to Indiana, but he worried there wouldn't be enough work for them. They were bent on a life in Kansas, where McCabe and others had made the way straight for them, arduous though it was. Voorhees had heard but interpreted what he heard through a pathology of Black people not needing more than the bare minimum they might have acquired in places like North Carolina.

One of the few witnesses called from Kansas was Benjamin "Pap" Singleton, whose reputation was well known. After escaping slavery to Canada and then Detroit, Singleton became excited by the prospect of colonizing the West. In his flyer that attempted to entice Black people to move there, he proclaimed that all should be "in pursuit of Homes in the Southwestern Lands of America at Transportation Rates, cheaper than ever was known before." And with a familiarity and comity that McCabe never quite had, Singleton encouraged all who read that flier to call him "old Pap." His company, the Edgefield Real Estate Association, organized land much as Nicodemus's founders, Hill and Smith, had done, carving out the outline of the townsite of Dunlap and divvying it up to parcel it out to newcomers. He had to determine who to recruit, who was willing to live off rations while they sowed, tilled, and watered in anticipation of a harvest that would feed the new residents of the town, as McCabe had done.

Singleton's testimony ran counter to the image of Black life in the South and the motivations for Black exodus that Voorhees crafted. Singleton, indignant, looked at the committee and articulated his plan: "My plan is for [Black people] to leave the country and learn the South a lesson; the whole of America—this Union—will have a lesson when cotton is forty to fifty cents a pound, and you can't get it at that." His initial desire, however, had not been to abandon the South but to teach it what it would lose by not treating its Black residents properly. He told the committee, "We don't want to leave the South . . . but we are going to learn the South a lesson. I have talked about this, and called a convention, and tried to harmonize things and promote the spirit of conciliation, and to do everything that could be done in the name of God." For Singleton, Black people had left not for greed but in desperation—after trying and failing to reconcile with their white counterparts.

Singleton wasn't the only Black person intimately familiar with the Exoduster march to Kansas. Charlton Tandy, a Black man from the St. Louis area, had shifted from his law practice to cataloguing the dangers that befell Black people from the South who stopped in St. Louis on their way to Kansas. And it wasn't the first time a Black man had made such an appeal, despite how the committee made it seem that way. Tandy traveled to Washington to testify in 1879, but he also came with a letter addended with select affidavits from 101 Black people who had passed through St. Louis on their way west. Tandy summed up what he saw as people who had survived the "vilest atrocities."

Tandy, whose mild-mannered, bald, long white-bearded portraits belied the brass-knuckled politicking he was known for in his home state of Missouri, kept his words sharp, even calling Frederick Douglass a "fawning sycophant" of the Republicans and for leaving the fight that Tandy had enjoyed so much to accept a job as a U.S. marshal just two years earlier.

Fourteen years before his trip to the nation's capital, he saw the Civil War come to an end as a captain in the Union army. In that same year, he began what was known as the Missouri Equal Rights League, the first of the state's Black political movements. He wanted what seemed nearly impossible: holistic rights—voting, equal treatment in housing, general welfare, and employment. Dreams that became pipe dreams when his fellow Republicans told him that they "would not be dictated to by any damned nigger."

"They have come by steamboats up the Mississippi River, from chiefly the States of Louisiana and Mississippi, and landed at St. Louis, Mo, a great number of colored citizens of the United States, not less than twenty hundred composed of men and women, old and young, and with them many of their children," Tandy wrote in a letter to Voorhees. These affidavits were delivered, uninvited and unrequested, to Congress by Tandy himself. "The condition of the great majority is absolute poverty," he told the committee. "They are clothed: in thin garments for the most part, and while there have been supported to some extent by the public, but mostly by private charity. The older ones are the former slaves of the South—all now entitled to life and liberty."

Tandy, who could read and write, along with his partner, James Milton Turner, collected and transcribed their words and synthesized them into compelling prose that conveyed what their journey had been. But the reality was that their journey was not over. They had come this far on faith—and opportunity lay beyond St. Louis. If they could just make it to Kansas, there would be a new beginning for them, the end of the old world. "This multitude is eager to proceed to Kansas, and, without exception, so far as we have learned, refuse all overtures or inducements to return South, even if their passage back is paid for them," Tandy wrote.

Even bad weather would not deter them. "Unusually cold" is what Tandy called the Missouri winter during the stop in St. Louis these Black folks made. Those from the South were inexperienced with the ice and snow that greeted them. Not "a single kind remembrance of their sunny Southern homes" remained, Tandy wrote. This would, in ordinary circumstances, be the factual basis upon which the committee would convene and become educated about the exodus. But this committee, under Voorhees, was more interested in ignoring the facts laid out by the very people involved in their own exodus.

Voorhees ignored the conditions of the actual exodus and fixated on a relatively fake one. Despite the 153 witnesses called, a reading of the reports and affidavits provided by countless Exodusters, and a pedestrian recitation of life on the ground for Black people, the committee's majority was still unmoved.

Primarily, they only looked at a small sample of North Carolina counties, not the whole of the state or any other place that Black people actively left. Those Black witnesses the committee called were often people who already held land in the area and had achieved some level of economic stability. So it was no surprise that the committee found "no county or district in the South where [Black people] were excluded, either in theory or practice, from their share in the management of county affairs and of the control of county government." They were so convinced that opportunity existed for Black people to succeed in the South that it must have been McCabe and others who were involved in a conspiracy to paint the South as something that it was not. In the committee's majority opinion, led by Voorhees, "whenever [Black] votes were in a majority, we found that the officers were most generally divided among black people, or among white people of their choice." In other words, Black people did not experience any differences in the way justice was carried out in the South. No evidence to support this claim was offered.

On the matter of political outrages committed against Black people, the committee found that that couldn't have been enough to trigger Black people to leave en masse. Why? Political exclusion and outrage had been, as the majority put it, "the staple of complaint for many years against the people of the South." It had become white noise, easy to ignore, especially because the committee's investigation "found nothing or almost nothing new. Many old stories were revived and dwelt upon by zealous witnesses, but very few indeed ventured to say that any considerable violence or outrage had been exhibited toward the colored people of the South within the last few years, and still fewer of all those who testified upon this subject, and who were evidently anxious to make the most of it, testified to anything as within their own knowledge."

When they reflected on the American West's Black politicians, the

committee's majority, led by Voorhees, constructed a hearing to reflect that Black politicians in the West had made it their "business . . .
to stir up feeling between the whites and blacks; keep alive the embers
of political hatred."

McCabe, who had already emerged as a political leader in Kansas,
would rebuff these claims. His career was developing such that he
was currying favor with both Black and white politicians, arranging
business deals not just with Black people but also with many white
people keen on working in Nicodemus and Graham County. As a notary public, clerk of the county, and co-head of the burgeoning Hall
and McCabe, Locators and Surveyors, he had a bead on the economic
and financial opportunities just beyond the horizon.

While Nicodemus was predominantly Black, McCabe and other
town leaders knew that attracting diverse homesteaders and entrepreneurs would increase the likelihood that their town could become a
train depot, a hub for commerce.

To Voorhees and his Senate colleagues, Senators George Pendleton
of Ohio (who voted against the Thirteenth Amendment, which out-
lawed slavery) and Zebulon Vance (the North Carolina senator who
had a vested interest in recasting North Carolina life for Black people
in the most positive light possible), Black people were not yet civilized. In fact, the three men end the committee's report with the conclusion that "friendship and harmony [on the part of Black people
with their white counterparts, or as they put it, 'neighbors' in the
South] once fully attained, there is nothing to bar the way to [Black
people's] speedy civilization and advancement in wealth and prosperity."

But for the Black people who came to Kansas, as Voorhees put it,
"cultivating the friendship of their white neighbors" in the South had
come to no avail. Instead, they left and started anew because they
were already "civilized" on their own, and far more than those who
sought nuanced ways to enslave them. They believed that the only

path to prosperity was severing themselves from the people who demanded friendship after doing nothing in policy, in practice, or in business to demonstrate that they understood the humanity of Black people, let alone demonstrated any measure of friendliness.

As the lone voice of dissent on the committee, Senator William Windom of Minnesota summed up the proceedings as "utter absurdity." But even Windom asked rhetorically, "Why take [Black people] from North Carolina? Why import them from a State where the Republicans hope and expect to carry the election, when there were thousands upon thousands ready and anxious to come from States certainly Democratic? Why transport them by rail at heavy expense halfway across the continent when they could have taken them from Kentucky with any expense, or brought them up the Mississippi River by steamers at merely nominal cost?"

Which is exactly what many Exodusters did. Not dependent on a government that seemed bent on ignoring them, they fashioned their own exodus and hailed ships to give them rides, even if those ships were meant to carry only goods, packages, and letters.

Windom continued, "Why send twenty-five thousand to Kansas to swell her 40,000 Republican majority?" His answer: "These considerations brand with falsehood and folly the charge that the exodus was a political movement induced by Northern partisan leaders." The goal of the entire investigation, in Windom's opinion, was to defame the North, when in actuality it wasn't just the North, it was the work of Black people committed to building lives on their own terms that was being maligned.

It wasn't just that Black people had left behind less opportunity in the South, as Windom pointed out. In the report of the Republican minority, he admitted that it is "impossible to enumerate all or any considerable part of the causes of discontent and utter despair which have finally culminated in this movement." For Windom, the committee was at risk of repeating "a history of violence and crime which for fifteen years have reddened with the blood of innocent victims, many of the fairest portions of our country; to do so would be to read the numberless volumes of sworn testimony which have been carefully corded away in the crypt and basement of this Capitol, reciting shocking instances of crime, crying from the ground against the perpetrators of the deeds which they record."

For Windom, the reasons for Black people leaving the South were clear: "Abridgement of their rights of self-government; second, their disadvantages as to common schools; third discriminations against them in the courts; and, fourth, the memory of Democratic outrages." Tandy put it more succinctly: "There is no political freedom for negroes in the South . . . 'If I vote the Republican ticket,' quoting a recent Exoduster, 'I wakes up the next morning in the graveyard.'"

Black people wanted to begin again on their terms. That was a more compelling reason for exodus than any cause Voorhees could invent, any cause Windom could understand, or any complaint Tandy could lodge.

They wanted to begin again.

11

Representation Matters?

TOPEKA, KANSAS, 1880–1881

The freedom and well-being of blacks is still sought, but black group autonomy, to the extent that it is favored, is viewed as only contingently related to black flourishing. Accordingly, if black interests can be adequately advanced through multiracial associations or within a multiracial polity, then this too would be perfectly acceptable.

—TOMMIE SHELBY, *We Who Are Dark*

McCabe wrote in the *Herald of Kansas* "in vindication of myself and in reply to the Rev. Fulbright, who, I have been credibly informed, took occasion at the recent State Convention of Colored Men to intimate that I had sold out my people."

McCabe penned this article in the state's Black paper of record, but he directed it not just at another Black man known as Reverend Fulbright. From what McCabe had heard, Fulbright blamed him not only for why the Exodusters, some supposed twenty-five thousand of them, didn't have money, land, food, or other necessities as they thought they would. He also said that Fulbright claimed that McCabe had "prevented [Black Kansans] from having a colored man selected as a delegate to the 1880 National Republican Convention in Chicago."

But McCabe made clear that whatever version of Black national-ism would be forged, it would not be forged apart from white people but from interaction and confrontation with white people. He wrote, "Had the reverend gentlemen been one-half as jealous in working to have a fair number of colored delegates as members of that [Republi-can, not Colored] convention, as he has since been to be captious and fault-finding the effort which I made might have resulted more favor-ably." McCabe wanted to be clear that he still believed in representa-tion being a key to power, but that the sheer number of people needed to be higher to secure more opportunity for Black people.

In McCabe's estimation, sequestering Black people in a Colored Convention—not working in partnership with those holding power—could be a key to wresting power away from white people and redis-tributing it to Black people.

In April 1880, Charles Henry Langston—older brother of John Mer-cer Langston, the Black abolitionist, U.S. congressman from Virginia, and Virginia State University president—was elected as president of the Kansas Convention of Colored Men. In his estimation, "colored voters in Kansas had been treated too long as a mere voting machine," and that needed to change.

The *Herald of Kansas* recorded that Langston "wanted to see the State, county and city [electoral] tickets have a little color on it by having the names of some able and deserving colored men on the same." But for Langston, "in the past the colored voters had allowed themselves to be wound up on the day before election like an old clock, and after the election he was left to run down and rust until another election."

McCabe didn't attend the convention and instead sent a letter, co-signed by other Nicodemus leaders—his best friend, Hall, as well as

Fletcher and Granville Lewis—that indicated that while he was minding the keep in Nicodemus, the people who convened in Topeka could "count on our hearty co-operation in any plan which you may decide upon that has in view the amelioration of the condition of the race." But his note wasn't without admonition: "We trust that your convention will be attended by a large number of the intelligent, thinking colored men of Kansas; that your deliberations will be marked for their dignity and importance, and be followed by only such results as your fondest fancies may suggest."

There was doubt among McCabe and his colleagues that conventions of Black people would amount to anything useful. They believed that talking about leading, instead of actively leading, wouldn't result in the advancement of Black people. But it was time for Black people at every level to reach for a role in Kansas government. And McCabe had been hatching his own plans for political office.

In fact, McCabe framed himself as a problem solver and a doer, having already been elected to run Graham County and Nicodemus. His appearance in the pages of newspapers and community bulletins in Nicodemus and beyond had become more common. His church, for which his company had located the land, was a frequent destination for the state's governor during his campaigns.

Politicking was a new skill that McCabe had acquired, but it was one he took to deftly and that enabled him to be at tables reserved for those whose skin was far lighter than his. But the peril of being at those tables was that McCabe began to become the target of attacks not just from white political leaders, but Black ones as well.

⊰⬤⊱

At the time of the 1880 Colored Convention in Kansas, the Republicans of Kansas had been meeting to discuss who would represent the state at the Republican Convention in Chicago in June.

It was a confrontational time. Democrats, it seemed, could win the state and roll back whatever gains Black people had made. Because of the split among Republicans—between those who wanted political appointments based on merit, political appointments based on patronage (who helped whom during the political campaigns), and those who wanted to restore the efforts forestalled by Reconstruction's demise—there was a chance that a divided party could affect the election's outcome. It forced both Black and white Republicans to ask themselves, "Who can we bet on? Which faction can best consolidate the rest of the party leading into the November election?"

McCabe was elected by the residents of Graham County to attend the state's Republican convention. Presented with answering that question, he implicitly posed others: Which one of these factions can I get to include some dispensation for Black people? Which one can I get to advocate for us? He knew that he would have to go back to his constituents and explain why he was putting his support behind one faction and explain why he would support a man to be nominated for president on the Republican ticket at the national convention in Chicago.

McCabe took Hall with him to Topeka, where the Kansas State Republican Convention was held. There they connected with William Bolden Townsend, the former obstructor of John Niles's bid to recoup aid for Nicodemus. Known as W.B., Townsend was one of the most formidable forces in state Republican politics. After studying law at the University of Kansas, he had run the post office in Leavenworth and soon had come to be known as the "Afro-American Diplomat" for his slate of accomplishments. His proximity to the state's locus of power—a five-to-six-hour ride to Topeka—made him a useful connection for Hall and McCabe to have. So the three of them corralled enough votes to ensure that Townsend's name was nominated to the list of representatives from Kansas for the Republican National Convention.

But McCabe wasn't done yet. He wanted political assurances that Black people wouldn't be left behind. He expressed an almost implicit understanding that representation alone did not matter enough without sufficient guarantees. He wanted those guarantees because it wasn't certain that Townsend would actually land on the delegate ticket. McCabe took it upon himself to begin navigating that three-way split in the party. He felt that it was in his best interests to back the most moderate candidate, the one who had a reputation of favor-trading and aligning with conservative causes, ones that split from advocating for a return to the Radical Republicanism that gave the nation the Thirteenth, Fourteenth, and Fifteenth Amendments and Black people some greater purchase in a society that had devalued them.

Despite the lobbying McCabe did, Townsend was not offered a delegate seat—just an alternate, which Townsend took as a metaphorical slap in the face and turned it down. Such behavior angered people like McCabe and Hall, who felt that they had squandered their political capital backing his nomination. Crestfallen, McCabe wrote that "while there [I] strove hard, single-handed, to secure a representation for my race, but without avail."

But there were complications. McCabe had chosen to attend the Republican Convention over the Black one and didn't get as much as some members of the Black convention believed they deserved. At the Colored Convention, they discussed what to do about the Exodusters. At the Republican Convention, McCabe chose to lobby white Republicans in whom he thought power lay, with limited success. The other problem was that Reverend L. Fulbright of Shawnee stated for the record at the Colored Convention that even though McCabe was at the Republican convention, he had not done enough to get the "claims of 25,000 colored people" recognized and sorted by his Republican friends and colleagues on the state and national levels. In other words, they believed McCabe had abdicated his role of representing Black people.

This enraged McCabe as soon as word reached him.

"I am proud of the record which I made for my race and self at that convention," McCabe wrote. "I regard such attacks" from people like Fulbright as evidence of "envy or spleen—I am undecided which." For McCabe, public divisiveness was corrosive to a community so nascent in its acquaintance with freedom and power. So, "It is his weakness," McCabe continued, "and he is so small a factor in our political economy that no harm can possibly accrue to me or mine by indulging him in it."

McCabe wanted his comrades to see beyond the present and beyond the political-economic footprint of the Colored Conventions to realize that they were part of an electorate so powerful that it could dictate the outcome of every election.

But instead of stopping there, McCabe moved toward what would become a habit, ad hominem attacks on critics who found fault with his political style: "The race, at least a portion of it which is domiciled in Kansas, has so many of these crabid dyspeptic individuals among it, who are wholly unfit to take the lead themselves, and yet are jealous of other and better men going to the front, as to seriously impede its progress." He told everyone—from readers to his political friends turned enemies like Fulbright—that he was both a better man and that he was heading to the front ranks of leadership. In other words, he was coming for their spots.

He criticized the Colored Conventions further, writing that "instead of having granted to us our just dues from the political organization with whom it affiliated [the Republican Party] we must beg, and hold State Conventions [Colored Conventions] and resolute, in hopes of securing our rights." His focus was and would continue to be politics. In his view, "the reverend gentleman [Fulbright] has evidently outlived his usefulness." In McCabe's mind, what use was a minister who organized Colored Conventions when that was not where power and influence were located? "Looking back on a mis-spent life is endeavoring to drag down to his level someone to share his misery. Perhaps a course of light diet will lengthen out his span of life. Stronger food than what I have given him would hurry him to an untimely grave, unwept, unhonored, and unsung."

McCabe was quickly pushing beyond the station in which many thought he belonged. And he did not care.

1882: The Year of "His Black Politics"

PARSONS, KANSAS, 1882

Several propositions will be laid before [your] consideration. But I will only speak of mine . . . [I] propose to ask—not a gift, for sure, to[o] proud to beg (as beggars)—for a loan and the privilege of entering the Oklahoma lands, and settling down for once. Where we can train our children in religion and virtue, and develop our own manhood, and do our part in making America a second Eden.

—REVEREND W. B. AVERY'S ADDRESS TO THE CONVENTION OF
COLORED MEN, APRIL 27, 1882, IN PARSONS, KANSAS

The anti–St. John faction wanted to load the ticket down with a nigger," the *Garnett Journal* reported along with a collection of other newspapers around the state. It was 1882, Governor St. John was running for reelection, and this time McCabe joined him on the ballot, as the Republican candidate for state auditor. The ambitious McCabe, it seemed, was being used as a pawn by white elites to duel with one another. The governor wanted McCabe to run to draw Black votes to the Republicans and nothing more; the governor's opponents, meanwhile, wanted McCabe to repel white votes.

Even at the Republican state convention where he was nominated,

McCabe was humiliated by St. John. He and his supporters admitted later that they had "only designed [McCabe's candidacy] to be a 'compliment' for it has always been held by the Republicans of this State that a nigger was too heavy a load for even that party to weigh down the ticket with." The governor even tried to backpedal and support McCabe publicly—only for those who hated St. John to give McCabe even more votes. The thought was that if McCabe was on the ticket, St. John would surely lose in the general election.

McCabe almost secured the nomination on the first ballot, but there was just enough opposition to it that St. John's team adjourned to give them time to determine how to remove McCabe's name from nomination. But as onlookers remembered, they "failed utterly to prevail on the anties to let up on McCabe. They wanted to stuff [the] nigger down the throats of the St. John men, and they did. This is how McCabe got on the ticket, and the reason why he was not kicked out."

The goal of St. John's men was to feign support for Black voters and their issues without having a Black person on the ticket. William L. Eagleson, an owner and publisher of the *Colored Citizen*, the first Black-owned newspaper in Kansas, and a Black hell-raiser in the state—who had escaped slavery to get to Kansas—tried to publish all of this in more mainstream press outlets. He approached one white-owned newspaper after another, only to be rejected each time.

The consensus among Kansas Republicans was that McCabe on the ticket would destroy St. John's chances and those of the Republican Party. For McCabe, this was a surprise. But it shouldn't have been: It was just another unfortunate consequence of being Black, political, and ambitious. For Eagleson and for McCabe, it was an indication of what was to come in November.

It was also a glimpse of the challenges Black politicians faced across the country—challenges that they knew could not be resolved until they forged their own political path. For Eagleson, the events of this nomination process, his waning confidence in the Republican Party, and his evaporating belief in Kansas began to cast the prospect of some-place new—like Oklahoma—in a rosier shade.

And he wasn't alone. Black people around the state were beginning to hear whispers of what it might mean if Kansas turned out not to be the promised land they once thought. Perhaps it was time to consider what kind of politics would lead to the creation of their own promised land.

—◄━►—

Kansas was full of ambitious Black people who believed that they were their own Moses. And that ambition provoked an increasing tension when it clashed with the intentions of others—particularly white others.

However, it was clear that the leaders of Kansas's overwhelmingly Republican political establishment—many of them veterans of Bleeding Kansas—wanted a free Kansas in their definition, not a Kansas in which Black people had an equal share of power and a say in political decision making. So they placed formal and informal limits on just how diverse Kansas's political leadership was going to be. This led to two divergent options for Black Kansans with political ambitions. The first was to do like McCabe and eschew politicking within the Black community, which he referred to as "petty squabbles" and "fights for young men with small dreams," in order to gain acceptance within the white political establishment and hope that Black people would sup-port the Republican ballot on which he hoped to see his name. It was a strategy that successful Black predecessors like Senator Blanche Bruce of Mississippi and Congressman John Mercer Langston of Virginia had used. And to some great extent, McCabe saw a viable path.

The other option was for McCabe to leave Kansas and move again to a new potential Eden: Oklahoma.

1880 was both the year of the Republican convention at which Mc-Cabe tried and failed to nominate W. B. Townsend for a delegate seat for the upcoming Republican convention and the year of McCabe's own defenestration at the hands of Black politicians in Kansas who felt he hadn't done enough to advocate for Black people in the state. Colored Convention attendees in Topeka had lambasted him and attracted a reaction soaked in outrage. They ridiculed him for doing what they wanted him to do—supporting and advocating for Black candidates. He simply had not been as successful as they wanted.

While on the surface this may have ended McCabe's involvement in the Colored Conventions, his popularity among Black people remained steady while his recognition among some white politicians actually increased.

When he visited Topeka, McCabe took the opportunity to mingle with not just Black politicians and voters, but white Republican kingmakers as well, even casting nominating ballots for Preston Plumb, a veteran free-stater U.S. senator who became a friend of McCabe's and a co-conspirator about a Black Oklahoma. McCabe also threw his support behind one of Kansas's wealthier bankers, State Senator Perry Hutchinson, whose railroad, milling, and banking interests were netting some $400,000 per year ($12.8 million in 2024 dollars). His bank had quickly ballooned to average deposits of $450,000 per year (nearly $14.4 million in 2024). John A. Martin, a popular former Civil War general, also befriended McCabe at the state Republican convention just a few short years before Martin successfully ran for governor.

As McCabe continued to learn how the political game was played, his friendships and rising profile made him a household name among decision makers. The hard-nosed politicking that he was lambasted for at the Colored Convention was what distinguished him in the state's white politics and decision making.

In her book *Whose Black Politics?*, political scientist Andra Gillespie argues that Black politicians often have better chances at winning statewide elections when they first lose lower-office elections for being perceived as not Black enough. Gillespie uses the example of Cory Booker losing his 2002 bid for mayor of Newark, New Jersey, to Sharpe James, a staple of New Jersey's Black political elite, and Barack Obama losing his first race for Congress against Bobby Rush. These losses made both candidates, who had pristine academic credentials and pasts that didn't necessarily comport with the narratives of what some might consider "typical" Black politics, the kind of Black politicians who were "inoffensive" and "nonthreatening." Obama, with his biracial identity and his handful of years working on Chicago's South Side, could not beat the bona fides of "Blackness" that Rush carried in his community as a Black Panther. Obama's loss in Illinois's 1st Congressional District communicated to voters in places like Oak Park, Peoria, and Joliet, communities with high concentrations of moderate white voters, that while he was Black he was not so bent on advocating for Black issues that he would prove unacceptable to them. Like Booker, Obama became more palatable to white voters with the loss.

The same could be said of McCabe. Even more, McCabe differed markedly from the version of Black politician most white people in Kansas had become familiar with. Think about Leavenworth, Kansas, where his colleague W. B. Townsend lived. It was said of Leavenworth that "if race relations were ugly in Kansas, they were especially ugly in Leavenworth and in surrounding Leavenworth County." It was known as a "sink-hole of iniquity," according to historian Brent Campney, and a center of racist violence. In contrast, McCabe represented the antithesis. He hailed from a part of Kansas considered remote, away from where many Black people had concentrated and from a town, Nicodemus, noted for its interracial makeup, its open calls to Black and white entrepreneurs alike to settle.

McCabe's political losses, his race, and his adopted hometown all became ingredients in a recipe of a meteoric political rise.

◄━►

McCabe's talent for converting the apparent loss into a potential win was aided by the nature of campaigning in Kansas.

At the time, primaries weren't door-to-door, close conversations between hopeful officeholders and potential voters. State parties would hold conventions, and at those conventions power brokers would send delegates (often themselves) from each district or county to nominate candidates for governor, lieutenant governor, attorney general, and at-large congressman. Statewide elected office didn't require McCabe to spend time appealing to the masses so much as it demanded that he travel around the state to be interviewed by regional leaders who held political sway—often showing up to local Republican conventions to extract commitments to do as they wanted once he was elected. Getting a party's nomination required a majority of support from state convention delegates, which required diligent efforts by a network of supporters to sway the majority of precinct committeemen in enough counties to win a majority of delegates. The entire process remained far from actual voters.

County by county, newspaper by newspaper, politician by politician, and delegate by delegate, McCabe made his case: Entrust him with the responsibility of becoming the ultimate clerk, Kansas's auditor.

◄━►

But in the Parsons Convention of Colored Men of 1882 that invited Black people from all over the state, the hope to exercise power within the Kansas political system was waning and the voices to abandon the effort to make Kansas into a promised land for Black people had grown louder than ever.

The invitation from W. B. Avery and others, dated March 24, 1882, read, "A large proportion of the present colored residents of Southern Kansas have arrived in this State during the last three years from Texas, Louisiana, and Mississippi. Most of them have been cultivators of the soil before coming here." The inviters wanted it known that the Black newcomers to Kansas did "not possess the requisite teams, farming implements, etc., to properly engage in it, or carry it on successfully." They were telegraphing their disappointment to the state, its governor, and philanthropic leaders that they had been derelict in their stated duty of securing the general welfare of its Black residents.

But Avery was not done. "Some of the best white friends of our race think they have a plan in view" that would require "the blessing of God and our own faithful individual efforts, to improve our pecuniary condition." It was for that reason that they called a convention to discuss what could be done to ameliorate their own condition. They invited delegates from "each colored church of any denomination in any locality" and "each community of five or more families of colored people," which were to send "one man for every one hundred of their men, women, and children."

Avery and the other men who gathered at the opera house in Parsons, Kansas, had lost patience with the promise of Kansas and believed their opportunity lay farther south and west. While McCabe wasn't yet convinced that Kansas was no longer viable—his political career was on the rise, after all—other Black men cast their eyes wider.

◄—►

As prepared as McCabe should have been for the rigor of a political campaign where he had to sell himself as the most viable candidate to an almost entirely white audience, he never expected the support and the pushback that he received.

Each newspaper that interviewed him placed bets on whether he could be elected. The *Atchison Globe* wrote that "[McCabe's] friends predict that he will make a strong race" and called him "capable, trustworthy and deserving." They felt that McCabe, "a colored man of letters" made the best candidate because "[he] has so little colored blood in his veins that it can only be detected with a microscope"—a signal to readers that he wasn't *too* Black. His interviews led papers to emphasize his regionality more than his race, an attempt to ensure that the Republican Party had greater representation from a part of Kansas often overlooked. The *Kirwin Chief* made the case that "the western papers continue to warm up in the cause of E.P. McCabe for Auditor of State." To emphasize his capability and to warm him up to white power brokers, the paper touted, "Mr. McCabe is a competent gentleman, and in the name of a large class of true and staunch republicans has a right to seek a place on the state ticket." The reason: "Republicans of the State will do well to recognize the claims of the west, and also the race to which Mr. McCabe belongs."

To say that the Republican Party dominated Kansas at that time was an understatement. Since the state's admission to the Union some thirty years before, its legislature and governor's office had been controlled by Republicans and the Republican Party. And part of the way the Republicans' power solidified was not due to some peculiar stranglehold the party had on the moral and political impulses of its constituents. It was outreach—in word more than deed—to the state's newcomers, Black voters included. It was so ingrained that it was understood that Governor John Pierce St. John's ascendancy would continue.

McCabe's rise was accelerating with every newspaper endorsement he received. The accumulation of endorsements prompted the *Millbrook Herald* to dedicate its entire second page to throwing its weight behind McCabe by listing as many announcements as could fit on its pre-convention edition of the paper. The editorial team of the *Herald* started by stating that "the *Millbrook Herald* presents E.P. McCabe, of Graham County, for auditor of state, and vouches for his fitness." The *Abilene Gazette* and the *Leavenworth Times* on two different sides of the state echoed one another, offering the same assessment: "He is a well educated colored man." The *Beloit Gazette* touted how bright McCabe was. The *Stockton Record* opined that McCabe was so qualified that he might as well be called "a smoked Irishman"— signaling to their white readership that he didn't have too much of what they might consider to be the stain of Blackness on him, while also negatively assessing Irish immigrants, conveying that at least McCabe wasn't worse than them. His "rare intellect and ability," which no doubt meant to signify a differentiation from most Black people, added the *Logan Enterprise* to his endorsement collection. Most of these endorsements came after local and county-level Republican conventions were held and McCabe's endorsement was secured, and he or his surrogates and allies made the case for him by letter or in person.

His endorsements didn't hail just from Kansas. The *Chicago Conservator* weighed in to attest to McCabe's expertise and fitness for the office of auditor. The *Conservator* used its pages to express how electing McCabe would improve Black Kansans' chance to seize the electoral and political power they had yet to embrace fully. As the editorial noted, "Kansas has a colored voting population of nearly or quite 18,000. They comprise an easy one fourth of the Republican party of that state and yet there is not a single colored man today holding an office higher than county clerk within her borders. There should be at least three representatives and one state senator in her legislators, representing by their identification with the race of colored voters, and the position sought by Mr. McCabe." Black Kansans had been denied their political due long enough. But the writer made sure to indict the Republican Party, which had benefited from the fealty of its Black supporters while failing to adequately include them in its electoral representation. Both internal and external pressures positioned McCabe as the near-inevitable choice.

⸺◆⸺

There were just two problems: First, Governor St. John had already served two two-year terms. And second, racism.

McCabe, even if he got the nomination for state auditor, would be running on a ticket that was garnering skeptics as much as it was gaining support. Governors in Kansas didn't have much power: Much of it rested with party bosses at local and county levels. And St. John had grabbed hold of one of the most divisive issues of the day—the temperance movement that wanted to ban alcohol. All of that could have been overlooked, except that Kansans had an allergic reaction to the notion that a governor would serve a third term. Party insiders and Democrats lobbied against it and began clamoring for term limits for governors. Without much power to do more than to curry favor with voters (and party bosses), St. John's candidacy was beleaguered, because many Republicans alleged reelecting St. John to a third term would amount to "bossism" and "third termism," a political position that lobbied against the creation and running of a political machine.

St. John knew that he would get the Republican nomination for governor. But winning the election in November began to feel like a much more difficult challenge than it had a few months earlier.

So how could St. John solidify his electoral strength?

By throwing his initial support behind McCabe to shore up Black support during the general election, without any intention of having McCabe on the ticket.

During the Republican state convention, McCabe did, in fact, secure the nomination as state auditor. White Republicans like then-congressman Harrison P. Kelley were said to be so moved by the race-forward actions of the Republican Party to nominate a Black man that he waved his hat for what a reporter said was some twenty minutes. "He said it is the happiest day of my life!" But in its report on the convention by the *Parsons Daily Eclipse* in Parsons, Kansas, a reporter wrote that "St. John had promised that the darkeys should be well taken care of, but he never intended that McCabe should receive the nomination." One of the antagonistic Republican leaders, George W. Reed, thought it was "the most hilarious nomination he ever knew of, giving the negro the auditorship when he should have had lieutenant governor, because the auditor has access to the treasury at all times and admission to the money vaults when he sees fit to do so." The meaning was clear: You couldn't trust the Black man with the state's money. If St. John wanted to make sure that Black people were well taken care of, he should have offered McCabe the largely ceremonial position of lieutenant governor. Giving a Black man the responsible job of auditor, regardless of his two decades of experience, was a step too far.

Reed wasn't alone in this assessment. "Many of the best men in the convention and among lobbyists," the *Daily Eclipse* reported, thought it better to stick to issues like securing voting rights for women, prohibition, and legislating the creation and promotion of more railroads. In their words, adding "a colored man on the ticket the party has a load to carry that will make it groan seriously," casting doubt on the viability of McCabe's electability. And even as his nomination was in reach and the votes in the primary collected, the convention was not without controversy, indicating to McCabe how limited his remit might be should he be elected and how limited his influence might be in a third St. John term as an ambitious Black man. That perhaps it really was time to start anew, as the men of the Parsons Colored Convention had recommended.

One of those most faithful Parsons Convention conveners was newspaperman William L. Eagleson. As Hall moved away from the combative political life in exchange for journalism, Eagleson became McCabe's closest political chum.

Maybe McCabe's cavalier approach to politics was what drew Eagleson to McCabe. Maybe it was that McCabe saw the Republican Party the way Eagleson did: as a vessel, albeit a weak one, to exercise power on behalf of Black people in Kansas. Eagleson didn't see the party as strong enough on Black issues. And this wasn't his first tangle with politics. In 1878, he tried and failed to get a Black man, T. W. Henderson, nominated by the Republicans for lieutenant governor. He realized then that the Republican Party saw him and others like him as a token, something to be cashed in at election season and otherwise forgotten.

Perhaps what drew Eagleson to McCabe was the realpolitik with which they both approached the task of elevating Black people and their power. They came to play the game of politics. Like McCabe, Eagleson wouldn't remain quiet about the chicanery he witnessed within the Republican Party. So while he lobbied Black attendees of the Parsons Convention to pursue the Oklahoma colonization project, he chronicled the activities of McCabe before and at the convention.

As much of a drag on the ticket as many feared McCabe might be, Eagleson did not.

Should McCabe win in the general election, for the first time in state and national history, every one of the state's financial transactions—from paying out war bonds, to overseeing capital outlays for railroad investments, to administering state tax collections and revenue distributions—would be signed by a Black man. Never had a Black man reviewed, approved, or denied tax assessments.

To some, this might seem like a significant escalation of responsibility for McCabe. But for McCabe this was yet another clerkship—albeit one with far greater implications and consequences than he ever had known. If he were to win, it would be without the limitations that he found in New York or in Chicago. This time, he would be captaining his own ship, a statewide office with autonomy. His job would be to hold other officials accountable and ensure that they didn't write checks they couldn't cash. As much as McCabe's naysayers wanted to blame him for the mired political straits of St. John at the top of the ticket, St. John was a weaker candidate than they could have imagined. And the vote tallies in November showed by just how much.

Elections of the period could take days, sometimes weeks, to tally. Precinct election committees would report in to district committees. District ones would report in to county committees. The counties would take out billets in the newspapers and community bulletins to report their numbers immediately after sending reports to the state—intermittently reporting data from precincts, towns, and counties as newspapers received them. The entire ordeal was tedious and time-consuming, and across the state newspapers would pensively await results. And in these numbers, Kansans began to clarify what they thought about McCabe and his effect on St. John's campaign for a third gubernatorial term.

13

"His Black Politics" in Exile

TOPEKA, KANSAS, 1887

Translated from judicial activity in racial cases both before and after *Brown*, this principle of "interest convergence" provides: The interest of blacks in achieving racial equality will be accommodated only when it converges with the interests of whites.

—DERRICK A. BELL, JR., *Harvard Law Review*, 1980

While down in Wyandotte County, McCabe was asked by a reporter, "Are the colored people satisfied with the Republican party?" It was a question meant to position McCabe as the sole and most important voice to speak for what the white public might have assumed to be a monolith. The year was 1883, one year after he was successfully elected as state auditor on the St. John ticket, but with a year left before the next election. Now it was McCabe who reporters were constantly asking whether he would publicly trash the Republican Party.

By now McCabe had become adept at playing the political game. He deftly answered with the optimistic vagueness of a seasoned politician. "We are always satisfied with the Republican Party," he said.

When they asked him to opine on the qualities of his new boss, Democratic governor George Glick, McCabe said, "Personally, I like Governor Glick, and the colored race can have no reason for dislike for him except that he is a Democrat."

In the 1882 election, Governor St. John had not just been outperformed by McCabe; he'd been soundly beaten by his challenger. Glick had been clever. Eight Republican governors had been elected before this election. And although a Democrat, Glick had promoted himself as a proponent of good governance who was less interested in big promises or prohibition efforts and more interested in managing the state without patronage, which voters assumed would be rife with it should St. John be given another term. And unlike national Democrats or southern Democrats at the time, Glick wasn't an outright enemy of Black suffrage. He even actively pushed for women's suffrage.

Voter tallies didn't include the number or percentage of Black Kansans who ultimately voted for Glick. But we do know that Glick's campaign represented a sea change in the way Black people positioned themselves within Kansas politics. St. John was increasingly seen both by Black people and by his political opponents as unrepresentative of the people and as a party machine. In places like Tammany Hall in New York, nineteenth-century American party "bosses" ran their fiefdoms imperiously, only checking in with Black, white immigrant, and poor voters when election season came around.

Before the 1882 Kansas election, advertisements and columns were taken out that encouraged Black people to bolt from the Republican Party and cast their ballots for Glick. "The henchmen of St. John are bending every effort to have him reelected," one writer in the *Burlington Independent* wrote. "The anti-bossism faction of the Republican party of that State will vote for Glick, the Democratic nominee, as a rebuke to St. John and the machine. Now what course should the colored people of Kansas pursue?"

"Ought they to support St. John," the writer continued, "simply because he is the Republican nominee—nominated because by a dexterous manipulation of the primaries, densely packed in his interest, men were sent to the Topeka convention in his interest, and thereby override the will of the people?"

The question clearly referenced the hysteria of the Republican convention, the volleying of McCabe's nomination as a political controversy. McCabe was used to whip up support among Black people, only for them to realize that St. John only saw McCabe as a tool, not a comrade. A man from Kansas City named Nero who was known for organizing Black voters wrote in the same article, "No, the colored voters of Kansas must not forget on election day that prior to the Topeka convention St. John, to get their support, promised to have a colored man placed on the State ticket; that that promise gained for him the colored support; that after his nomination, treacherously, he used his influence against the nomination of McCabe; that McCabe was nominated, not by St. John men, but by the anti–St. John men; that St. John is not the choice of the people but of the machine; and that the St. John men will scratch McCabe on election day, while anti–St. John men will support him."

Nero wanted readers to understand that St. John was not loyal to Black interests or even to the Black candidate he supported to get more Black voters. If he couldn't be loyal to the interests of a Black candidate on his own ticket, Nero and the *Burlington Independent* suggested, then he couldn't be loyal to the Black people who had helped give him two consecutive terms.

This helped distance McCabe from St. John. Now, a vote for McCabe was a vote against the establishment, the party bosses who did what was in their self-interest and not in the interest of the people. A vote for St. John became a continuation of the status quo, which had the potential to worsen.

Two days after the ballots were cast, the *Parsons Weekly Eclipse* reported that "McCabe beat St. John in Parsons by a hundred and seventy-six votes," though McCabe was far down the ballot. In communities like Cowley County, where St. John showed up on the ballot in fifteen districts versus McCabe's twelve, St. John received 1,517 votes and McCabe 1,400. McCabe beat St. John in Oswego, a predominantly white community. In Mitchell County, McCabe received nearly 35 percent more votes than the governor. In Ellis County, St. John got 11 percent fewer votes than McCabe. El Dorado gave McCabe a resounding win, beating his other competitors for the position of auditor with over 81 percent of the vote and a voter turnout 10 percent higher than St. John. And there were virtual ties between the two in Bunker Hill and Franklin, Lyon, and Rice Counties.

As more results came in, it became clear that McCabe was surging beyond expectations. When the vote went to the people, the people—Black and white—sent him to the state capital.

—◄═►—

When the newly elected state auditor left Nicodemus for Topeka, he could not know that he was leaving the remarkable town forever. In Topeka, he was once again busy trying to craft a promised land—not just in Nicodemus, but across the whole state. Buzz about Oklahoma continued to swirl, but the prospects of a Black Oklahoma paled to the promise of opportunity that McCabe had experienced as the Old West's first Black statewide-elected politician, the keeper of the state's coin.

By the end of 1883, McCabe had to campaign for another nomination to keep the job he already had. But with supportive opinion columns—such as from the Topeka correspondent of the *Kansas City Times*, a Democratic, white-owned newspaper—it seemed as if he would sail to another nomination. His management and administrative skills seemed deft and the leaders of both parties seemed to realize that. As prognosticators of the *Kansas City Times* had it, "it is very doubtful whether [McCabe] has any opposition. He has performed the duties of his office so well, and with such utter abandonment of tentation or proud feeling, that to go back on him now would be a deadener to the Republican party." In other words, the Republicans would be doing themselves an electoral and moral disservice if they did not renominate McCabe.

The Topeka correspondent continued, "When the precedent was established last year of giving colored men a recognition, and Mr. E.P. McCabe was nominated for Auditor, hundreds of people predicted that he would be a failure"—not the least of whom were scores of St. John supporters and St. John himself. But "in the face of every obs[t]acle and misgiving, he took hold like a man, has conducted himself as a man of ability, and is deserving to be renominated."

McCabe was renominated and reelected without the fanfare and embarrassment that the Republican Party suffered under St. John, despite Glick losing reelection to the Republican candidate, John A. Martin.

Perhaps it was inevitable that in McCabe's eyes the job of state auditor became old hat. Approving railroad expansions, issuing reimbursements, overseeing the financial management associated with the creation of state university charters, paying state employees' salaries, providing warrants, selling land for school building developments, and conducting surveys of population and landscapes had their limits. McCabe had become a fixture not just of Republican politics, but of Kansas governance.

That is, until a confrontation prompted people to wonder if he had overstayed his welcome.

◄—►

McCabe's record as auditor had become practically unimpeachable: Promising nothing but efficiency, he gave few interviews and abandoned weighing in on political issues like temperance. Even so, he found himself in the unfortunate plight of running for a third term, which that year became a political lightning rod. It was no accident that of all the officials doing so, it was McCabe, the sole Black official, who drew the most criticism.

As the nominations were being sought in May 1886, McCabe was lumped into the small club of politicians who had attempted to be elected to a third term. In the *Osage City Free Press*, the editors wrote, "General Grant was defeated for a Third Term even after he had been out of office four years. Are [State Treasurer Samuel] Howe and McCabe better men than Grant?" The hope was to start a conversation in which people—powerful party leaders and average Kansans alike—would begin to question McCabe's renomination. "St. John was nominated for a third term, and the people rebelled and defeated him at the election. Messrs. Howe and McCabe should profit from his misfortune," the editors wrote. McCabe should share the same fate, they thought, if he chose to seek another term. The allegation was clear: "If they loved the Republican party half as well as they love office, they would step aside without an invitation."

But McCabe wasn't there for the Republicans or for the Democrats. He was there for himself and for those who looked like him. And being state auditor got him that much closer to realizing his own ambition. When the *Gate City Press* of Kansas City, Missouri, came to his office two years earlier for an interview that the *New York Globe* would later carry, he reveled at the opportunity to demonstrate what he had done in the office, how it had been reorganized, how he and his clerk, De Randhomie, had arranged the large stacks of papers and records into alphabetical order. "Every one" both "white and black," the reporter alleged, "spoke touchingly upon Mr. McCabe's administration." The sentiment was "unanimous." The reporter, who had traveled all the way to Kansas, wrote that McCabe's success spoke for itself and that each person was "unexcelled." The reporter left with the impression "that a renomination and election should be set down as a matter of course, being but a fitting expression of our appreciation for the labors of a worthy public servant."

Such words might ring familiar to the complaints lobbed at St. John. But there was one difference: St. John had been attacked with allegations of machine politics, big promises, and bigger letdowns. With McCabe, there was no such criticism. McCabe was being punished for the *lack* of success of St. John and the appearance of a political machine. What was animating these accusations against McCabe was that his skin was darker than it could've been to secure the confidence of men. Underlying the idea of "third termism" was an unpleasant subtext: If a white man in a state that had been Republican since its founding couldn't secure the deed, then a Black man could have no bigger hopes. The concerns of third termism were being used as a veil to jettison McCabe's campaign and to whiten the ranks of Kansas's elected officials.

Take the Republican campaign for the third term of Samuel T. Howe, the state's white treasurer. Howe had the kind of sterling work record that resembled McCabe's. Yet his skin was white, and, even better, his blood was blue. Howe could easily trace his family's ancestry from England and making their way to Massachusetts on the ship *Truelove* in 1635. Among his family were congressmen and lawyers. McCabe was called by opponents a carpetbagger. But Howe, though truly a carpetbagger—having moved to Kansas seeking political office after having served in Republican politics in Ohio—never got that label. Maybe this is why the charges of third termism missed Howe and hit McCabe.

And although it had taken four years, the accusations that McCabe was part of the political machine were beginning to stick. Going into the Republican state convention in July 1886, McCabe was seen as a beleaguered candidate. Now there were a sea of other candidates interested in securing his job. These challengers wanted to take down a prominent Black official, but they also wanted to usurp the mantle McCabe had claimed four years before: the anti-establishment, anti-machine candidate.

Unlike the first and second times that McCabe ran, he came to the convention with no certainty of what the future held. In the lead-up, Wyandotte, a county in which McCabe had received more votes than St. John in the 1882 election, refused to put McCabe's name on the slate to even be considered. The next several months became a function of managing decline, for McCabe hung his hopes for renomination on that of Howe, the wealthy state treasurer. He told his waning number of supporters that he was "confident that in the case Mr. Howe is nominated for treasurer [McCabe's] claims for auditor will be duly considered." Put another way: If it could work for Howe, perhaps the voters might overlook the third-term issues lobbed at McCabe and make him the Republican nominee again.

"Does Mr. Howe smile any prettier or any oftener than Mr. Mc-Cabe that the Harvey County republicans prefer the former for a Third Term and reject the latter?" asked one columnist in the *Osage City Free Press*. "Or, is because Mr. McCabe is a gentleman of color?" And yet this writer was no supporter of McCabe. According to him, McCabe had not gained his position because of his talents, experiences, or abilities; instead, the writer leaned on the idea that "McCabe was nominated in the first place for no other reason than his color." Attacking both McCabe and Howe, the writer drew on the Old Testament to sharpen his condemnation of them both: "The Jonahs must go overboard together—pitching one of them overboard won't quiet the storm." Even here, the writer continued to deny McCabe's equality and worth. After all, Howe had to go because he sought a third term; McCabe, meanwhile, didn't deserve to be there in the first place, as he had gotten there thanks to his race, not his ability.

Disagreeing with McCabe's pursuit of a third term had the veneer of evenhandedness—an attempt to ensure that McCabe would not fall prey to the bossism that hurt other Kansas politicians. Discouraging his third term could be cast by his opponents to be a call for greater fairness, equality, and a fairer distribution of electoral power. But what it really was, according to the *Wichita Daily Eagle*, was "rot, hog wash, and demagogical."

The Democrats and Republicans who organized against McCabe's third term had supported other candidates who had held four to six terms, which they failed to mention. Party bosses often would nominate and elect a candidate in one county, then move that same candidate to another county to ensure that they wouldn't have the stain of overstaying their welcome. The anti-machine anti-bossists were in fact bosses when they decided that the Black man holding state office had overstayed his welcome and pushed ahead of what elite Republicans had decided was appropriate. It is for that reason that McCabe's supporters alleged that those who opposed McCabe while supporting other third-term candidates "are not loaded down with principle, even if they are 'good fellows.'"

There was not much difference between McCabe and these other men who had served far more than their terms at county levels, except that McCabe was a Black man who had ambition and talent. He had become too bright a sun, whose orbit might interrupt the white-led machine politics of the Republican Party of Kansas.

⊷⊶⊷

Try as he might, McCabe lost in November. The postmortems were uniform in their assessment as to why. The *Philadelphia Record* wrote, "In Kansas, too the 'colored man and brother' was emphatically laid on the shelf." Put another way, Kansas, once considered the Black promised land, had reverted to a type of wilderness, a prolonged one that contained the full lives of thousands—one where Black people could be accepted as refugees, and maybe even citizens, but not as leaders of all people.

McCabe found himself not just out of office, but out of a job, out of work. A long list of jobs immediately awaited Howe—who also lost—along with the financial foothold in America's political establishment his family left him through their invention of the solid-head pin and the profitable Howe Pin Company. He soon became a prominent real estate owner in Topeka and—as McCabe's supporters warned—shifted from treasurer to arguably the most important commission in the state: the state railroad commission, which the Kansas legislature had juiced with capital, talent, and authority. McCabe received no such sinecure.

For a man so ambitious, returning to Nicodemus seemed untenable, both in fact and feeling. So instead of heading back, McCabe quickly went forward, busying himself finding his next move.

It seemed that McCabe's political career had come to a quick end—a meteoric rise and an Icarian fall. The failure of his third bid for state auditor came at the precise time that his friend Eagleson and others had garnered greater support for the Oklahoma scheme. As a matter of faith, Black Kansans began to convene "Oklahoma Clubs," small collections of Black people who could, like McCabe, feel the weight on themselves crafted by white politicians who capped Black ascent. Admittedly, life in Kansas for many members of these Oklahoma Clubs was not as bad as it was for many throughout the Jim Crow South. But the task migrated to trying to survive instead of working to thrive.

McCabe's political loss was not the end of his world. Rather, it was the beginning of a new chapter. But until the Oklahoma colonization scheme became outlined in detail, McCabe would have to test out the strategy among the men who held the power over Indian Territory.

And that road led to Washington, D.C., where politicians were asking yet again, what would come of this new world?

For McCabe, what he thought was his promised land— Oklahoma—was beckoning him long before he could decipher the details of his part in shaping it. But McCabe, like the Exodusters, was his own Moses. And like Moses, exile gave rise to a path to a new promised land.

PART III

TAKING THE
(UN)PROMISED LAND

We have met, not as paupers, but as men—tillers of the
soil—homeless, but not hopeless; strangers in a strange
land; but not without friends, tried and true! We are
here to deliberate, to [decide], and then to act! Will you
help us? Will you make common cause with us, and say
to this nation that the house has come and you must
meet it? Several propositions will be laid before you[r]
consideration. But I will only speak of mine . . . [I] propose to ask—not a gift, for sure, to[o] proud to beg (as
beggars)—for a loan and the privilege of entering the
Oklahoma lands, and settling down for once. Where
we can train our children in religion and virtue, and develop our own manhood, and do our part in making
America a second Eden.

—W. B. AVERY'S ADDRESS TO THE CONVENTION OF
COLORED MEN, APRIL 27, 1882

14

"No Man's Land"

THE KANSAS BORDER, 1889

The dream was especially espoused by Kansas blacks. When it became apparent that Oklahoma would open to settlement, Kansas newspapers such as *The American Citizen* (Topeka) urged every black who wanted 160 acres to prepare and watch diligently for the opening.

—DANIEL LITTLEFIELD AND LONNIE UNDERHILL,
"BLACK DREAMS AND 'FREE' HOMES"

Prairie schooners—covered wagons drawn by teams of horses—lined the outskirts of Arkansas City, Kansas, a sparsely populated town just over three miles north of the Oklahoma Territory. Inside these wagons, the newcomers—once-settled farmers turned unsettled seekers—could see into the lands that had been designated as "Unassigned Lands," which was code for lands taken from the Indigenous nations exiled from the East by the U.S. government. Now the territory *appeared* empty. This is why these settlers had drawn up their horses and wagons, waiting for these newly declared "public lands" to be formally opened to settlement. The transit stop at Arkansas City was hardly the only one developed to capitalize on the lands newly dispossessed from its Native inhabitants. It was just one of the closest outposts to the lands themselves. In fact, around the country settlers were gathering, preparing to make their own journeys into this territory. These settlement communities emerged soon after President Benjamin Harrison signed a proclamation on March 23, 1889, making 1.8 million acres of the Unassigned Lands—some of the most desirable land for cattle grazing—available to nearly anyone.

The lands of Oklahoma Territory were an opportunity for people across America to reconsider what their life could become. The Indigenous nations who had fully occupied the land were faced with questions of just how much of their land and their way of life they would be forced to give up. What hunting practices would be upended, what religious practices would disappear if they had to cede land and autonomy to the U.S. government and in turn to the people the government would open these lands to? This was the last stop of Native people's forced migration—or that was how it had been pitched to them during and immediately following the Indian Removal Act. But every promise the U.S. government had made to them had been broken. For poor whites—some of whom had believed that freed Black people had robbed them of opportunities in the South and the North—Oklahoma seemed a last desperate chance for opportunity and autonomy. For the formerly enslaved, Oklahoma was a last opportunity to embrace what America might offer. For some richer whites, it was a place of speculation: land sitting atop untold opportunity. For the federal government, Oklahoma remained a relative unknown—an opportunity to extend America and its imprint farther south and west.

This expansion of public lands was achieved by Harrison using two weapons: the threat of brute force, and racism. When Harrison became president in 1889, he was forced to deal with the complex issue of the Cherokee Outlet, a land found to be rich, but whose boundaries and ownership were due to broken treaties and the horrid displacement of Indigenous peoples. Grover Cleveland, his immediate predecessor, had not done nearly as much to get Harrison what he wanted: these lands in government hands.

Early in his presidency, Harrison made it clear to his administration that the Cherokee Nation and other Indigenous nations needed to embrace the inevitability of the expansion of the United States and that their lands would be co-opted into the expanding American frontier. In the time to come, it would be presented to the Cherokee Nation as a choice whether to earn some cash by leaving the land voluntarily or to be steamrolled off it violently. Publicly, Harrison's Cherokee Commission, also known as the Jerome Commission, placed a high priority on negotiation, but only toward the end of Indigenous autonomous ownership of those lands. The result was never in doubt, only the method for achieving it.

Ultimately, the United States bought the Cherokee Outlet on the cheap, for $8.5 million (approximately $297 million in 2024 dollars). In so doing, the government enabled itself to give a powerful, growing subset of the broader American citizenry a chance to get what most of them had never had access to before: 160 acres of land for themselves. The acreage lay available for them so long as they were willing to travel to the territory and develop it by cultivating it for five years. Mythmaking grew as quickly as their ambitions let them. Lionizing their ambitions, settlers would boast of what they would do and what they would achieve.

Just over the border from Arkansas City, Kansas, in the dry duskiness of Oklahoma's red dirt, sat a school. Created by a formal act of Congress in 1882, the Chilocco Indian Agricultural School conscripted school-age Indigenous children. It is possible that the families of settlers, just a few miles away, might have seen those children for what they were: prisoners; forced child laborers; children without a voice, being compelled to "civilize," leaving behind all that made them who they were.

Some may argue that many white families looking toward Oklahoma Territory were just as destitute as the Indigenous families of these child conscripts. In fact, they seemed destined for economic and social decline. But public policy is nothing if not a collection of choices made by people. Now, with a signature, some people's lives were about to improve, and some were about to be shattered yet again.

That land in which those schoolchildren lived, ate, and labored was the last bit of land the Cherokee Nation held in Oklahoma Territory outside the lands assigned to them to the east in what was Indian Territory. It was the throwaway acreage the U.S. government offered to the Cherokee Nation after they forced the nation onto the Trail of Tears. The Cherokee land stretched 60 by 225 miles, just south of the Kansas border in what is now north-central Oklahoma. For how much the United States had assaulted the Indigenous peoples by forcing them first off their ancestral lands in the Southeast and then onto this land, the Outlet enabled the Cherokee Nation to graze their own cattle and even generate revenue by leasing their land for the grazing of cattle by others.

But all that changed with Harrison's proclamation.

This was a crucial first step in removing the Cherokee from the land the U.S. government had given to the nation in perpetuity and selling it to homesteaders from the North and East. In a history of tragedies suffered by Indigenous nations at the hands of the federal government, this was a new chapter. When the Indigenous peoples, primarily the people of the so-called Five Tribes—the Muscogee Creek, Cherokee, Choctaw, Chickasaw, and Seminole (along with a bevy of smaller tribes)—were forced to leave their ancestral lands in the eastern United States, these autonomous groups were given a treaty that promised this would be the last time the U.S. government would force them to move. Most came from the Southeast during the administrations of Andrew Jackson and Martin Van Buren in the 1830s. Many fell ill and died and thousands lost loved ones along the eight-hundred-mile trek west.

At their hands, Indian Territory was created as destination of last resort. As much land as they had lost, and as much hardship they faced moving from the southeastern to the southwestern part of their country, this area, Indian Territory, would be theirs for all time.

It lasted only five decades.

Each of the Five Tribes had its own process of distributing land, which was often held communally. They also had their own practices for governing themselves, with their own legislative bodies and diplomatic arms. Each had their own ways of determining citizenship, arguably more comprehensively and accommodatingly than the United States did. Especially in the case of the Cherokee, Creek, and Seminole Nations, Black people whose ancestry was interlinked with these nations could find reparation and citizenship in nations that once held Black people as slaves, others as adopted citizens, and others as full, never-enslaved citizens. While the United States failed to muster the moral courage to integrate Black people into the country at large, these Indigenous nations did not bestow their citizenship by skin tone. Part of governing themselves meant creating greater opportunities for themselves and expanding who got to take part in the work of creating their own futures.

Even the Civil War did not infringe on their sovereignty, at least on paper. Each of the so-called Five Tribes involved itself (often begrudgingly) in the Civil War to varying degrees. Some, like the Choctaw and Chickasaw, allied primarily with the Confederacy, while others, like the Creek, Cherokee, and Seminole, split loyalties between the North and the South. At the conclusion of the war, the United States exploited the fact that some nations and individuals had fought for the Confederacy to extract further concessions, obtain more land, and rewrite treaties. Yet the nations still remained nominally independent. And the bulk of the land was still theirs. The next blow came with the loss of over 1.8 million acres and the leaving open of the Unassigned Lands, lands that once held their memories, practices, and homes.

Less than two decades later, the nation's capital again turned its attention to the territory. Although there were differences of opinion on how to carve the lands, the government's knives were out.

Senator Preston B. Plumb of Kansas, a supporter of McCabe's, wanted to open up Oklahoma for seemingly idealistic reasons. When he moved to Lawrence, Kansas, in 1856 at age nineteen, after being a newspaperman in his native Ohio, Plumb believed that Kansas represented an opportunity to stop the spread of slavery and a chance for anyone to put down roots, create a family, and invest in the building of what would soon be a state. He saw the same possibilities for Oklahoma Territory.

As he argued on the floor of the Senate, Plumb believed that the Indigenous people had had their say and had moved aside, ceding their lands. He believed that the Indian nations had already given up the land and that it should be left for new generations to till, build, and develop.

Most important, Plumb wanted a fairer distribution of lands on the frontier. He did not want speculators to control how land was distributed. Kansas had seen enough examples of such men—like the speculators who founded towns like Nicodemus—who had invested in towns and then disappeared, making thousands of dollars in profit (millions in today's dollars) off the hopes of the little guy. In fact, the Kansas legislature sent an urgent request to Congress, delivered by Plumb, asking that town developers for Oklahoma not be the ones to take over the state, but actual settlers—those who wanted to build homes and lives on land there. Such settlers, according to Senator

Plumb, could be either white or Black. Both Plumb and Kansas wanted Oklahoma to be a symbol that every man could make it, even if enabling every man meant canceling out the existence of the Indigenous nations whose land it was.

Plumb's and his colleagues' seemingly progressive eyes saw the Indigenous not as people living on land they owned in perpetuity but as pawns to move, civilizations that could be lifted and replanted by fiat. Plumb wanted a single territorial government for the entire region that would give him and his colleagues—and the men they would appoint—collective discretion to manipulate the territory for their own ends. He cared about efficiency, hoping to streamline governance and consolidate it in white hands.

His colleague Senator Henry Dawes of Massachusetts fancied himself an even greater humanitarian, telling his colleagues at the Conference of Friends of the Indian at Lake Mohonk in New York State, "[The Indigenous] must take his place where you have undertaken to put him, or he must go a vagabond throughout this country, and it is for you and me to say which it shall be. He cannot choose for himself, and he does not know where the ways are." Dawes thought that it was the U.S. government's job to "fix the Indian problem" and disagreed with Plumb's idea. He favored identifying by his own standards who was "Indian" and by what degree on his own terms and allocating land, not communally but individually to people who were Indian.

Dawes won.

As McCabe was poised to lose his state auditor's election in 1888, the U.S. government had been reorganizing how it treated Indigenous people after the passage of the Dawes Act of 1887, which broke up reservations and tribal lands into limited allotments to individual Indigenous peoples. The Indigenous, Dawes and others believed, could be forced to shed who they were, what they owned communally, and what they believed. Using the blunt instruments at their disposal—such as the privatization of land, the relegation of beautifully ornate ways of being, and creating citizenship requiring spot checks and Euro-American citizenship genealogical tests, along with a heavy dose of racism that sounded more "scientific"—the government would wrest control of Indigenous land.

The tragedies of this "help" are numerous. The enactment of the Dawes Act enabled the U.S. government to determine citizenship using the brutish tactics of shoddy genealogy in these Indigenous nations, determining who qualified "by blood" or "mixed blood" or freedman status, often by uneducated guesses. It enabled the government to relegate families to private land, a concept long rejected by the spiritual constitution of these nations and their people. It enabled the United States to take much of those lands and create "twin territories" from them—the theft of some hundred million acres and the relegation of Indigenous peoples to the central part of the territory as the *new* Indian Territory and making the original land "Oklahoma Territory."

The government broke its promises to these Indigenous nations because its leaders believed that Indian Territory was always up for the offer, open to the experimentation of the U.S. government. Because while it may have been named "Indian," it was U.S. territory.

◄─◆─►

In his 1889 proclamation, President Harrison chose the lives of those who wanted to settle over the lives of those who had been conscripted to being resettled there. This was why Arkansas City, Kansas, and other towns like it were filled with horses and prairie schooners ready to cross the border. It was also why the town itself was now booming, filled with tobacco salesmen and liquor brokers and preachers, all ready to profit from these new settlers: the formerly enslaved; the big-city hucksters; the brave and the scared.

How can a land be both promised and devastated? Many Black people found promise in the treaties that reconstituted the size of the land held by the Indian nations, in the wreckage of obliterated promises. The lands of the Oklahoma Territory were being opened up with scant details offered about what would happen to Indian Territory. And any mentions of what protections would be available to the Indigenous would be quickly flung on top of the heap of literally hundreds of other broken treaties.

Plans for opening up the land started to be hatched despite the problems and challenges. And this seemingly inevitable—yet entirely avoidable—tragedy set in motion a collision. But that collision was between people who, though wholly different from one another, shared one common trait:

They had all been disinherited.

15

Moses in Pharaoh's Court

WASHINGTON, D.C., 1889

Let it then be understood, as a great principle of political economy, that no people can be free who themselves do not constitute an essential part of the ruling element of the country in which they live . . . A people, to be free, must necessarily be their own rules: that is, each individual must, in himself, embody the essential ingredient—so to speak—of the sovereign principle which composes the true basis of his liberty. This principle, when not exercised by himself, may, at his pleasure, be delegated to another—his true representative . . . He must possess within himself the acknowledged right to govern: this constitutes him a governor, though he may delegate to another the power to govern himself.

—MARTIN DELANY, "POLITICAL DESTINY OF THE COLORED
RACE, ON THE AMERICAN CONTINENT," DELIVERED
TO THE NATIONAL EMIGRATION CONVENTION OF
COLORED PEOPLE, AUGUST 1854

There never was a more favorable time than now for [Black families] to secure good homes in a land where you will be free and your rights respected," William Lewis Eagleson wrote in 1890 in a flyer for the Oklahoma Immigration Association. "Oklahoma is now open for settlement. Come in and help make it one of the best states in the union. The soil is rich, the climate favorable, water abundant and there is plenty of timber. Make a new start. Give yourselves and children new chances in a new land, where you will not be molested and where you will be able to think and vote as you please."

In previous decades, Eagleson had been an influential booster of Kansas for Black settlers. Now, seeing that Kansas was abandoning its Black residents, Eagleson was beckoning his readers into a new "Exodust": Oklahoma. And he knew what to say: Although his appeal might seem broad, it was actually targeted to resonate with concerned Black people across the country, but especially in the South. Check it, he told them: in Oklahoma, "You will be free."

The spate of elections throughout the South, the further decline of Reconstruction's advancements, and the retrenchment of Jim Crow—era laws made it such that Black people did not feel free no matter how much on paper some said they were.

And yet, like Niles and Hall and even McCabe, Eagleson might have been a true believer, but he was also a promoter. Even though he had not even traveled through most of Oklahoma, he still wrote confidently that "the soil is rich, the climate favorable, water abundant and there is plenty of timber."

It was a clear appeal to Black farmers. One need not be an expert in anything but their own ambitions. One hundred and sixty acres, free, with only the requirement to cultivate it and develop it for five years—just demanding of sweat equity. Oklahoma, via the U.S. government, was calling for any kind of worker to populate the territory and build it up for their own economic productivity. Not only would their economic and financial futures be secure in Oklahoma, Eagleson argued, but their political freedom would be assured as well: They wouldn't be bullied, bulldozed, or pressured into voting a particular way or kept away from the voting booths. No, their votes would matter just as much as anyone else's.

Eagleson's tone was invariably pugnacious. The *Los Angeles Sentinel* wrote of him, years after his passing, as a "pioneering editor" who "didn't mince words" as he wrote to attract Black people by arguing that the Black people who came to Kansas would not be forced to accept whatever any party might give them. In fact, beneath the masthead of the *Colored Citizen* were the words "AMERICA Our Country! We Toiled for it in 1776; We Fought for it in 1812; and we saved it in 1863!" And he routinely said, "We would not advise an affiliation of the colored voters as a whole with either party," because they were prone to "take blacks for granted." The *Colored Citizen* became the nexus for vocalizing Black perspectives on all the issues of the day, short though the paper's two-year life may have been.

Moreover, Eagleson had long been McCabe's biggest supporter. His perspectives were widely perceived to be more radical than McCabe's carefully considered, more placid public statements. When McCabe would discuss the state of affairs for Black people up until this point, of moderate Republicans he would resort to moderate stances and careful statements. Eagleson's writings, by contrast, would lambast the South as an abominable place where Black people were made to become "targets of white men." He reflected on his affiliation with the Republican Party with caution because he found his and his people's Republicanism to be purely transactional, called upon only when a critical election was imminent and their votes could swing the race one way or another.

But the opening of Oklahoma lands gave Eagleson not only his chance to separate from the whims of powerful white people. For Eagleson, Oklahoma was what he called the "Coveted Prize." So coveted, Eagleson told the *Kansas Democrat*, that "we are determined to take it" because as he saw it, it was a place that Lincoln had offered Black people but had never delivered on. Eagleson claimed, the reporter wrote, that "there are 1,100 colored families in Topeka" alone who were ready to make the move.

Reporters seemed convinced of Eagleson's conviction that Oklahoma was "the land of promise for the [Black] race," because it would be the "panacea for every ill now affecting negroes in the south."

A plan was coming together among the aspiring Black colonizers of the Oklahoma Territory. The most distillable components emerged as:

1. Talk up Oklahoma.

2. Call it a promised land.

3. Write about it in whatever newspaper would accept it.

As similar as that was to the Exoduster scheme in Kansas, Eagleson had a new idea for Oklahoma, one that would end up most important for McCabe:

4. Appoint a Moses.

⸺◆⸺

When thousands of settlers poured over the border from Kansas into Oklahoma in the 1889 Land Rush, Eagleson was in Topeka, starting the Oklahoma Immigration Association. His goal was to raise funds—"metallic sympathy"—to funnel Black settlers into the new territory. At that time, McCabe was in Washington, D.C. He and his wife, Sarah, had been dealt a series of blows to their ascendant political life in Kansas. Fresh off of this electoral loss, Sarah needed a medical procedure, and McCabe had determined that the nation's capital would be the best place for both of them. He hadn't lived in Nicodemus in some time, and Washington's proximity to power made returning untenable. Kansas government had lost any statewide representation of Black people. Plus, McCabe and other Black people had gotten a glimmer of what seemed like hope through his brief term.

For McCabe, the election of Benjamin Harrison might soothe the sting of his own defeat. Perhaps by dislodging himself from Kansas politics, McCabe could elevate his influence and profile at a time when both houses of Congress had swung toward the Republicans; his remaining relationships with the Kansas delegation in Congress and throughout the administration represented the best chance to emerge as a power player to protect Black people in the South, advance their interests in the North, and use political patronage to make himself a member of the elite political class.

◄━●━►

As Eagleson began using his organization, namely the Oklahoma Immigration Association, to promote Oklahoma as another promised land for Black settlers, he wrote to McCabe. Surely, such a venture was right up his alley.

After corresponding with Eagleson, McCabe wasted no time in gathering enough Republican bona fides to land a job in the Harrison administration developing the Washington, D.C., branch of the movement to Oklahoma.

He set up his family in the District and went about soliciting investments and donations (called subscribing) from elite Blacks and sympathetic white political power brokers to finance the operation. As he worked, he received updates via telegram from Kansas to keep him apprised of what was happening as people prepared to enter the territory. By return telegrams, he gave them details about the entry of Oklahoma as a new state. Before 1889 was over, McCabe had invited Eagleson to come to Washington to pressure politicians to make Oklahoma Territory a Black state. McCabe also used his base in Washington to communicate with Black organizers in the South to encourage them to consider moving to a land they had never visited but could make their own.

The advancement of Black people, McCabe believed, might be best achieved in Oklahoma. He also dared to imagine—and Eagleson proclaimed—that he would do more than simply lead those Black settlers or represent them in a local legislature. Given McCabe's political skills and his experience as state auditor, he might one day lead the entire territory.

Harrison had yet to appoint a governor of the territory. At the time, governors were chosen directly by the president and the governor would select his territorial cabinet and in some cases would oversee various offices in the counties. While these territorial governors may be forgotten now, their impact extended for generations as these gubernatorial appointments were pro forma before the territory was admitted to the Union as a state. So the governor of the Oklahoma Territory would be first in line to become governor of the state or maybe even a U.S. senator.

McCabe had already eyed these larger gains and saw that a Black Oklahoma for the United States could lead to him becoming Governor or U.S. Senator McCabe.

Others were less grandiose in their selling of the Oklahoma Territory to Black people, in part because their ambitions were not McCabe's. People like S. H. Scott moved to Oklahoma during the first Land Rush in April 1889 and brought many Black North Carolinians as well as other Black people with him from Fort Smith, Arkansas. The same could be said of John Young and D. B. Garrett, who both came from Kansas and created a town in Kingfisher County, Oklahoma, that they affectionately named after President Abraham Lincoln. And as promising as these non-McCabe Black efforts were, none had the audacity to say that they'd be the best or that they'd be the leaders of the territory. None of them spoke with the clarity that their presence as Black towns would crowd out white settlers.

While McCabe was in Washington angling for a seat at the table as he clamored for support for Blacks migrating to Oklahoma Territory, he kept his statements conciliatory, genial, and noncombative. "Brash" was not a term that applied to McCabe during his time in Washington. But with the prospect of his ambition taking hold in a new state, an opportunity to create the world on his terms, his true motivations emerged.

A reporter from the *Rocky Mountain News* observed on March 3, 1890, that McCabe's influence among Kansas Republicans in Washington, D.C., and the wealthier Black residents of the nation's capital was growing. At the time, McCabe had reported to the paper that he had already sent some three hundred families from North Carolina and five hundred families from South Carolina directly to Oklahoma. Those families, the paper reported, "are now comfortably situated, some of whom will go to the neutral Strip." That part of the territory hadn't been formally opened yet, but Black families already had started gathering.

McCabe had also been currying favor with both of the U.S. senators representing Kansas, John J. Ingalls and Preston Plumb. The two already supported McCabe's efforts, including the notion of a Black state. Morally, they were for full Negro suffrage and publicly condemned the deplorable treatment of Black people in the South. Edward Funston, a congressman from Kansas, lent his support to the efforts to migrate Black people. Oklahoma, as a state, would be the solution to the "Colored Problem"—one that non-Black people had been trying to solve without the consent or involvement of Black people. But solving this problem McCabe's way would create a state with a Black governor, members of the House of Representatives, and senators appointed by a Black governor.

Finally, McCabe got his meeting with President Harrison on March 2, 1890.

Born in Ohio and trained as a lawyer, Harrison, a lover of law and process, questioned why McCabe had been so busy trying to convince Black people to move to Oklahoma instead of trying "to populate a Southern state." McCabe told the president, "We desire to get away from the associations that cluster about us" there.

As distant as McCabe's life had been from those of Black people in the South, he linked their destiny with his own. He knew that in his meeting with Harrison, he had to paint the South as bad as Black people saw it and disabuse Harrison of any notion that life there was acceptable and livable for Black people. "We wish to remove from the disgraceful surroundings that so degraded my people and in a new territory in Oklahoma show the people of the United States and of the world that we are not only good, loyal citizens, but that we are capable of advancement and that we can be an honor to those who broke down the barriers of slavery," he said.

His plea to the president was clear: Give us a chance in a new place that we are masters of.

It was in this way that McCabe was beginning to earn a reputation as a modern Moses. To him, the White House was just another Pharaoh's court, except the plea was not "Let my people go!" The plea was "Let my people begin again!" It's a plea of enduring resonance and familiarity today.

Harrison was seemingly a less callous Pharaoh, and it was well within his power to support the endeavor to begin again in Oklahoma. McCabe, familiar with the ways of Washington's power brokers, could hold court with Pharaoh. Like Moses, he could tell the story of the people he hoped to lead while positioning himself as worthy of the role: "Some of us have names borrowed from our masters, some of us have the blood of those who owned us as chattels but disowned us as sons and daughters."

"We are willing to abide by that decision," McCabe said, signaling his willingness to put aside the ways in which the United States had allowed his people to be enslaved, but with a caveat: He would accept what happened to Black people in America only if they were allowed to live and prosper "in a new country, on new lands, with a climate suited to our race." And to beat Harrison to the inevitable question about whether Black people could do it, McCabe said, "We desire to show you that we are men and women capable of self-government."

◄—◆—►

Word in Washington had gotten out that McCabe had met with the president, and like a game of telephone, the finer details—such as Harrison expressing neither strong support nor condemnation for the move—didn't take hold nearly as much as that McCabe spoke clearly about why Oklahoma should be secured for Black people. While Black people waited for Harrison's decision, McCabe and Eagleson continued to work.

McCabe had to recruit those who wanted to embark on freedom and tell them the plan going forward. Eagleson knew that they couldn't depend on the U.S. government or the emerging territorial government of Oklahoma for help. The Kansas government had shown him that all they had to depend on were the solicitations of metallic sympathy from white philanthropists. So the new recruitment message that rang out sounded different: "Come Prepared or Not at All."

As Eagleson and McCabe plotted a strategy to identify what some success looked like, they started to dispatch people to go, hatching talking points to distribute among Black people in the South. They built the dream in the hopes that masses of Black people would come.

McCabe had learned firsthand what it took to build up a town and what would be required to recruit people into the unknown Old West. The clarion call rang out across the South when Eagleson printed in his Immigration Association adverts "Come"—a throwback to their Kansan comrade Pap Singleton, who painted wondrous pictures of the opportunities in Kansas if Black people came with the willingness to work.

The desired outcome was clear: With enough Black people moving west, McCabe could present himself as the natural person to lead this "new" territory and its eventual status as a state admitted to the Union. For McCabe, this territory was a tabula rasa. It was an opportunity to begin again, except he hoped that this would be the last time. If the land was full of only white people and a modicum of Black people, then McCabe might find himself again as a Black token or political chit used by white people. But what if Black people made up most of the new settlers of the territory?

As exciting as these questions were, they led to other less optimistic questions: Would their white counterparts allow this to happen? Would the Indigenous nations who had been banished there with a promise that they'd not be moved again take this lying down? Would both white and Indigenous people sit by while a Black man and thousands of Black people rewrote the historical legacies and political lives of America?

McCabe hoped the answers would all be "yes."

16

Come to Oklahoma!

GUTHRIE, OKLAHOMA, 1890

The dugout, the shack and the sodhouse are being rapidly re-placed by beautiful and comfortable homes for man and beast . . . There is a large Afro-American population in that portion of the territory, many of them worth their hundreds of thousands of dollars. The Afro-Americans have settled in some parts almost to the exclusion of the whites. Langston City was founded by E.P. McCabe . . . The streets, avenues, and boulevards of Langston City are named in honor of prominent Afro-Americans . . .

. . . It is possible that when the [Oklahoma] territory is admitted to the Union it will have an Afro-American popula-tion of some 100,000.

—*New York Sun*, AUGUST 23, 1894

The *New York Age*, one of the most acclaimed Black-owned newspapers in the country, carried an article that also ran in several mainstream newspapers. The editors wrote, "There is nothing at all alarming or disturbing over the prospect of a Negro state." The writers asked the reader to consider how a Negro state could be alarming when the state of the Black people in the South was so dire. "In the South the Negro is generally dependent of the whites, who own the lands and from whom the indispensable corn and bacon must come; but a new Territory settled by industrious and comparatively intelligent colored men who own their own homes and who go there to assume the responsibility of ruling a State, will give the first true test of the capacity of the race for self-government . . . Give the blacks a chance."

That was what McCabe was asking for: a chance. His bid for the governorship of the territory might have been part of a larger scheme to promote himself to a position of greater power. Even so, he believed that his selection as governor could be a vote of confidence from people or a country that never gave Black people the chance to build confidence in their abilities. Every time a Black person ascended to a position of leadership in any field, that person was expected to represent a diverse racial group.

And people all over the country had begun to believe that McCabe could become governor. New York financier and businessman William Waldorf Astor promised $500,000 to endow a university in the area if McCabe and Eagleson could add $100,000 for buildings. Ever the real estate visionary, McCabe began trying to entice Blacks with means to purchase large claims in Oklahoma with promises to develop them. Some of the claims totaled $500 to $1,000 (approximately $17,250 to $34,500 in today's dollars).

The Black population of Oklahoma reported by McCabe and Eagleson would continue to climb from twenty thousand, topping out at one hundred thousand within several years of the first waves of land runs. No one could say for certain: Rather, hope served as the gloss.

For that was what Eagleson and McCabe were offering: hope. Some might call it aspiration—so much aspiration that at the beginning of 1889 Eagleson declared to the press, "We are determined to take it and make [Oklahoma] one of the greatest states in the Union."

To do this effectively and make himself the likeliest choice to lead it, McCabe demonstrated that he had learned how to make himself and Nicodemus matter to state government. He had learned the lesson in his early days of trying to put together a base of power in western Kansas. Nicodemus was multiple days' ride from Topeka—a day's ride from the nearest county clerk. That's why McCabe and his friend Hall spent their time convincing the governor to appoint them to clerkships and move the county clerk's office closer to them. But their political capital remained sparse because they were so far from where decisions were made. As a result McCabe was tokenized twice over, once by race and once by region. This time, he would not make that mistake.

So when it came to Oklahoma Territory, McCabe went right to where the power was. The capital of the Oklahoma Territory was Guthrie—a town bustling with railroads and a depot that overflowed with people looking for whatever Oklahoma had in store. Guthrie itself was changing and filling out quickly. Just eleven miles away, McCabe and Eagleson planned a new town that they hoped would serve as their power base and a home for thousands of Black settlers: Langston.

Originally, Black people who came to Guthrie—in segregated railcars—would wait until the train got to "The Elbow," a small outpost adjacent to Guthrie. The image could, if not careful, convince a Black newcomer that this was all there was to it. But they read in papers, heard from preachers and agents of McCabe that there was a plot just beyond the squalor of The Elbow called Langston, named after a successful Black politician and legal scholar named John Mercer Langston, which had been founded just for them. A short two-hour horse ride away would reveal a town that was, in fact, built for them, with land occupied and cultivated by Black people, and more to spare. They'd see the early makings of schoolhouses, a new university on its way thanks to McCabe's persuasive skills. They'd see grist mills, and churches, and streets named to revere Blanche Bruce, the first elected Black U.S. senator and McCabe's political chum. They would not see impressiveness, but they would see themselves in the midst of a land that McCabe called promised.

The first land runs in Oklahoma didn't welcome only the hopes and dreams of white settlers, but the wild dreams of Black colonizers, too. They weren't there grabbing allotments hoping to live a nice life. No, they were there to establish a colony, Langston, which would be incorporated as a town on the lines of the passageway to lands set to be opened up in the second land run—the launchpad nearest to the soon-to-be-opened lands.

The outlines of Langston were much like those of Guthrie. It became a resting station for the weary traveler looking to occupy the reallotted lands of the territory.

For his efforts, McCabe had attracted more people than his naysayers thought possible. And he didn't limit himself to Langston, though that quickly became his power base. He began populating other towns, founding them under his name. Towns like Liberty, some thirty miles north of Langston—a touch closer for migrants coming from Kansas. It also attracted Black people coming from places in the South like Texas and Mississippi. But more important, founding that town was another chance for McCabe to position Black people to take advantage of the opening of more lands for settlers just north of Liberty.

Moreover, McCabe knew that he was set to "make a barrel of money out of his scheme." These weren't his words, but those of the *Daily Leader*, the local newspaper in Guthrie. As a speculator who would stake the lands opened at rock-bottom prices, he'd then sell each parcel for a tidy profit to families looking for a new land. He never had to truly develop the land, but instead encouraged families to bring shovels and a tenacious work ethic. He was, in an important sense, carrying forward the work he had done in Kansas. He also worked with railroad agents who made a commission on tickets sold to get Black people to Oklahoma. This not only provided financial gains for those agents and for him who proselytized about the great opportunity in the West, but it also gave him cultural currency with the people who carried the message forward to Black people boarding trains.

It wasn't long before the town of Liberty, which had less of the bustle potential of Langston, got a boost. Black people, scores of them, poured into the town of Perry first. But that town was built not so much for them.

Oklahoma was on the precipice of transitioning from a place known for cattle ranching to one that would transform the world's economy and make the state the oil capital of the world. Its oil was first discovered in 1859 in Cherokee Nation lands and decades later would overflow in Osage Nation lands. The prospect of finding an abundant resource of oil and gas underground was an enormous opportunity. But one group with whom the Osage did not work well were the Black people who had come to Oklahoma and Indian Territory looking for opportunity. The Osage despised the new Black people, and the only place to which Black people could think to go was "McCabe's new town, Liberty, a few miles north of Perry."

These towns—Liberty, Kingfisher, Langston, and soon more to come—were the promised land for those who had been told they did not belong. The promise was that when they came, they would be welcomed with the warmth of opportunity. Whatever harshness they experienced on the land might fade if they focused first on the hope for what might arise.

But in coming, they didn't escape the scourge of racism. As they boarded trains in Georgia and Alabama, Texas and Arkansas, they were reminded of their position, told to find the "Race Car." The journey to Oklahoma was a stark reminder that they would always be separate as the Atchison, Topeka and Santa Fe Railway was said to have Black people on every arrival into Oklahoma. And Black people would have to struggle to become equal. They were quickly disabused of the notion that equality was within reach.

The very reason towns like Lincoln, Langston, and northern parts of Tulsa and Kingfisher, like Liberty and even the colored towns of Indian Territory to the east of Oklahoma Territory, existed was that the separation of the races was so implied that it felt intentional. Oklahoma mattered because it was the call to whoever needed to hear it that it was a chance to begin again. The nearly unanimous approval of Congress, the sign-off by the president to create a new territory to settle signaled that unlike shipping Black people to Haiti, Liberia, or Panama, America approved of this chance for a Black man to join in the effort to recreate a new America.

But reinvention of America is difficult work. It requires anticipating that many people would be bringing with them *not* the intention to reimagine America but the desire to reproduce the social, racial, and political dynamics of the places they had left, whether from the North or the South.

⊰◆⊱

By 1890, Eagleson declared that the territory would soon have one hundred thousand Black people settling there. And as much as colonization had hurt Black people in the past, it now was the tool they saw as the most viable path to securing freedom. And it wasn't just white people who found this plan suspect.

A Black man, John Paul Jones, interviewed in the *Daily Oklahoma State Capital*, made it known that he did not think McCabe had the support. "When we got up a colony last spring to get homes [near

Kingfisher, Oklahoma], McCabe refused to join it or assist us in our efforts," Jones told the editor. Because McCabe "said Kansas was good enough for him," Jones said. He had been busy in D.C. lobbying the politicians he hoped would help him become the territory's governor. "If Oklahoma, without the hope of an office, wasn't attractive to his eye, we don't want him to pick up and come here now, carpetbag in hand."

The reality was, they all were to some extent carpetbaggers. It's just that Jones saw McCabe as a token and said as much. Reflecting on McCabe's success in Kansas, he continued, "It became necessary for Republicans to have a colored candidate in recognition of the colored vote. McCabe happened to stand where the lightning struck." Jones's opposition, despite having spent time learning about McCabe earlier in their careers, stemmed from his belief that the only hope for Black people rested not in elective office, but in owning land, maybe a farm, and having a few dollars to invest in the future of their families. He had become resigned to the limited lot in life Black people had been offered, whereas McCabe refused the offer. Jones said of McCabe, "If he is coming here with the honest and noble purpose of getting a home"—which Jones thought the culmination of success—"all colored people will welcome him and so will the whites."

McCabe could have found a sinecure in Washington, D.C., or returned to Nicodemus and continued his successful real estate practice. But his ambitions wouldn't let him. For Jones, "The colored man who thinks of coming here to get an office had better stay away. He will get disappointed." It wasn't so much that Jones was casting aspersions on McCabe, it was the worry that McCabe's hopes might outpace reality.

And the *Atchison Globe*, which ordinarily wrote favorably of McCabe, had a dour scourge in its March 10 edition: "For months [McCabe] hung by the eyebrows at Washington, hoping for a place. Finally, in the face of opposition of the Kansas delegation, he began a boom for the governorship of Oklahoma." The writer noted, "The other day he returned to Kansas . . . seedy and thin, but full of hope, and the people of Oklahoma greatly fear that he will be appointed governor." The headline of the article made it clear what the editors thought of McCabe. "[He] talks too much," it read.

Without sourcing and without attribution, the editors wrote, "He simply aimed high, in order to pose as the representative negro of Kansas, and thus be in position to demand the secretaryship of the territory."

And the writer concluded, "In his bowels Mr. McCabe has no such hope."

———◄—◆—►———

McCabe likely believed that the Republicans would give him the support he wanted. It's why he went to President Harrison looking for permission to enter Oklahoma as if it belonged to Black people. But no matter how committed he was to the party and how much organizing he had done, Republicans didn't uniformly support him, not the least of whom was President Harrison himself, who unilaterally proclaimed that the lands of Oklahoma Territory would be opened. In fact, since the 1870s, McCabe's best friend, Eagleson, had foretold that Black people shouldn't rely on Republicans or any party for that matter.

Texas and Missouri papers carried rumors of McCabe's response to having been rejected as leader of this new territory. "It would be unwise to recognize the colored element in that manner," the *St. Louis Globe-Democrat* and *Galveston Daily News* both carried.

McCabe said that such negative sentiments were rumors. He called them "simply idle gossip" that he would not "partake of the character of a bluff." McCabe continued to play careful politics, telling one reporter, "If I should be appointed Governor I would administer the laws of the United States without fear or favor to white and black alike." McCabe was trying to distance himself from claims that he would be a Negro supremacist. Dispatches from Oklahoma and Washington, D.C., indicated the reactions he'd received—that whites might formally and forcibly rage against any attempt by him and his allies to make Oklahoma a Black state, according to the *Atchison Globe*.

It was at this point that McCabe began to receive targeted accusations of Negro supremacy for vying for office and recruiting Black people to the territory. Frustration spilled over into newspapers. "That character of balderdash may do south of Mason and Dixon's line. Insulting the insinuations of his leadership[.] But we go to the Territory to put an end to that kind of politics."

It was a clear statement that his leadership of the Oklahoma Territory would prevent the extension of the South into the Old West. Because that was what was at stake: Would Black lives in this colonized territory be subject to the limited and relegated life of the past? For McCabe, the South was just a hodgepodge of "stuffed ballot boxes or shotgun policy," and his promise was that such a practice would be "relegated to the South, where it belongs." His stance risked angering the thousands of southerners and southern sympathizers who went to Oklahoma to find new lives of their own.

That line in the proverbial sand earned McCabe a nickname in the *Milwaukee Journal*. They called him "the One Who Would Be the Moses." McCabe was trying to make Oklahoma "the New Canaan of the Colored Race" and to secure "its Future Status." The paper described McCabe as "one of the most persistent of the applicants for a post in the new territory."

The plan for McCabe to recruit as many Black people as possible to the territory started to align with the emergence of a rumor about what Harrison did or did not agree to in his meeting with McCabe. The newspaper wrote that McCabe "has insisted on the appointment of governor, and it is given out by his friends that the president has

promised to appoint him if he can prove that a majority of the inhabitants of the territory are negroes." If these rumors were true—that
Harrison would look at the future of Oklahoma and its Black people
as nothing but a question of electoral math—then McCabe's persistent efforts to recruit Black people en masse make even more sense.

There was a race afoot to build enough of these towns as quickly
as possible in this rapidly transforming land. The goal was to demonstrate enough presence and momentum that it would convince everyone that the Black people building these towns had greater purchase
on the eventual statehood of the land.

What makes even more sense is the wide variation in the numbers
of Black people migrating to the territory. Sometimes McCabe said
that he expected one hundred thousand Black people to be in the territory. In other newspapers, he was quoted as saying thirty thousand,
fifty thousand, and sixty thousand. The first census of the territory
was scheduled for 1890, and the appearance or even assumption of
the amount of people could lead to the understanding that there was a
Black "majority." McCabe returned to the salesmanship he had learned
in Chicago, delivering what he hoped the customer—in this case, the
president—wanted to hear.

McCabe used these interviews to make clear how successful the
movement for Oklahoma was. He left reporters like the one from
the *Milwaukee Journal* with the belief that he was confident that in
less than three months Oklahoma would have anywhere between fifty
thousand and seventy-five thousand Black people. "If [McCabe's] plan
carries a year hence there will be a negro state with two black senators and a representative in congress," the *Journal* wrote.

McCabe argued that these Black people would be a reliable voting
bloc for the Republican Party, which worried that an Oklahoma populated strictly by southerners and southern sympathizers could become a Democrat stronghold. But the reporter demonstrated just how
deft he was at predicting what might happen: "The administration

can have the time to consider what is best to be done for the interests of the grand old party which of course always are to be considered before the claims or the rights of the colored people who want to make it their home and govern it."

McCabe's job was to demonstrate that the interests of the Republican Party and Black migrants to Oklahoma were the same and that he could be the bridge to make their connection of interests clear.

That was difficult because the party focused on what was best for the white people who ran it, not the Black people who were counted on during elections to deliver a victory. And it is for that reason that McCabe's ambition represented a threat within the party. The *New York Times* wrote that McCabe's rise was leading to "rapidly growing anti-negro sentiment caused by the aggressiveness of the blacks whenever they are strong," and that somehow this worked to "unite the whites irrespective of party."

Such aggressiveness was a matter of perspective. Six-shooters sat in the holsters of many white cowboys as their horses galloped through the territory, but somehow that wasn't aggressive. Somehow it wasn't aggressive when white men threatened those who eyed the same land they did. The Portland *Oregonian* reported, "In Oklahoma will possibly be seen the beginning of a race war" triggered by "negro society, 'The First Grand Independent Brotherhood,' crowding people in settlements in sections where the lands [were] already taken by whites."

McCabe was singled out both by his supporters as their Moses and by racist antagonists who sought to have him assassinated. Similar threats and actions made the assassination feel more like a promise than a threat. White Boomers, settlers who pushed for the opening of the Unassigned Lands for settlement, often ransacked Black settlements along the Kansas and Oklahoma border or engaged in fights with Black people. At the time, the rush into Oklahoma and the crowding of a growing number of Black people of means with those without means made it seem to the *Oregonian* reporter that Black people began to "expect [McCabe being appointed governor] will be the outcome."

As time passed and the hour of the appointment of the governor grew nearer, Black people began to voice the concern that McCabe wouldn't be appointed. Those in Oklahoma began to wonder if this would be just "another 'grievance' that will bind the black race together, and secure united action." What they knew for sure was that they, led by McCabe, according to the *Oregonian*, always had in view "to found a new state where they themselves will have full power."

◄━━◄━━►

To some, McCabe seemed like a guaranteed lock on the appointment, particularly as he was from Kansas and Kansas senators and congressmen had done their fair share to boost him and the idea of opening the lands south of their border.

But the *Guthrie News* carried a two-word, mockingly solemn headline on May 12, 1890: "Poor Kansans." The *Kansas Democrat*, no friend to President Harrison, reported, "Harrison has knocked E.P. McCabe and the colored cohorts out of time, in refusing to give the colored element any representation in the new government of Oklahoma." The *Fort Scott Tribune* wrote, "This is the first and only time that the colored people have asked recognition in the territories, and they have been snubbed. The administration, evidently, is not favorable to extending the colored man's power in the territories—nor anywhere else, for that matter."

Kansas was snubbed, but even more specifically Black people were snubbed. Instead of appointing McCabe as governor, President Harrison chose George Steele—a former Union officer, a fellow Indianan, a friend, and a former U.S. congressman. Harrison's former law student Horace Speed was appointed attorney for the territory. Seemingly to appease the South, Warren Lurty from Virginia was made marshal over the territory.

In the wake of this defeat, McCabe licked his wounds and chose a relatively short time for reflection and strategy. Eagleson, by contrast, went on the offensive. When asked if he was disappointed that all his work had not resulted in the appointment of McCabe as governor of the state, he said, "I am not disappointed at all. It is only what might be expected of Harrison. The president is a small man in more than one way. He did not get all the negroes at the national convention and he is now taking out his spite on the negro applicants. Had the name of E.P. McCabe been presented to Grover Cleveland with the endorsement of his race nothing could have beaten him for the appointment . . . There the colored man's usefulness ends."

17

The Land Run

For the master's tools will never dismantle the master's house.
They may allow us to temporarily beat him at his own game,
but they will never enable us to bring about genuine change.

—AUDRE LORDE

Sunday, September 20, 1891, was no kind of Sunday at all. A free-for-all was afoot. Into the Oklahoma Territory—by train, by foot, by horse, by buggy, by wagon—people had been coming. "Each day's crowd of arrivals being larger than that of the day before until now every train comes in four and five sections of ten coaches each loaded to the guards," a reporter from the *Wichita Eagle* covering the land run recounted. In Guthrie, the capital of the territory, the roads—yet still new—were packed with crowds atop horses, pulling ponies, belongings, and mementos from the places they had left behind.

Guthrie was just a pit stop. It was where the new inhabitants of this territory came before redirecting their wagons to the roads crafted to take them to their new beginnings. They came with hopes of embracing a new vision of America, but in no way was it new, or at least it wasn't new to many. It was deeply American, as American as one could get. Black people came with the hope of building anew, after hearing the tales about what McCabe had been up to on their behalf. For many of them, this Sunday would reestablish what they all knew: America—even the parts that were just territories, not even states— would be a recapitulation of the status quo where Black people would take a back seat.

Guthrie's land office became an encampment of these newcomers' dreams, while its steps and bordering streets became their eateries, their beds, their living spaces. The collective anticipation cleared out restaurants, saloons shut their doors, and local newspapers shuttered— only temporarily. Even the printers setting the type for the daily news declared that they, too, "are in it." The owners of these stores closed their businesses to join the thousands of others in the streets. Because nothing would be the same after September 22.

They saw that just beyond this night, at noon the next day, rifles and handguns would fire in towns across the western territory. Thousands would depart Guthrie, pushing east under the pretense that everyone had a "fair field and no favors." They came from lands where the fields were far from fair and where trading favors was a means of survival. White men and women, children and elderly parents in tow, felt beleaguered under the perception that they needed to marshal their resources if they hoped for a better life. The calm belied the "waiting expectancy" and the "happy anticipation of how much better off" they might be if they made it, because they all felt as if they'd make it— they all knew that they would make it.

One *Eagle* reporter wrote of that calm, "It is the night before Christmas, the eve of election, the night before the crossing of the Red Sea into the promised land." They knew of this land, its size, what word scouts had sent back about how many homesteads could be established.

The contract was simple. Find land. Stake your ground. Develop your land and stay on it for five years, and though you might have had only a nickel to your name, that land, 160 acres in total, could be yours, your family's land. It could be the stake in tomorrow because nothing about yesterday inspired the slightest optimism.

The next day, the second Land Rush was set to begin.

━━◆━━

Perhaps the advantaged were the ones who slept peacefully under the stars the night before—some twenty-five thousand in total. But not all the twenty-five thousand slept. Some stood watch, waiting for word from surveyors and government scouts, and the Sac and Fox Nation, and the Potawatomi, and the Shawnee who came back with word that some "surveyors are suffering for water." That parts of the land, especially around the Chandler townsite, remained "the poorest that could have been found in the territory, rough and rocky, with deep gullies and ravines through the town, and with absolutely no water within two miles."

Some optimism had found its way into the advertisement of this land run—"That there will be a race fully as exciting as the famous English Derby . . . except that it is free for all; black and white and Indian will participate." "Black and white and Indian will participate" was understood only as an addendum that found its way there by members of Congress pushing the issue. And it turned what would have otherwise been a whites-only land run by edict into a white-preferred one, in fact and in deed.

In special dispatches from the *St. Louis Post-Dispatch* and the *Lawrence Daily Journal*, reporters wrote, "Gamblers are here with their outfits, and 'sure thing' games of every description are being loaded and forwarded to the young towns." Despite what governance had been installed into these lands, "Winchesters and six-shooters will be freely used if occasion requires," the reporter wrote. "Everything is wide open."

The advantaged could pay a citizen of an Indigenous nation who had a long history in these lands to tell them where the most prosperous spots might be, which valleys lay low and which ran with streams ideal for fishing, which were closest to potable water and most distant from danger. Some advantages went to those who could pay people to just break the rules and adopt the role as "Sooners," rushing into the land before it was allowed, cornering the best parcels, getting kicked out by U.S. soldiers only to return at a different entry point to find new places that weren't all that new.

Still, in a race to get land, bad things were bound to happen. It made the apparent calm dangerous.

———◄━►———

By the evening of September 18, Black people were at the starting line, Eagleson being one of them.

Word had it that this land and the land around it had been broken in—that the soil around it was productive—unlike the red dirt that typified parts of the territory and mystified newcomers to its viability. In the southern valley, fruit could grow, cows could graze, fertile farmland was plentiful, according to news reports and scouts. It rested directly in the center of the valley, with nearby rivers that flowed with water for drinking. In the slopes north of the Cimarron River, lush forest provided "timber of the finest quality" as well as land suitable for growing "grain, cotton, and vegetables of every kind," with promises that flourishing there would be easier than anywhere else they had known. People looking to build homes wouldn't just have to rely on timber. "The finest building stone is found, and hundreds of springs produce a never-failing supply of water." And as an exception, one could buy up the land at $1.25 per acre and could get full ownership of the land under their feet in fourteen months, not the usual five years.

There was promise in these lands, but the promise was twofold for the Black colonizer. On the one hand, he had the promise of making the land under his feet *his* because the law said so. On the other hand, that promise would read like a threat if you thought that ownership rid you of the discrimination you could find in the rest of the Union, particularly the South.

The land was deeded to no man, and it wasn't only Black people of Langston who had their eyes set on it.

So did the newly arrived white cowboys. Whiskey and beer had intoxicated them that night, bringing out a liquid courage that tested the mettle of the Black people of Langston—their ability to shake off threats and corral the rabble-rousing, while never giving the impression that they wouldn't defend themselves. Sober or intoxicated, the cowboys made their promises clear, as a reporter paraphrased their sentiments: "Any negro who attempts to settle there will be killed." Even more starkly, the *Chicago Daily Tribune* wrote, "A gang of cowboys from the Cherokee strip have their eyes on this locality and say that any negro who attempt to settle there will be a dead nigger." A familiar tone from the world many of these Black people had left was struck—one where lynching occurred where the state didn't want to execute justice, where hopes of Reconstruction had been dashed, and an equal chance at *making it* seemed a fiction.

Even more familiar were those who rode uninvited into Langston to shoot at Eagleson just two nights before the lands opened. By this time, Eagleson had a reputation of making headlines about how the land was promised to any Black family who wanted their chance to begin again. Given Eagleson's prominence, the cowboy's grim logic made sense: And so they sprayed shots into a crowd of Black Langstonians.

Somehow, Eagleson managed to get away unharmed. But others were not so lucky: Their wounds testified that these white cowboys would be back, as one reporter put it, "swearing they would return . . . and wipe out the town." They'd need to protect themselves, as all the deputy sheriff's office in Guthrie would do was announce that a race war was brewing.

Two days later would be the land run. And cowboys would be coming for McCabe himself.

———◄—●—►———

Tuesday, May 5, 1891

Opening lands in America nearly always turned violent. But a few months before, that violence had been not between Black and white settlers, but between Black settlers and Indigenous homesteaders. Scenes of marginalized people pitted one against another are peculiarly gruesome, not because it is inhuman for people to disagree, but because such disagreements represented painstaking work to set them against one another for no other reason than to consolidate power.

On Tuesday, May 5, 1891, the land of Oklahoma witnessed one such disagreement that should be read as an example of what happens when lives of abundance are on offer to everyone who's white.

Oklahoma Territory had been designated primarily for white settlers in the western part of the present-day state, while the eastern part, Indian Territory, was reserved temporarily for Native American tribes. Many parts of both territories possessed the ruggedness to match the myth of the West that hardened its supposed pioneers. But by Gooseneck Bend, the topography tells a different story—one of a lush, green land of plenty. The streams curve between the towns of Fort Gibson and what would become Braggs—key areas during the Civil War. The mountainous terrain provided shade, and the tall trees and grass left open opportunities not just for grazing, but of timber for homes in which those logs could light fires. The counties of Muskogee and Cherokee contained the bend, with trails that wound around sprawling pumpkin patches that sprung up wild.

The U.S. government was continuing to force concessions of land from the Cherokee Nation, but Gooseneck Bend was still Cherokee-held land, as long as they could keep it.

Maybe it was the fertility of this ground, or its proximity to the waters, or its protection by the Cookson Hills at the lower part of the Boston Mountains that attracted people who were not Cherokee, Creek, Seminole, or Sac and Fox. But the call issued by McCabe to the Black people to come west was too alluring not to take him up on it.

Many stopped short on their journey to Guthrie and then Langston to their haven of Black life and took it upon themselves to make this land theirs—the land of Gooseneck. And their presence was resented most by Chief Joel B. Mayes.

On May 5, tensions boiled over. Black people who had been told by McCabe's agents that they'd be received well were called "intruders" and "negro squatters." Some two hundred had begun putting down roots in Gooseneck after repeated dictates by Cherokee Nation leadership to stand down, retreat, and return. But the Black people observing the activities of the white people who also made landfall in parts of the territories thought they could be just like white people, that their powers of colonization would count for just as much. That they could arm themselves with Winchesters and a brass cannon and ignore the requests of the Cherokee.

With each demand from Chief Mayes, the aspiring Black residents of Gooseneck in Indian Territory called on more Black people to join the effort—to brandish their weapons and show that they wouldn't be moved. Papers like the *Manhattan Mercury* called the effort of the Black people a "negro assault." And it was.

The U.S. Interior Department refused to intervene, because it already had more than enough complaints from other parts of the twin territories of hostilities breaking out. This certainly wasn't the only one. So the U.S. government told both the Black people and the

Cherokee that "it would be not well for the parties concerned" if the government settled the issue. Put another way, the government admitted it knew this was a problem of its own making, so perhaps doing each other in was the best path forward.

Many Cherokee—both Black and not, given that at least 10 percent of all Cherokee who came to Oklahoma during the Trail of Tears were Black, many of them called Freedmen (a blanket term for people listed in the Dawes Rolls as descended from the formerly enslaved even if the ancestors had not been enslaved)—began to question why Mayes's posture toward the Black people was so brutish. "Had the Mayes administration inaugurated its crusade against the Gooseneck negro intruders at some other time instead of the present, it would have looked more like they intended to do something other than electioneer," wrote the *Indian Chieftain* of Vinita, Oklahoma. The allegation was that the Black Cherokee and the Black people they deemed "intruders" might try to work their ways into Cherokee citizenship and affect Mayes's chances of getting reelected.

Ultimately, that was the only way the standoff was settled. Chief Mayes, instead of starting a battle that would have cost many lives and much property, sacrificed the property and put up for sale the land upon which the Black people sat. Ike Rogers, a Cherokee Freedman (and relative of humorist Will Rogers) took to the papers to say that the sale of the land was a violation of existing treaties. Confused and angry, he wrote, "It was not our intention to run over the country, to kill people and destroy property," as was reported. "All we ask is peaceful possession of the homes we now occupy." Continuing, he said, "We are law-abiding people, yet we will protect ourselves when we cannot get protection through our laws." His protests and pleas fell on deaf ears.

Mayes proceeded with the sale of what Black people had—Cherokee or not—along the Gooseneck. It angered the Black people, but Mayes conceded to the U.S government the evolving nature of the circumstances. The land wouldn't be Black or Indigenous. It would soon be for the highest bidder.

—◄—■►—

Only a few months later, Eagleson and other Black settlers were shot at just before the territory opened. Whether in Gooseneck or the Cimarron Valley, and across the lands, Black settlers would not be welcome.

At the same time of Eagleson's near miss, the *Topeka Daily Capital* published an unusual series of articles with an argument to present: that the sudden advent of "poverty-stricken negroes" into the Indian Territory would prove to be a boon not just for newly arrived Black people, but for the Territory. It was the territory that stood to gain most from the then-exodus from southern states into Oklahoma.

Writers from the *Norman Transcript* surmised that residents of Norman, Oklahoma, disagreed. Not only would Black people not improve the territory, the editors wrote, but Black people didn't belong there at all.

A Kansas reporter, the residents warned, even "lauds McCabe, the founder of the bogus town of Langston and the originator of the exodus scheme, to the skies instead of giving him the censure and thorough showing up that he so richly deserves for the part he has played in [e]nticing these poor deluded people into a strange country to be at the mercy of the wintry blasts and sharks like himself." The paper believed that this "new" world was for them and those who looked like them alone, not McCabe, and not the thousands of Black people he brought with him.

If there was anything the residents of Norman wanted of McCabe and those like him, it was to return, not just to the states where they came from, but to the stations in life they believed God had designated for them.

The *Norman Transcript* was not alone. Impassioned pleas rang out from newspapers like the *Arkansas Democrat*, the *Topeka State Journal*, a Washington reporter for the *St. Louis Republic*, and the *Lewis County Journal* of Missouri to prevent the territory of Oklahoma from becoming a Black state or even allowing a government at the state or local level to be established where Black people would lead. The *Lewis County Journal* threatened, "There are white men there who entered the territory in good faith to take up homes and build up the country." The *St. Louis Republic* carried the same report, but added, "If the negroes attempt to capture that territory they will have to fight for it."

The *Democrat* even quoted an unnamed Iowa Republican who'd emigrated to Oklahoma. He was no friend to McCabe's plans for Oklahoma. "I am a republican and have always been a Republican," he told the paper, "but we will not tolerate a negro government there."

The aspirations of McCabe, then, were dangerous. "If McCabe is appointed governor and ventures to enter Oklahoma as such," the Iowa Republican continued, "I would not give five cents for his life." He made his point most clearly when he told the paper, "I am told that 'dead niggers make an excellent fertilizer,' and if the negroes try to Africanize Oklahoma, they will find that we will enrich our soil with them."

The day of the land run was, for McCabe, almost business as usual. Like any other day, he worked on behalf of the territory's governor as its treasurer of Logan County. This meant riding between Guthrie and Langston. But on this day, his typical horse ride to Guthrie was met with that most classic of events on the prairie: a challenge by gunmen.

The cowboys who greeted McCabe were white. And they did not

view him as a man on his way to work but as an impediment to them and their view of their promised land. The night before, another set of white cowboys had fired warning shots at Eagleson. Now, if they shot McCabe, it would become the third reported unprovoked attempted killing of a Black man in two days. Loudly, they told McCabe to return from whence he came, only to be disappointed, befuddled even, when McCabe returned their demand with a denial—a no.

The cowboys' reported 1873-model Winchester rifles—the ones that "Won the West"—fired. They would have to wait quite literally until the smoke cleared to see if McCabe had been killed. But as the powder and dust began to dissipate, they could see that McCabe was no longer astride the horse. Their deed—it seemed—was done.

But they missed.

With the pommel of his saddle grazed slightly, McCabe had fallen off his horse and hidden behind nearby carriages. His comrades, not far off, had heard the screams, the yells, and the gunfire, knowing McCabe had been headed home. The Black men took up the same guns the white men had, Winchester 1873s, to defend their own version of the West and the Moses who had led them there.

McCabe survived, escaping narrowly, but not without the warning that achieving his dream would mean laying his life on the line. His dreams—and those of his followers—were as dangerous as they were alluring.

"Too Much Political Ambition"

LOGAN COUNTY, OKLAHOMA, 1892

O*ctober 6, 1891*—Negro Supremacy

"At present the Oklahoma blacks will work in harmony with the Republican party," said the *Daily Picayune* in New Orleans, "but that as soon as they are strong enough they will have a new party, that of negro supremacy in at least one State, with negro State and county officers, and negro Senators and Representatives in Congress."

This dispatch, ringing out from the paper of record for New Orleans and arguably the state of Louisiana, stoked a fire that only amplified the aspirations of some Black people and ignited rage and fear among white settlers of Oklahoma. The article's electrifying headline? "Black State."

A few weeks before, McCabe had escaped being shot at on the opening of the Land Rush, after losing his bid to be appointed territorial governor of Oklahoma. But when this article appeared in the *Picayune*—which highlighted him by name—McCabe seemed remarkably undeterred.

He had been busy building up towns in Oklahoma, not just Langston, demarcating what he hoped would one day be under his governance. Langston had already held municipal elections, electing a host of McCabe's friends and colleagues to implement the strategies he developed. The plans began to take shape, transforming it from a sodhouse- and wagon-lined outpost into a community that represented the self-contained dreams they hoped to scale upward. "A hotel, dry goods store, drug store, grocery, meat market, livery, cotton gin, and grist mill, as well as a building contractor, a barber, a doctor, and several lawyers and real estate agents," according to Daniel Littlefield and Lonnie Underhill. Dreams were becoming reality.

"McCabe professes to be thoroughly well satisfied with the results so far attained," stated the *Picayune*, "and asserts that within two years the negroes of Oklahoma will outnumber the whites two to one." The numbers here are approximate and skew more aspirational than factual. Guthrie, had in fact, ballooned to over ten thousand people upon the first day of the first land run. After all the efforts Mc-Cabe put into building a Black state, the plausible amount he actually attracted—some eight thousand—also felt like a reach then and now. But that didn't prevent him from estimating the number far higher, toward fifty thousand, with a goal of one hundred thousand by the end of the year.

Guthrie had become the center of gravity for the territory. And as self-contained as McCabe had hoped Langston would be, he had to balance that despite his hope for what Black people might have, Guthrie was still white, as was Oklahoma Territory.

In fact, every day more white people were arriving in the territory, only to see—with surprise, if not outright hatred—the numerous towns established by Black people. If their eyes were open, they'd witness every achievement McCabe made—getting to Langston, supposedly convincing some two thousand agents to proselytize a new day dawning, thousands of Black people moving into the state, a well-organized town, with more towns coming, subscriptions of hundreds of northern white sympathizers sending money, a grist mill, a school, doctors, lawyers, real estate developers, and more plans. This was McCabe pushing ahead of and beyond what his supposed station should be.

Perhaps this is why McCabe, according to the *Daily Picayune*, argued that Oklahoma was the place for not just Black people, but for the country to solve its "colored problem." But his solution was not just exodus. It was the offer of a beginning, a different one than his white counterparts anticipated or wanted. The *Picayune* warned that "the white people living in Oklahoma and in the newly opened Cherokee strip which will doubtless be territorially attached to the former, will have something to say about the peopling and politics of the new state." This meant that McCabe wasn't so much solving the "colored problem" as he was making Black people a problem in the West.

The stakes were high not just for white people whose sympathies didn't support the cause of a Black state or their living for the first time as an afterthought in the construction of American society. They were higher still for McCabe. "Another Hayti in the heart of the American Union, in the form of a sovereign State, would be constantly cheering and instructive to those religionists and politicians who have so earnestly desired to the whites of the Southern States under the dominion of the negroes," the *Picayune* continued. "This has been denied them, but the spectacle [of] a negro State may be yet vouchsafed."

Haiti—a revolutionary Black nation with an ethic steeped in the tradition of resilience and Black empowerment—represented far more than a school or a grist mill. It represented the chance for Black people to govern themselves and create a government in their image. The creation of a Black state could be "necessary as an object lesson to educate the American people as to the capabilities of the colored brother. It would give the negroes themselves an opportunity to show when left to themselves whether they are capable of creating and maintaining any higher civilization or better political conditions than their race has established in Hayti and Liberia," the *Picayune* wrote.

No longer was McCabe's message one of fulfilling the Republican dreamscape of a big tent only during elections. No longer would McCabe prize equality but rather a nationalism, a supremacy of his race over matters in the state he hoped to make theirs. No longer would he campaign to be a governor who would honor Black and white citizens equally. Now he was determined to build "another Hayti."

◄━►

Not long after George Steele was appointed territorial governor of Oklahoma, he made known that his tenure would be short-lived. Before long speculation rang out whether McCabe would quickly ascend. Before the end of Steele's term, Black papers began to push McCabe's candidacy again. The headline "Why Not McCabe?" even appeared in the *New York Age*.

At this point, few in the territory could rival McCabe's accomplishments prior to making it there and his preeminence in Logan County. McCabe had been serving as treasurer for the county that contained the capital of the territory. He had founded townships. He had added colleagues to his roster of supporters—both Black and white. He reported the financial dealings of the capital county of the territory directly to its governor, who'd held office for less time than McCabe had. He marshaled resources from Black people locally and from the Northeast-based advocates of his cause of Black abundance and autonomy. He had presided over a migration and colonization scheme that, while it hadn't resulted in a Black state *yet*, offered a glimmer of hope that it would.

Republican Party politics had become old hat to McCabe. He had played at the most local levels of party politics—in Nicodemus, in statewide party politics across Kansas—and national party politics in Washington, organizing for his own political aspirations and the collective pursuits of Black people in the West. So the activities of the Logan County Republican Convention should have been relegated to the perfunctory, just proceedings to affirm the platforms of the territory's Republican Party and leadership that affirmed the platform of the national positions of the party. Whatever disagreements erupted, they would have been petty squabbles. As much as McCabe should've been able to anticipate the sentiments expressed during the convention, he had been shot at, and his township was surviving solely by his grit and that of the Black migrants who came. To some, McCabe and the cause of Black colonizers were becoming signs of neglect in Oklahoma Territory writ large.

Of the numerous items on the agenda of the Logan County Republican Convention of September 1892, nothing caused as much of an issue as schooling.

Kingfisher, fifteen miles west of Logan County, had seen catalytic growth once the Chicago, Kansas and Nebraska Railway connected through it. This area had always been in McCabe's mind as a potential location for even more Black people to settle, almost as an overflow from the actual capital, Guthrie, and the de facto Black capital, Langston. Black people had settled some of the towns surrounding Kingfisher but were not included in the county that shared the town's name.

The growth of the Black population and the prospect that that growth would spread to all parts of the territory and the growing assumption that both Oklahoma Territory and Indian Territory would become a unified state struck some white residents with fear. And they used the *Kingfisher Times*, the town's local paper, to place that fear in literal black and white—for both Black and white.

McCabe and his fellow Black Republicans who attended the county convention became the subject of fixation for the *Kingfisher*

Times. "The republican Convention in Logan County is a fair sample of what it will be here next time," the paper announced. Put another way: One way or another, the Logan County Republican convention would be replicated. In other words: Beware.

◄—◆—►

Many of the people in Logan County were landowning Black people and came from all parts of the country. Here, at the edge of the frontier—and long after Reconstruction's end and Jim Crow's rise—these people decided they wanted to get ahead of the territory's Republican Party by prioritizing the creation of "mixed schools"—schools that were racially integrated. Undoubtedly this would be a polarizing issue and nobody knew exactly where it would lead. Yet the residents of Logan County made their best pitches at the county convention. The new territory need not resemble the worst ills of the South, they argued; instead, Oklahoma could actually be a forerunner in redesigning a future they wanted all of America to adopt.

Objections rang out from the editors of the *Kingfisher Times*, who spoke, they felt, for a large contingent of Oklahoma's white population. Although the county convention was by all accounts orderly, the *Times* warned that there was a problem: "The negroes ran the whole concern." With Black people running things for perhaps the first time, white observers concluded that Black people gave "the whites a few crumbs to prevent their bolting the ticket." The Logan County Republican Convention, the paper lamented, "shows that the dominating element in the party here are negroes and that their low tastes will hereafter find expression in the measures proposed in the platforms."

It was a signal to McCabe, who advocated for these educational reforms, that his aspirations for a state run by Black people or even equitable treatment in the West might exhibit too much political ambition. The hope was that there would be a fusion of opportunities, especially educationally, for Black and white people, which did not mean a true blend of ideas from both Black and white residents but rather contrition on the part of Black people for even endeavoring to secure equitable treatment for themselves. Fusion was simply an agreement to allow Black children to attend the same schools as white children.

Any future divisiveness was now squarely the fault of Black people, trumpeted the *Kingfisher Times*, since it was they who advocated for equal education. "It also brings forward the question of race distinction and makes it the leading question in the territory"—precisely what the white territorial residents would've rather avoided. "It drives men to take sides one way or the other"—even if without advocating for themselves, Black Republicans and white Republicans would have different opinions. In this moment, Black people were not just cast as unsettling to the future of colonization, they were made to become a pollutant. "It shows that negroes rule the board despite the vote of the whites. It also shows that republican rule means negro rule and that a vote cast for that party is for the domination of blacks of the whites." They equivocated the likelihood of casting their lot with Black politicians with Negro supremacy and the limiting of white male influence. The fear was that if Black people got mixed schools, it would "affect the future peace and contentment of our settlers and have a permanent effect upon the character of the future emigration to Oklahoma." In other words, too many signals of progress might bring to fruition McCabe's plan of Black colonization—and colonization on the terms of Black abundance.

The fear increased, the coverage of the events spilling into other columns in the same edition of the paper. "What is the difference between voting for a negro and voting for the man the negro controls?" another piece in the *Kingfisher Times* asked. "If you believe in the principle of mixed schools and negro rule in this country, you must accept . . . negroes in office. Negro politicians mean negro officials, and negro officials mean negro supremacy." Negro supremacy for McCabe wasn't a statement of enhanced social status of Black people over white people or the need to take away the rights white people enjoyed. It wasn't the notion of trying to have more than white counterparts in a society of deficit. Rather, it was the notion that Black people would take up the mantle of leadership for themselves, if given the chance, without encumbrance and interference by white people. But Negro supremacy was but a threat for white politicians.

As such, McCabe's ambition represented a threat to the new world that America was creating atop Indian Territory, which many whites were bent on making similar to the South they had left.

——◆——

McCabe understood this. As the Republican county convention drew to a close, mounting frustrations for Black people swelled inside McCabe, who had come to a realization he would've preferred to ignore. His hope in the Republican Party was evaporating. His frustration over the misalignment between his desired pace of progress and that of his white Republican colleagues had been simmering in the background. He did more than hint at his indifference to the Republican Party when it came to what he believed Black people needed and demanded. He came to Oklahoma to advance the causes of the Republican Party as they propelled forward the causes of Black people and the potential for self-governance. And he hinted two years before the frustration became too much that his eventual departure from the party would come one day.

But the quiet threats of a supposed departure from a party in which McCabe had become a national name seemed to remain just that, no matter how much McCabe telegraphed that this threat was a promise. It took little time for convention-goers to hear the escalating sound of the rumor of McCabe's desire to leave the party and take people with him. McCabe wouldn't be satisfied to leave the party quietly, but he knew that part of his power as either a token, in the cynical view, or as a power broker with an active Black base, in a more honest view, could spark a conversation that would otherwise have no chance of happening.

Even though privately he had left the party, McCabe showed up at the convention and ran afoul of norms. He hadn't just bolted from the Republican Party, he made a bolt for the stage to make a speech. The convention resembled in no way the conventions in Kansas—the ones that convened Black men. The men in Oklahoma were primarily white, many of whom had come to know McCabe as an effective county treasurer and assistant auditor for the territory, but not without taking exception to his scheming on behalf of Black people.

The head of the convention loudly declared McCabe out of order and told him that his time had expired. To some extent, it seemed that his time in the party was over. But at this point, McCabe was on the stage, ready to make a speech.

His Black colleagues, all delegates from different parts of Logan County—many of them brought to the territory by McCabe's calls for a new beginning—also jumped onstage, struck defensive postures, and surrounded him, as McCabe's castigating words tried to be heard over the ruckus rustled up by the convention-goers who had no interest in hearing him. The police and the county sheriff rushed the stage at the McKennon Opera House turned convention hall, brandishing their clubs to ward off people coming to fisticuffs, though a tussling scrum did break out, tossing in its fray the convention chairman, whose status didn't make him impervious to the controversy.

Before his eyes, McCabe saw that his chances of a Black Oklahoma were waning—if not dying, then trampled literally and figuratively by the racialized fear of the white attendees.

19

Things Fall Apart

GUTHRIE, OKLAHOMA, 1907

To those of us who lived back yonder in the yesteryears, when a black man of the type of E.P. McCabe was assistant territorial auditor; when we had a Negro board of regents at Langston and when it was the custom to elevate Negroes to membership on the Republican State Central Committee, the times are sadly out of joint, and we remember too well how many, who prior to statehood and democratic rule, professed to be our friends, turned their backs and joined in the program of passive acquiescence in our demoted citizenship.

—*Black Dispatch*, DECEMBER 30, 1926

On January 1, 1908, Oklahoma hadn't been a state for a month. Aside from the citizens of the Indian nations, the people in its most senior leadership positions were all relative newcomers. There were several train lines that could bring these newcomers into town. However, of most concern for McCabe became the Atchison, Topeka and Santa Fe Railway, who he had recently taken to court for discriminating against Black passengers. The least treacherous way for people to cross the state was by rail. Commerce happened there, and love letters made their way by the rail. The railway was the highway that moved life from one place to another. When William Jennings Bryan came to Oklahoma to extol the populist virtues he believed in, he took the rail. So, too, did Booker T. Washington. But if Washington— the man who in 1905 drew thousands of people, Black and white, to hear him speak—came again just two years later, he would have come in a segregated railcar.

Remarkably, the first bill passed by the Oklahoma legislature, on December 6, 1907, was to impose segregation on its citizens. This was an imposition, since the railways had previously had no laws constraining passengers by race.

"JIM CROW CARS" read the headline of the *Norman Democrat-Topic*, "Railroads Are Preparing for Separate Accommodation of Races." The headline was carried with some approval, with the clarification that "separate accommodations will be provided at the depots for the present, in many instances by designating the general waiting rooms to 'whites' and 'blacks.' In other cases where but one waiting room is provided partitions will be erected."

──◄►──

When a state is first founded—as Oklahoma was formally in 1907— what ought its legislature focus on first? Perhaps the answer lay in neighboring states.

In 1861, Kansas passed a voluminous set of laws called "General Laws of the State of Kansas." They covered items ranging from the issuing of bonds to defraying expenses the state accrued in its infancy. Despite Kansas being organized in the throes of the country's most divided time—the Civil War—legislators spent the time worrying about making sure they appended the country's founding documents and affirmed them.

Texas joined as a state in 1845. Ever bent on its independence, Texas spent its first years in the Union working to adapt its preexisting constitution—from its days as an independent republic—into a state constitution. Eventually, like Kansas, it adopted a set of general laws that governed the state. Each one of the states surrounding Oklahoma came into existence at a time when the U.S. Constitution articulated a degraded status for Black people. So it should come as no surprise that Texas and Arkansas (which became a state in 1836), both states that joined the Confederacy, affirmed a limited status for Black people.

Decades later, Oklahoma might have been different. After all, it was founded after the Civil War. More important, many of the territory's towns had been founded by Black people, and its Black residents could be counted among its historical and contemporary leaders. But in spite of this progressive history—or perhaps even because of it—Oklahoma swung far to the right in its founding. In so doing, the new state told McCabe just how little its leaders valued him.

The state didn't waste any time implementing its number one priority: segregation. The rules took effect immediately. The state activated its Corporation Commission to ensure that separate depot waiting rooms would be created, and the Railroad Commission commanded that each railway had to continue services without any interruption.

This unexpected Christmas gift wasn't received with indifference from Black people throughout the state, not the least of whom was McCabe.

‹———›

Delegates from the state's capital were making their way to Muskogee on the Kansas and Texas railway when they passed through Redbird. The town had been founded in eastern Oklahoma as an all-Black town and followed the template established by McCabe, sending out invitations throughout the South for Black people to come to build a better life. Some four hundred people had founded the town years earlier and it grew eventually to encompass its own schools, general stores, churches, and the like.

State leaders who came through had been riding in their whites-only carriage after the sun had fallen. State Senator Reuben Roddie was standing in the aisle, and his colleagues State Senator Henry Johnston and State Representative H. G. Stettmund were seated. The state senate and house had been busy passing laws at a rapid pace, and the three men were on their way to Muskogee on state business. They were nearly in Muskogee, just seven miles away, when the windows shattered, sending glass all over Johnson and Stettmund, who suffered a flesh wound as the coal rock that had shattered the glass struck him. The residents of Redbird made their dissatisfaction clear without raising a voice, lodging a complaint, or implicating anyone, because before the passengers or train attendants could figure out who had done anything, the protestors disappeared into the darkness.

Satirically, the *Boley Beacon*, a Black newspaper based in Boley—another Black town that had followed the McCabe playbook—wrote, "It's now in order for the legislature to enact a curfew law for the Negro, compelling all Negroes to stay indoors after dark and by the way, another law that Negroes shall not eat biscuit and grape nuts except by authority of the governor, countersigned by the secretary of the state and Attorney General." Perhaps another Jim Crow law, in the estimation of the *Beacon*, would've prevented Black people from stopping the so-called "Royal Train."

Moreover, it wasn't a shattering of the windows by large lumps of coal. No, the *Beacon* called it "[hearty] applause from the citizens" of Redbird, who presented not "coal" but rather "diamonds and such other jewels as they could find along the railroad right for-way." Jokingly, the publisher of the *Beacon*, Ernest D. Lynwood, wrote, "The royal party complained of this sort of reception but did not seem to understand the situation."

McCabe's case and his profile quickly garnered the attention of

William Henry Harrison Hart, a Black attorney and then-dean of Howard University School of Law's Criminal Law Department, the same law school that the namesake of McCabe's town once served as dean of.

By February 26, 1908, Hart had descended on Oklahoma. His trip lasted longer than the very reason for his visit—or rather his own form of protest that drew him to Oklahoma. McCabe had filed an injunction in federal district court in Oklahoma against the state and against the five railroad companies, chief among them the Atchison, Topeka and Santa Fe Railway, but he was swiftly denied, allowing train services to continue segregating passengers. Hart refused to take the train because it would force him to endure the same fate that the thousands of Black people in Oklahoma were now subject to—riding in the Jim Crow Car, as it became known. As soon as Hart crossed the Kansas-Oklahoma border and reached Fallis, Oklahoma, a Pullman porter greeted him and demanded that he enter the Jim Crow Car, which Hart flatly refused to do.

Instead, he was met with an automobile that drove him slowly across the vast landscape all the way to Guthrie. When he arrived, he was greeted by Black people who were looking for their own knight to lead their cause in court. Not only did Hart possess credentials that dazzled Black and white audiences, but unlike McCabe, he claimed that he had in his pocket a letter written and signed by President Theodore Roosevelt urging Judge John H. Cotteral, who had dismissed the injunction, to reconsider his position.

But Hart came to town to fight what most believed would be a losing battle. "If I had not been employed in the case I should have insisted on coming to Guthrie on the white section of the train, but I could not afford to take any chances on laying over in jail for fighting the constitutionality of the law," he said.

Hart's education, qualifications, and ambition proved no match for a state government that had been given the right to do as they pleased. What's ambition in a state if America has decided to let the state double down on racism? The case was dismissed by the judge.

—◄●►—

McCabe still believed in the system, or at least his actions spoke to that effect. He took up the case and pursued it further when more reports came in from across the state of the demeaning conditions for Black people in train cars. Samuel Robert Cassius wrote a pivotal account, "Jim Crow as I Saw It." In it, he wrote, "This closet," not a true waiting room in the Ardmore area, "is the most filthy place I ever saw, in even a village. The sitting room is small and devoid of all regard for comfort . . . It seems that it is used by bums and toughs of both races as a place in which to drink boot-legged whiskey."

The Jim Crow Car transported Oklahoma backwards—back to the South, back to the worst of America, back to making a Black state an impossibility, not an outgrowth of McCabe's political ambition.

And the state was just getting started. Soon, the state passed bans on interracial marriage (only between Black people and everybody else), implemented poll taxes, limited Black people being able to serve as electors from various precincts and counties. Democrats openly applauded themselves as they delimited Black life to near electoral meaninglessness.

—◄●►—

The actions that empowered the white Oklahoma politicians to flatten McCabe's dreams were all driven by the same principles. First, that Black people were inferior. Second, that America had given the leaders of Oklahoma who thought Black people were inferior permission to make Oklahoma into their image, and that image was distinctly white.

Governor Haskell, House Speaker William Murray, and their supporters appropriated the same cries the heads of Indigenous nations bellowed: that the federal government shouldn't interfere in their local decisions because the rallying cry for this new state's government aggravated the governor. Haskell fumed that Oklahoma was admitted to the Union under the auspices that Guthrie would become the new state's capital, keeping it at the center of the state's commerce, politics, and power.

In Guthrie sat McCabe, but not just McCabe. Logan County contained the greatest concentration of Black people, many of them landed, many of them educated, and they were joined by thousands of white Republicans. There was always a concern among the likes of Haskell that Black people would get too big for their britches— britches he believed white people had bestowed upon them. There was a place for Black people, and for Haskell it wasn't at the center of decision making.

In one short year, Black people had been stripped of their equal status under the law. Republicans who took for granted that the Black people who powered that party recognized that they and their electoral power were sliding down the slope of power and abandoned them. The grandfathering in of these sorts of laws led to A. C. Hamlin, Oklahoma's first Black state legislator, from Logan County, and a noted friend of McCabe, losing reelection after many Black people lost their guaranteed right to vote. But even in their abandoning of the Black people who had powered their party for decades, the Republican Party also became a useful object for target practice by the Democratic Party, Haskell in particular.

As much as the Republicans and the Black Oklahomans had lost in several short months when Oklahoma transformed from a territory into a state, they still could, in many ways, control the power center of the state. The capital was theirs.

Haskell favored a muscular state that monitored corruption and the financial dealings of the banking sector. He was no friend of the

common man, if that common man was Republican, and certainly if
that person was Black. He took up his de facto headquarters in the
Tate Brady Hotel in Tulsa, run by W. Tate Brady, a noted member of
Oklahoma's growing contingent of the Ku Klux Klan. As above reproach as Haskell presented himself, his dealings made clear that his
animosity toward Guthrie wasn't just about race, but also about personal profit. A collection of Oklahoma City–based leaders processed
a payment of $20,000 (approximately $660,000 in 2024 dollars), newspapers found, for Haskell—a veritable incentive to move the state's
capital from Guthrie to a whiter, less diverse part of the state.

In short order, campaigns were waged, and there was a well-
financed advocacy campaign to move the state's headquarters from
the diverse Logan County to a whiter part of the state, Oklahoma
City, which was passed in 1910. What hold Black people had on the
center of power had been dislodged by a governor whose contempt for
Black people ran deep and by an electorate overwhelmingly whitened
by depressing the Black vote.

—◄—◆—►—

"PASSING OF E.P. M'CABE," the *McAlester Capital* on August 27,
1908, carried as a headline. Without immediate explication, those
who read it could've been convinced that the man who built up Oklahoma (or at least Black Oklahoma) had died. Written as a nearly
feature-length obituary, the subhead read, "Story of Negro Politician
Which Is Full of Human Interest."

But it wasn't true. It was an attempt to dishearten supporters of
Black equality who might run across the headline while luring them
to consider lending their support to the Democratic Party.

The *Guthrie Leader*, unlike the *McAlester Capital*, wasn't in the
pocket of the Democratic Party, and it wasn't in the business of

spreading lies when it came to Black people. Their actual headline read, "M'Cabe Soldier of Fortune Kicks Dust of Oklahoma from Feet After Varied Career." The paper suggested that McCabe had become a "Victim of Treachery and Broken Promises: After Long Years' of Service in a Republican Party He Is Turned Down." McCabe had given up on Oklahoma because in his eyes Oklahoma had given up on him. He made contact with his old political pal, who was also likened to Moses, Benjamin "Pap" Singleton, and hatched a plan to leave, first for Chicago, but then quickly for British Columbia.

The article took pains to detail each one of McCabe's ambitions and how they were dashed, how each time, Oklahoma and even Kansas gutted him:

1. "Appointed by President McKinley registrar of the treasury. Name withdrawn at behest of Senator Plumb"—the very man who encouraged his Oklahoma endeavors in the first place, a man McCabe would consider a friend and political ally.

2. "In 1898 appointed assistant auditor of Oklahoma, holding that position until November 16, 1907"—only to be unceremoniously removed the moment Oklahoma entered statehood.

3. "1908"—perhaps his last-ditch effort to embed his ambitions into the future of Oklahoma and perhaps the future of Black people in the state—"Applicant for member of Creek lands commission. Turned down by McGuire."

As he watched his political career incinerate, McCabe and his wife were racked with grief as their daughter Edwina died while seeking better medical treatment in Chicago, and his other daughter, "Dimples," was dying as Sarah, his wife, waited by her side.

Whatever wealth he had built from his jobs and his real estate dealings had dwindled to his home. He sent what money he had left for Chicago to his wife and used whatever money he could to pay off the debts he had accumulated when he banked on the future of a promised land that never was.

He even owed the *Guthrie Leader* ten dollars. He paid it, but on his way out after paying his debt he confirmed to them, "Yes, I'm leaving," as "tears glistened in his eyes." "I want to be even with the world," he continued, "I'm settling everything I owe. I love Oklahoma, but the new state has grown too fast for me. I must seek other fields."

The fields that awaited him were in Canada, which had already tried to stem the heavy tide of Black people flooding across the border from Kansas, Oklahoma, and a handful of southern states seeking not even a promised land, but a chance to live without the constants of life dissolving into an abyss of racism. He closed the chapter on his ambition when he told the paper, "I gave the best of my brawn and brain to the cause of Republicanism, but I did not expect when I really needed assistance, that the men whom I have assisted to offices of preferment for nineteen years would throw me down."

Ambition wouldn't let that be the last word. "I shall not complain. And I have no advice to offer my race. Oklahoma has been good to the colored people and it always will be as long as they are orderly and law-abiding. But the colored people cannot depend on Republican promises."

Is Oklahoma Even Worth It?

GUTHRIE, 1907 & OKLAHOMA CITY, 1910

As a rule, [Black people] are failures as lawyers, doctors and
in other professions. He must be taught in the line of his own
sphere, as porters, bootblacks and barbers and many lines of
agriculture, horticulture and mechanics in which he is adept,
but it is an entirely false notion that the negro can rise to the
equal of a white man in the professions or become an equal
citizen to grapple with public questions.

—WILLIAM "ALFALFA BILL" MURRAY, PROCEEDINGS OF THE
CONSTITUTIONAL CONVENTION OF THE PROPOSED STATE OF
OKLAHOMA HELD AT GUTHRIE, OKLAHOMA, 1906

I t is most gratifying to note that for the most part there is peace
and good will among the races," Booker T. Washington told
some ten thousand mostly Black people raucously gathered at the
Brooks Opera House on November 23, 1905. The self-proclaimed finest theatre in the Southwest, the Brooks sat adjacent to the popular
Royal Hotel in downtown Guthrie. The arrival of the best-known
Black celebrity of the time had been the obsession of newspapers, both
Black and white. He came to view the prosperity of Black people in
the western territory. Not everyone who wanted to hear Washington

speak could even get in. An estimated five thousand waited outside, hoping to behold the orator and Tuskegee Institute president.

Washington had a message he stuck to that made him the darling of many white fans and drew criticism from some Black people and adulation from others. The message laid out a prescription for what America might do for Black people—which was limited—and more so about what America's Black people might do for themselves. It shifted the burden of uplift from the party who did the stepping upon to those who were fodder for making the lives of America's white people easier.

"In order for us to grow and exert and influence for the good of all," Washington told the massive crowd, "we should never lose sight of the fact that, in a large degree, we should become owners of property in city and country."

McCabe would agree, as his plan had offered the West as the ideal area for Black people to acquire land, and those ten thousand Black people who listened to Washington were the direct result of that plan. Washington's message was in some ways directly aligned with McCabe's. Doing for oneself resonates with the efforts of McCabe: their own state, their own schools, their own towns, their own leadership.

But the similarities stopped there. "Here in the South both races labor under a disadvantage," asserted Washington, "because the bad that there is done among the whites and blacks is, almost without exception, flashed all over the country, while the worst acts of both races are seldom known beyond the borders of the community or state."

This magnanimous view wasn't just something that McCabe disagreed with personally. McCabe's entire prospect of creating a Black state hinged on reaching out to Black people in the South, people who faced prospects markedly worse than those of the most disadvantaged white person. And it wasn't just McCabe who thought so. Word of the worst treatment of Black people had traveled pervasively from the South to Oklahoma, which was currently experiencing a surge in violence, lynchings, and registrations for the Ku Klux Klan. Even as Washington was preaching, Black Oklahomans were witnessing the exportation of the South's worst tendencies into Oklahoma.

In the face of such violence, Washington focused on moralizing Black life in America, castigating, as reporters summarized, "the tendency of Negroes to buy unnecessary things," and asserting that Black people needed to learn where to "draw the line between the good and the bad, between the virtuous and vicious." Such moralizing was something McCabe and his colleagues never did. Perhaps this was why McCabe never had the sort of celebrity status that Washington did, even in his chosen home of Oklahoma.

After his speech, Washington went to nearby Langston, once McCabe's power base and the seat of Black life in the territory. There, he greeted students at Langston University, a school founded with the desire not to get along with white people but to do for one's own, under the leadership and vision of Edward McCabe. McCabe was not present, let alone celebrated. Instead, Washington was feted by Oklahoma's leading mayors. The smorgasbord laid out and the attention paid to Washington were evidence of the appreciation white and Black leaders had for him that McCabe never enjoyed.

A Pullman car—a railroad car designed for comfortable long-distance travel, offering amenities like private sleeping quarters and dining facilities—conveyed Washington to Guthrie, and in carriages he was paraded through the town McCabe founded. Washington was being feted in a way McCabe would never be. The car arrived at the town's decorated Banquet Hall. More than a hundred plates were arrayed around the space, and the menu had the opulence fit for the kind of man more interested in reconciling Black and white people than combating the truth that split them—oyster soup, fresh radishes and pickles, prime rib with sweet potatoes and chestnut dressing with mashed potatoes, lobster bisque, little neck clams, and more.

Washington came with his customary message that wouldn't un-
settle Oklahoma's white residents with notes of Negro supremacy.
Perhaps Washington didn't mean to do so, but his message of humil-
ity and conciliation was music to the ears of the territory's white establishment looking to finalize their control of this once-Black land.

◄━►

Still, all was not yet lost, it seemed. Throughout Oklahoma Territory,
beyond Langston, Liberty, Lincoln City, and Dustin, other towns like
Boley and Slick had been organized. Advertisements from Black towns
read, "Oklahoma is the best country in the United States for the Southern Negro . . . the liberty loving Negro of Tennessee, Mississippi,
Texas and Louisiana. If you want to breathe pure freedom, come to
Ferguson in Blaine County Oklahoma. If you are a businessman, come
to Ferguson, Oklahoma, and buy business lots and get ready for doing
business." It was clear that McCabe's ambition had coalesced into a
strategy for giving Black people what they couldn't find elsewhere in
America: ownership and control of their fate, no matter how ill-fated.

In Indian Territory, Black people, having seen the successes of the
McCabe project, began doing the same. Even the Black people of Indian Territory—many of whom shared some ancestry or a compli-
cated history of enslavement with these Indian nations—began to
promote Black migration to Indian Territory. These Black people in
the Creek, Cherokee, and Seminole Nations, in particular, had been
granted citizenship in 1866 due to treaties established with the U.S.
government that also ensured that all Black people who had ancestry
in these nations would be granted full citizenship. That citizenship
often came with land and the chance for full participation in the nation's politics and culture. Redbird, Rentiesville, Wybark, and more
towns talked openly of their Black mayors, law enforcement, mer-

chants, judges, and ways of living. That citizenship was constructed in the shadow of Jim Crow but was fortified by their own sinew.

By this time, McCabe had been the deputy auditor of Oklahoma Territory for nearly a decade. This was a far cry from the governorship he'd sought and was accomplished enough to manage. In fact, being deputy auditor was a definite step down from the high position he had in Kansas.

Still, he looked after the finances of the territory even while it was barreling toward becoming a unified state, ignoring the interests of the Indigenous nations who had tried to create their own state and call it Sequoyah.

He had witnessed nearly every part of the transformation of these two territories into a state. He had seen the explosive growth of the towns he founded. He had witnessed the creation of the university and had secured the initial private funding for it. He watched as Republicans and Democrats tussled in the territorial legislature for control of the soon-to-be state. And he saw towns that were once just heaps of grass become buildings connected by paved roads.

McCabe knew that his story would be integral to understanding the story of Oklahoma, whatever it may become. And without his story, there was no understanding of the West as he knew it. So these words of Alfalfa Bill, then-president of the Oklahoma Constitutional Convention, were disconcerting, alarming, and angering:

> As a rule, [Black people] are failures as lawyers, doctors and in other professions. He must be taught in the line of his own sphere, as porters, bootblacks and barbers and many lines of agriculture, horticulture and mechanics in which he is adept, but it is an entirely false notion that the negro can rise to the equal of a white man in the professions or become an equal citizen to grapple with public questions.

But McCabe and his peers could not say that these words were unexpected. Oklahoma was becoming the South, which is to say that Oklahoma was becoming a part of America where Black people were directed to accept separation and be satisfied with less than what they deserved. This was inevitable, and their anger raged at that inevitability.

—◄●►—

On November 7, 1905, the state's constitutional convention was approved by the people of these nations to seek one last time for Congress to honor the wishes of the Indigenous nations of Indian Territory. Congress swiftly denied Indigenous nations a state of their own and cast their wishes into the sea of forgetfulness. By the next March, tribal governments were going to end, according to the Curtis Act, which Congress had passed eight years prior. Under the primary leadership of the chiefs of the Choctaw and Cherokee Nations, and eventually Pleasant Porter, then-chief of the Creek Nation, and John Brown, Seminole Nation chief, leaders from all over the Indian Territory convened to decide how to create their own constitution that would admit the Indian Territory into the Union as its own state, called Sequoyah.

The looming March 1906 deadline created an urgency. The nations hadn't been interested in agreeing to further oversight by the U.S. government. The notion of becoming a state was settling to some extent. As historian Angie Debo points out in her seminal work *And Still the Waters Run: The Betrayal of the Five Civilized Tribes*, leaders of the Indian nations recognized what McCabe did not—that Congress would never approve a state that wasn't controlled by white men. By joining the Oklahoma State Constitutional Convention, the Indian nations tried at least to secure some semblance of their interests to attain better economic and political opportunities within the framework of a unified state.

So the change in course was the result of several collisions, as the U.S. government sought to increase its oversight of Indian affairs. And people like Charles Haskell, a wealthy white man who had no citizenship in any of the nations, had made their way into the Indian Territory and amassed their wealth in places like Muskogee. Alfalfa Bill found his way into the territory by marrying a Chickasaw woman and serving as a legal advisor to former Chickasaw principal chief Douglas Johnston. (The Chickasaw Nation permanently disenfranchised its Black members.) The two were named officers of the convention. Despite some eighty Black men who came to the convention as representatives of Black residents of the territories, only these white men and the non-Black citizens of Indian nations were appointed to official positions at the convention, many of whom espoused deeply racist views. Alex Posey, one of the best-known literary minds of Creek Nation history, publicly and openly hurled racial epitaphs at the Creek Nation's former Black chief, Legus Perryman. But what is to be expected when you minimize the land of people who had been marginalized since the arrival of white people?

The convention concluded with a disappointment, but an inevitable one, not dissimilar from the inevitable pains experienced by Black people in Oklahoma Territory. The two territories were to become a single state.

And the likes of Alfalfa Bill Murray and Charles Haskell would be elevated as populist heroes of the moment. These two Democrats had operated as cultural brokers between the Indian nations and the Oklahoma Territory. The beauty of being these two white men was that they claimed knowledge of the issues of concern to people who had been disenfranchised. It also gave them the chance to appear to their white counterparts in Oklahoma Territory as the most trusted and informed white people on the matter of Indigenous rights. It made Murray and Haskell the clear front-runners for crafting a constitution that would get through the approval processes of the new president, Theodore Roosevelt, when the time would come.

◄━●━►

At the time of the 1900 Territorial Census, Black people numbered over fifty-five thousand, with more coming seemingly daily. Some fifty towns had sprung up under the audacious title of "all-Black towns." As such, one would think that Black men—or at least McCabe—would be front and center in any discussions of a single state.

But not one Black person was invited to the 1906–1907 constitutional conventions. Their most significant presence was found in a petition from Black people in Wanamaker, Oklahoma, protesting the segregation of train coaches and stations. They were literally separated at the constitutional convention, both on paper and in the halls: They were observers, not participants. They could watch as their futures disappeared, without so much as a faint whisper of their voices inscribed into the historical record of the proceedings.

As much growth in the Black population of Oklahoma as there had been, Blacks were far outnumbered by white people, many of them southern Democrats who desired that there be nothing but segregation at all levels of government. Theodore Roosevelt, now president, threatened not to approve the new state's constitution that would separate Black people to that extent. No matter, the all-white Oklahoma Constitutional Convention pushed forward, glossing over the racism that spewed from Murray, the convention's president, who sought to relegate Black people to lives he and his white brethren thought right for them.

For his part, McCabe had to watch the world he had a hand in building fade in front of him. He had become the ball batted between

Republicans and Democrats to distance themselves from the causes of Black people.

No one had anything negative to say about McCabe's actual work. But as the territory became a state, the question of what kind of multiracial democracy there would be in Oklahoma became more of an issue. And Black people in positions of authority became a matter of debate, if not pure castigation. Thus the character of J. E. Dyche, the auditor of Oklahoma Territory, was indicted, because he oversaw McCabe. "The man who prefers McCabe to a white man or an Indian," opined the northeastern Oklahoma paper the *Vinita Leader*, "is liable to do queer things." Could anyone trust a white man who would appoint a qualified Black man like McCabe over a white man?

It was an echo of Alfalfa's sentiments at the constitutional convention that Black people ought not have professional positions. Others indicated their distaste for where McCabe's determination had landed him. The *Norman Democrat-Topic* wrote, "Negro McCabe today is holding the position of deputy auditor and a white girl stenographer is compelled to take this nigger's dictation."

Perhaps that's why when eighteen Black men protested the lack of consideration and the exclusion of Black people at the constitutional convention for the state they had helped to build, their complaints fell on deaf ears.

But this was only the beginning of the undoing of McCabe's dreams. The worst was yet to come. The convention may have written into the Oklahoma constitution that the state "shall never enact any law restricting or abridging the right of suffrage on account of race, color, or previous condition of servitude," but McCabe knew that his time in Oklahoma might be up.

21

Last-Ditch Efforts Require Turning Over Unturned Stones

WASHINGTON, D.C., 1913–1914

It is the old story of the lure of the fruit—sweet because forb'dden. Not warned by the well nigh extermination of the Indian by commingling with whites, nor the already apparent evils of white and black inter-association, they seek to make compu'sory what nature, speaking rac'al antipathy, abhors. The monopolistic conditions of present day passenger traffic would make racial commingling compulsory if segregation in public places is forbidden. What the plaintiffs [McCabe et al.] need is not a decree of court, but a sense of Gargantuan humor.

—*Morning Examiner*, NOVEMBER 21, 1913

McCabe may have left Oklahoma, but he could not leave it behind. And though many indignities had been forced on him and other Black people by the state, it was the 1907 "separate coach law" that continued to weigh on his thoughts.

So in 1908, McCabe, as the lead plaintiff, filed a case first in U.S. district court, suing not the state of Oklahoma for passing its coach law that required segregated railcars, but five railroad companies, the Atchison, Topeka and Santa Fe Railway Company chief among them, for complying with the state's demand to create separate cars for Black and white passengers.

The case had no chance.

To no one's surprise, McCabe's case fell on deaf ears. But finally, in 1910, the Eighth Circuit Court of Appeals agreed to hear the case. In 1911, the court released its decision; McCabe lost the case 3–0 before a three-judge panel. One of those judges was William C. Hook, a then-promising jurist with big ambitions. When Hook concurred with the majority opinion affirming the right of the state of Oklahoma to discriminate against McCabe from riding in the same cars as his white peers, he likely thought nothing of it. It passed along with the many other cases Hook reviewed and issued judgments on. The court found that McCabe and the other three plaintiffs hadn't actually received the injury because they hadn't ridden on the trains, nor had they been refused "equal" but separate cars—or at least the court didn't find their proof sufficient that they had been discriminated against.

The court fully acknowledged that the train cars for Black people had far fewer amenities, services, and accommodations. But all the train companies argued that Black people didn't ride the train nearly as much as white passengers did, so there was no need to provide them equal services.

It wasn't an unfamiliar legal argument advanced by the railroad companies at the time. Several other cases decided by other circuit court judges issued similar opinions and dismissed the claims of Black people. It should not have mattered if Hook dismissed these Black men's claims.

However, Hook's eyes widened as he took in the view of his own future—one that might place him at the door of the U.S. Supreme Court. And when people prepare themselves to occupy a seat on the highest judicial bench in the country, sometimes they forget that it's the details, not the major infractions, that trip up even the most highly qualified.

But on October 14, 1911, Justice John Marshall Harlan, one of the Supreme Court's longest-serving justices, died. His legacy rang out as a peculiar adherent to the principles of civil liberties being applied to all, not just some—a dissenter-in-chief, if you will. He even dissented in the legendary *Plessy v. Ferguson* decision, which ruled that states' segregation laws didn't violate the equal protection clause of the Four-teenth Amendment and therefore were allowed, which served as the legal basis for the "separate coach law." Harlan would have been the reliable "no" in allowing the law to remain in place. Suddenly, a plan was hatched to fill Harlan's seat. But for every political plan, there's also a person who waylays those plans.

But Hook could never have imagined that the waylayer of those plans would be Edward McCabe.

◄━●━►

President William Howard Taft had as many views on the political system as he did the legal system. A Republican from Ohio who had served as secretary of war under Theodore Roosevelt, Taft looked enviously toward the Supreme Court, a court he had long wished to join, and occupying not just any seat, but the chair in the middle—that of the chief justice of the United States. But before he could get there, he would have to contend with ever-worsening race rela-tions that were glazed over by the appearance of legal protection for Black people, even if that protection meant a separation of the races. A former solicitor general of the United States who in only two years had argued eighteen cases before the Supreme Court and won fifteen of them before he reached the age of thirty-five, Taft was an expert in matters of the law and had more experience than nearly any president in memory, with nearly three years on the Superior Court of Cincinnati and eight years on the Sixth Circuit Court of Appeals. And as much of a loyal Republican as he might have been, his loyalty to Republican victories and his own legal career often trumped the causes that Black Republicans supported—he spent much of his 1912 campaign running more moderately against Theodore Roosevelt and the Progressive Party, appealing blatantly to Democratic voters and interests.

None of this should have mattered to McCabe or his case before the court. But Taft was actively trying to hold together a tenuous coalition that had vaulted him into the presidency: southern white Democrats, northern Republicans, a growing population of westerners, and unpredictable Black voters who couldn't be counted on to vote in every state, given the rise of Jim Crow laws.

And Black people had cause to be distrustful of Taft. As president, he elevated Edward White, a former soldier in the Confederate army and believed to have been a member of the KKK, from associate justice to chief justice on the court. In the minds of some in Black Oklahoma, it imperiled the lives and futures of Black people.

Taft is "one of the weakest presidents the country has ever had," Black Methodist bishop Alexander Walters exclaimed to an audience in Boston at the National Independent Political League, "in view of the fact that he had remained silent in the face of continued reports of lynchings about the country." Supporters of Taft, like the *Messenger-Inquirer* newspaper of Owensboro, Kentucky, responded, "What could the president accomplish by denouncing lynchings? He could do no more than denounce. He is without power to put a check to it or to punish the members of a mob." These bishops, pastors, and church leaders held sway over the electorate Taft needed if he were reelected in 1912, just as Theodore Roosevelt was mounting a third-party campaign to recapture the presidency.

The number of lynchings increased during this time and the relative silence of President Taft, coupled with the Jim Crow laws solidifying across the South, placed into question whether Black people would turn up to vote for him. Walters's denunciation was one of many that piled higher than the Taft team had anticipated. The relative discounting of the Black vote seemed to be the tactic that might do in Taft's political future, which made his team's subsequent decisions a tricky game of chess.

This applied as well to the appointments he would make to the Supreme Court. With the death of Harlan, the voice of civil liberties and dissent, Taft would have to appoint a replacement. When loyalties are focused almost entirely on professional appointments and not core values, one finds oneself in a bind similar to the one Taft found himself in. If he appointed someone in the mold of Harlan, he might rouse the support of Black people whose votes he needed. But if he appointed another Harlan, he might also anger the white southerners he had already thrown political bones to with the appointment of Edward White to the chief justice seat. It was the classic quandary for a moderate: trying to appease everyone might end up with him angering everyone.

And with cases like that of McCabe's against one of the most prosperous railway companies coming to the court, the dance that Taft would have to pull off would require no missteps.

Enter William C. Hook. His bona fides were clear as he ascended the legal ranks from private practice to advising the city of Leavenworth, Kansas, to a district court judgeship, and eventually to the Court of Appeals for the Eighth Circuit. He had the sort of credentials that made an ideal nominee. And though a loyal Republican like Taft, Hook didn't let his personal values obscure his professional ambition. Having worked as an advisor to the Democratic mayor of Leavenworth, a town then-noted for it's "ugly" race relations.

When Harlan died, Hook found his name at the top of a list of potential nominees, as Taft watched his chances for reelection hang in the balance. To an antagonist to the advancement of equity between the races, Hook might have appeared to just be a qualified judge. But for Black people, especially reporters at leading Black papers like the *Washington Bee*, "Negroes are opposed to the Hook appointment on account of his alleged hostility to the equal rights of the race in traveling on the railroads . . . Judge Hook rendered a decision [in *McCabe v. Atchison*] positively denying Negroes of the same rights in traveling as other Americans, upholding, in effect, the 'jim crow' car principle." Hook, for Taft, represented a splitting of the difference—moderation in a time of polarization.

Taft received a letter from Kelly Miller, a dean at Howard University. Miller had been known to straddle both sides of the political fence, much to the chagrin of faithful Black Republicans like the editor of the *Bee*, W. Calvin Chase. His paper once wrote that "Miller is never known to come to a conclusion on any subject. He is the only man in the country who is able to ride two horses going in opposite directions at the same time." Miller praised Taft often, but had only unkind words for the president in his decision to dismiss the protests that came from the Black people who had learned of Hook's record on race and were against his nomination.

The ministers Taft might have depended on gathered at Ebenezer Methodist Episcopal Church, where the Black pastors of the Evangelical Ministerial Alliance met and issued this statement: "The Evangelical Ministerial Alliance, embracing the colored ministers of all denominations of Washington and vicinity . . . unanimously adopted a resolution protesting against the appointment of Judge Hook to the Supreme Court." They made clear their reasons: "The ground of objection was that Judge Hook, while presiding over the Eighth Judicial

District, rendered a decision denying Negroes equal accommodations in railway travel."

The proprietor of the *Lexington Leader* in Kentucky tried, unsuccessfully, to dissuade Black Republicans from bolting the party over Taft's nominations by listing every Black appointee Taft had made, but he admitted that on the matter of appointments and the fairness of their allocations, "We have no statistics at hand, but from our own personal knowledge we know that more Kentucky Negroes are now employed in honorable, remunerative positions in the Federal government service than ever before." It was the *Leader*'s view that Black readers would feel comfortable with Taft's appointment of the man who blocked their equal treatment on trains because the president had appointed more Black people than any other president. A veritable "but our best friends are Black" defense whose origins clearly reach back further than one would think.

◄ ◆ ►

McCabe wanted to know that whenever he rode the trains, if he had to occupy a separate car, that car would feel adequate relative to his white peers—many of whom no longer viewed him as a peer, but as an "other." Regardless of what one might have said in support of Taft, Hook's words in concurrence in the case were unmistakable: "Sleeping cars, dining cars, and chair cars are, comparatively speaking, luxuries, and properly enough no such imperative provisions are made concerning them as are made concerning the common and indispensable coach or compartment."

In short, no train service should feel compelled to give Black people the "luxuries" that were afforded to white people as part of their basic service. Put even more bluntly: Black people, like McCabe, were asking for too much. How could Black bishops, ministers, lawyers, average folks, and activists ever be expected to overlook something like that?

It became more difficult to imagine Black people settling for this nomination when Hook concurred that "the ability of the two races to indulge in luxuries, comforts and conveniences was so dissimilar that sleeping and dining cars which would be well patronized by one race might be very little if at all used by the other." Hook believed that if Black people couldn't afford such luxuries—which he clearly believed they couldn't—they shouldn't be offered them by requirement of the law.

Never mind that Oklahoma could boast of thousands of Black people with the means and needs to travel across the state for both business and leisure. Hook placed a cap on the degree of pleasure and comfort Black people should ever be able to enjoy.

Long after he filed suit, long after he sunk what remaining dollars he had in a case that would find its way to the Supreme Court in 1914 only to lose, McCabe was causing trouble that only a righteously obstinate *Moses* could create.

And for those troubles, he didn't pay the price, William C. Hook did. Hook's nomination to the Supreme Court sparked anger and outrage, and eventually was pulled by Taft, who felt bullied by the protests. McCabe and Black people didn't have the right to seek the comforts white people received by dint of doing just as white people had done.

McCabe might have been out of Oklahoma, but he left no stone unturned. As the *Guthrie Leader* would lament, "When [McCabe] left, Oklahoma lost a character and the colored race an honest champion."

22

Scattered and Peeled

CHICAGO, 1920 & TOPEKA, 2000

One by one, that brilliant group of pioneers who formed Guthrie's splendid black citizenship, are folding their tents and silently stealing off to other localities . . . We walk about the silent streets and think of that passage of scriptures which speaks "of a nation scattered and peeled, whose lands the rivers have spoiled."

—*Black Dispatch*, OCTOBER 13, 1921

I have built a monument more lasting than bronze,
higher than the Pyramids' regal structures,
that no consuming rain, nor wild north wind
can destroy.

—HORACE, *Odes* III: XXX, LINES 1–4, PUBLISHED 23 BC

For all intents, McCabe had gone dark after Oklahoma entered the Union, after he made his impassioned speech at the *Guthrie Daily Leader* in 1908, and as he set off to attempt to replicate his colonization society. Newspapers would occasionally ask: Where is McCabe? Some newspapers—mainly Black ones—would feign sympathy for his failures, and for the deaths of two of his children that bookended his quixotic move to Oklahoma. They'd wonder what happened to his hopes for higher elected office, and for a joint venture with Pap Singleton in British Columbia.

And what happened to his dream of a Black state?

The reality is that the Victoria colonization effort was shorter-lived than any of his others. When McCabe left, his family first stayed in Kansas and then moved to Chicago to await word that Victoria was ready for them—word that never came. Canada didn't want them. "Stay in Chicago" is the word they got until McCabe came back to join them.

McCabe came back to Chicago with no fanfare, just a collection of memories. When he arrived, he didn't seek out the newspapers, and once it had been reported that he was back in Chicago and was no longer pursuing the hopes of a Black colony or state, the news stopped seeking him. Until, that is, McCabe was spotted in a place that wasn't all too unexpected.

A summer resort not far from Chicago would be the kind of place where McCabe's narratives about the good old days wouldn't sound imaginary. In a summer hotel, one might expect to see him in a panama hat, glancing every now and again at his pocket watch, shining his once-signature gold-rimmed monocle on the lapel of his suit.

However, it was other men dressed this way that were being served by McCabe. He was headwaiter at a local social club. What claims he once had to popularity and fame had faded.

When he wasn't waiting tables, he was trying to find his way into mattering again. One doomed experiment involved Chief Alfred Sam, a Black man from the British colony of the Gold Coast (today called Ghana) who nearly a hundred years after white men had tried to repatriate Black people to Liberia would try again. Sam wrote to McCabe to convince him to lend what credibility he had left to the enterprise, so that McCabe's support would give Sam's program the imprimatur of seriousness. Sam convinced McCabe to solicit people he knew in Oklahoma, which angered local Black newspaper publishers, who alleged that Sam was a crook.

But as Black life in Oklahoma got worse and Black people began to sell their possessions with the intent to move to the Gold Coast, McCabe began to feel that perhaps his name still carried weight.

Ambition has a way of looking for bright spots when there's only darkness. With great doses of ambition and perseverance, Sam managed to engage a ship, and it set sail for Africa in August 1914. But Sam would soon learn the lesson that McCabe, Kock, and the ACS had learned before him: Ambition can't cleanse the stink of colonization or solve its practical challenges. Some died from malaria, even after being warmly greeted by Gold Coast residents. And local rulers did not find the notion of foreign ownership of land, especially without their consent, agreeable.

McCabe's once-clear memories now were drowned by a rasping cough and frail state, as he became a shadow of his former self. He no longer evinced the strength or resolve he once did. Reality had dealt its blows. Even those who escaped the Gold Coast to return to Oklahoma struggle to remember those days. "They too are plagued by the same symptoms, reflecting the challenges that lie ahead." But these survivors of the Chief Sam venture to the Gold Coast could likely barely recall the fervor of thirty or forty years earlier. Thousands rushed to cross an imaginary line, fiercely staking their claims. Towns materialized almost overnight, driven by ambition, hard work, and the fear of returning to the South. For a fleeting moment, the dream of a real Black state was almost within their grasp.

The intrepidity of these founders of the envisioned Black state that urged them to leave the predictable misery of the South for the untamed promise of the West wobbled under the weight of failure of unrealized dreams. Dreaming, as McCabe learned, has limits, low ones, that restrict the power and influence Black people could accumulate.

◄──►

Like all stories, the end lands not where anyone would have predicted.

On March 19, 1920, the *Topeka Plaindealer*, the paper that once carried the headlines of McCabe's big plans, wrote briefly of his death. "He never bartered or catered to the white man the rights of the colored race," the *Plaindealer* said, "and always stood up for his people." His heroism made it all the worse that no one cared for him in Chicago. These "new negroes," the *Plaindealer* said, "cared naught for men like McCabe who had stood up to advance the manhood rights of the race, still they ignored him." It was said, "They did not even give him a pleasant smile."

He had become nobody once again.

The man who came to Chicago in the 1870s with no friend returned to the city without a friend. No patronage was extended to him for political office. Toward the end of his life he fell sick, could no longer work, and died with debts. Some called him penniless.

He died in an almshouse as a ward of the state, relying on the very sentiment he had always avoided: the charity of white people. His wife begged friends of his in Kansas for enough money to cart his body to Topeka. Luckily, he had bought a family plot when his children died long before his financial straits worsened. His wife traveled to Topeka. She couldn't pay ministers, and what friends he had were scattered, so the pallbearers were the men who worked at the cemetery, the men who dug his grave, and the undertaker himself. They lowered the casket, and Sarah McCabe, the woman who had stood by the dreamer, watched as what little remained of his dream descended into the earth—penniless.

It might be hard to imagine how and why McCabe died in such squalor and how a man who preached Black opportunity and prosperity allowed his own family to descend into the outcome that he preached his followers to avoid. The reporters of the *Plaindealer* offered an explanation as a lesson that could be distilled into the familiar "Negroes, take care of yourselves."

"This should serve as an object lesson," they wrote, "to the men of the race who now have such excellent chances to carry life insurance and membership in lodges. All of these opportunities were not open to McCabe because "in his day lodges were an experiment." For McCabe didn't have access to "the life insurance companies of reliability" because they didn't underwrite "colored people."

For as much bluster and swagger as McCabe had in the worlds of politics and business, in the end he died in silence. And that silence began a washing away of his memory.

◄━━►

Lowell Manis could be found on the grounds of the Topeka Cemetery across four decades, wearing a cowboy hat and a smile. With his two hands and starting not long after high school in the early 1960s, he had maintained the grounds of the cemetery. As superintendent of the cemetery, he held the memories of those whose lives had been forgotten. His living was made by caring for the sites of the dead, the left behind and the forgotten. In doing so, he became the advocate for a history that told of a different America.

Manis had long heard the stories of McCabe, as many other Kansans had. He was a footnote to the great history of the state. But footnotes are not meant to serve as containers for people's lives. They're meant to validate larger stories.

In his capacity as the superintendent of the Topeka Cemetery, Manis knew who inhabited these lands. He'd cut the lawns and unclog irrigation systems. But most important to those who cared to visit the loved ones who had died, he maintained the headstones. Without family or some endowment, he warned, the inscriptions might fade, and with them the notion that the lives were worth remembering. As the writings on the headstones began to vanish, Manis became a zealous advocate for the memories of the people who lay below his feet. And he found allies in his advocacy—unexpected ones.

For all that Edward McCabe might have done and for all that he may have wanted to achieve, what remained of him was barely legible—"P. McCa" is all that remained on his headstone. The man who once eschewed charity had now become the target of it—his memory's survival enslaved to it.

Students from the Dwight D. Eisenhower Middle School in Topeka, under the direction of their principal, Steve Roberts, launched a campaign to save McCabe's memory. Roberts reached out to Manis, who had been telling whoever would care about the dilapidation of McCabe's plot and headstone (as well as others'). Roberts had worked with Manis in the past to raise money for the cemetery's general fund. But this time, Roberts had heard Manis's public pleas that McCabe's name could barely be read. Roberts told Manis that he had come up with an idea to save McCabe—one Roberts had used to help other grave sites in the past.

A pancake feed.

Roberts believed that Manis was struggling with two related problems: awareness and money. No one in Oklahoma today knew McCabe, and, as such, there would be no grand announcement of the establishment of an endowment to create a mausoleum in his honor, as was the case for Manis's successes in reviving the grave sites of some of McCabe's cemetery neighbors. But Roberts understood the system and how schools in Topeka could be the sites of ginning up support. He dispatched his students to tell parents and neighbors, friends, and churchgoers to come to the first pancake feed—pancakes in exchange for metallic sympathy, with all proceeds after costs going to building a new headstone for McCabe.

Manis told the Associated Press that he had tried "to raise money for a headstone." He had read newspaper reports about McCabe's humbling end. He had heard about his wife not being able to give him the funeral most felt he deserved for the sacrifices he made because what little money there was had been poured into sustaining his unlikely dream. So in the late 1990s, Manis decided unilaterally to hold a burial service. He called Reverend Henry Davis, pastor of the Emanuel Temple Church of God in Christ, to preside over the service. Manis invited an anemic crowd of local history lovers, journalists, and community members for what he called "a committal service." Before McCabe's belated funeral, Manis told a reporter, "[McCabe] was a tireless worker for black Americans." Michael Hooper, the journalist who covered the event, wrote as he reflected on what Manis had pulled off that McCabe was the "principal Black leader in Kansas." Manis had become convinced that McCabe's wife, Sarah, did not want the pomp and circumstance not because she couldn't afford it but because she did not want the people they once hobnobbed with in McCabe's halcyon days to see how poor the family had become. As the ceremony concluded, Manis told Hooper, "Never a slave himself, he was deeply aware of the damage of slavery and need to overcome the results of it. He was a true man of the time."

Manis established the McCabe Family Monument Fund and hoped that the committal service, the oratory of a Black pastor, and Manis's personal plea would net them the funds necessary to rebuild the headstone. Only $26 was raised. Later, some $200 was raised by the children of Eisenhower Middle School in a second feed to inscribe the new headstone.

McCabe's promised land had been scattered and peeled—a nod the *Black Dispatch* made to the biblical book of Isaiah to symbolize a time of distress and dislocation for a people. What adherents he had fled Langston, in large part to seek better lives in other Black towns and settlements. And from those places they did as McCabe had done, fleeing for inventions of other promised lands, only to learn that the land wasn't promised, just conjured by hope. In some important sense, McCabe had truly become a Moses—prophesying of a promised land without stepping foot in it.

Today McCabe's life and memory of what he tried to achieve are preserved by the pluck of junior high school students and their principal. Thirty-two inches wide and eighteen inches tall, easily missed in the compact historical section 19 of Topeka Cemetery—a part of the cemetery not far from the resting place of former vice president Charles Curtis, and a handful of other impressively memorialized headstones and mausoleums—sits Kansas's most permanent memorial to a man who tried to reinvent the state, create a new one, and lead it. The name "McCabe" is engraved on both sides. The names and dates of his kids on one side; on the other his and his wife's names and dates. Under his years, it is written, "State Auditor, 1882 & 1884, Sec. of Nicodemus Town Co., Founder of Langston, OK."

There lies the man they called McCabe—or as his followers, antagonists, and observers all called him—"the one who would be the Moses."

Coda

They bypassed us.

—ANGELA BATES, DESCENDANT OF A FOUNDING
FAMILY OF NICODEMUS

W hat address should I put into the GPS?" I asked Angela
Bates.

She giggled. "Oh, you don't want to do that." Ordinarily, the dissuasion to use GPS directions would have stopped me from continuing any trip before it started, no matter how important. I admit, I was just happy that I could fly from Boston to Chicago and from Chicago into Hays, Kansas—a town with a one-terminal, one-gate airport that serviced United Express (the dinkier, younger regional cousin of United Airlines) flyers and United Express flyers only. It was during a brief period when getting from Chicago to Hays didn't require flying past Hays to connect in Denver. From Hays, GPS estimates that it can take an hour to get relatively close to Nicodemus, Kansas. No structure appears on the GPS when typing it in, just a morass of greenish brown and a single Kansas historical marker.

The ambiguity of where it is and how to get there didn't matter because I was happy that the pandemic's travel restrictions had subsided. During the pandemic, getting to Nicodemus required either flying to Denver and then driving four and a half hours or flying to

Kansas City and driving some four and a half or more hours. Neither was ideal.

But after Bates finished giggling, she gave me her own directions. "When you get off the plane and get your car, you want to get to the main street in Hays—it's called Vine Street." As I hurriedly wrote down the street names in a town I had never visited, Bates continued at ever-increasing speed. "You're going to want to take that to the left onto 8th Street coming out of the airport. The next right will take you all the way through Hays. And then you take that to the town which is called Plainville." Hays sounds like a town, and so does Plainville, but those could very well just be street names, though she did joke that some of these towns are one-stoplight places—in fact, Plainville had two flashing yellow lights, not an actual stoplight. So what could be the difference?

She continued, "Now you're going to take a left onto Highway 18 going west again. You're going to want to take that about twenty-five miles over to the town of Bogue. And then when you get to the town of Bogue, you'll come into that town on the left-hand road and go a quarter of a block and you'll see Main Street. You want to go to the blinking right lane and go to the grey Honda sedan and the blue pickup truck and that will be me."

For the next several seconds, all that could be heard on the call was my heavy breathing as I tried to figure out how to get to a town that I had examined only in archives, oral histories, and historical mapping and real estate records. For Bates, a multidecade resident of this town into which she had been born and has now returned to, this was old hat. Giving directions was the only way to find Nicodemus, as any GPS navigation would overlook and bypass it.

———◄●►———

Someone at a county commission meeting—Michael Boyles, mayor of Langston, Oklahoma, couldn't recall who exactly—"asked about a zoning issue." As he remembered it, county commissioners responded rhetorically, with a battery of questions that disregarded Langston, once a town of Black preeminence, as a place worth taking seriously: "Well, it's just Langston, right? Can't you just do what you want to do there without any repercussions? There are no laws or anything like that, you know?"

The mayor recounted this story to me as he held court at a plastic fold-out table, his desk. He was flanked by his wife, Mary, and de facto chief of staff. The decor didn't evince the storied history of the town. The town council meeting room had a leaky roof. The city hall is the same building in which McCabe worked with newcomers who had come to register their land plots or get their marriages recognized.

The Boyleses wanted to tell all who would listen—at this moment just me—about their "Pave the Way" initiative. Mayor Boyles and his wife had picked through the histories they knew of or could recall communally from the remaining residents of the town to determine which streets held deeper history than others. The donor could get a street named after them and the donation could fix some streets that hadn't been repaved in decades. The streets of Langston tell big stories of grandeur that McCabe had wished this town would hold. An avenue named Massachusetts harkened to the importance of the New England Emigrant Aid Company that charted the path to a free Kansas that launched McCabe's political career. Bruce Street and Townsend Street told of Black political leaders who had achieved acclaim as contemporaries and pals of McCabe—Blanche Bruce, the first Black person elected to a full Senate term, and W. B. Townsend, McCabe's Leavenworth counterpart from his time in Kansas.

Before these streets had homes, schools, stores at any of their intersections, before people occupied these towns, and before McCabe had fully established himself in the area, the streets had been named and planned. Naming in these towns was an act of faith and a belief that Black people once built what Mayor Boyles called a "Black

Mecca in America." McCabe drew maps of this town to come—a town named after a Black congressman he admired, John Mercer Langston—in newspapers for distribution and heralded it as "The Only Distinctively Negro City in America," where he promised "Peace, Happiness, and Prosperity" for and by only Black people.

Driving these streets today might indicate that not nearly as much happened in the over 130 years since McCabe first placed advertisements about this town. The streets are in disrepair and no longer paved, rubble replacing smoothed asphalt. In some ways, the mayor and his wife have embarked on the same effort McCabe did some 130 years before.

They're selling the town's streets.

Commercial hubs have passed them by for towns closer to the Oklahoma City metro area, just some fifteen miles away. And with those commercial hubs, so have homes and stores. The population of Black people and people overall in Nicodemus has dropped by over 20 percent between 2010 and 2020 alone. And that atrophying has emptied the town's coffers. What most towns in America do for their citizens—pave roads, fill potholes, pick up trash—aren't financially possible here. So the town has to adopt the strategies of McCabe, except for different purposes: It's offering people the chance to buy into history.

----◄◆►----

Why should anyone care about these two fading rural towns? The answer is simple: Langston and Nicodemus were never meant to be rural outposts, where Black people would live strictly off the land. The design of Langston had much to do with Black dreams on the frontier. It was the expression of what they hoped could be achieved if they built their own Black metropolis.

In Nicodemus, Bates bemoans the tragedy she has witnessed over the decades. She reached into her many boxes of files and memorabilia, her own mobile museum, to pull out "Nicodemus Township Map 8," which displays who owns what. With perfect recall, Bates pointed to each plot, dictating how many acres are contained within each plot. She pointed to where her family set down roots. She pointed out where the churches are, where she'd spend her summers playing with cousins, where annual Pioneer Days were held to commemorate what once was and what the founders thought the town could be. Without taking many deliberate breaths, then-seventy-year-old Bates recounted details few city planners and historians of this region could have. She pointed at each one of the plots on the map and then paused to ask if I noticed what the shaded plots owned by her, family members, and friends had in common. "It's easy," she said. "The shaded-in ones are the ones still owned by Black people." Only eleven were shaded in a town built by and for Black ambition.

⎯◄●►⎯

Nicodemus, which once was a hub for Black political, social, and economic potential, has been called by outsiders a "ghost town." One doesn't have to imagine why: The town has some fourteen residents left. Bates herself does not even live in Nicodemus, but in the town adjacent to it, Bogue, where she runs a restaurant. As I sat in her home for what was supposed to be a brief introduction before heading to her family farm, it turned into a five-hour lecture about the history of Nicodemus and her history with the town.

Her point was not to regurgitate history but to apprise me (and, by extension, you) of the perils of overlooking this town, like the town of Langston and other places that we don't think about but that will tell us a great deal about the history of America.

As a town, Nicodemus had declined. But Bates seems undeterred

CODA   235

by that decline. What's of interest to her is all that she has done to keep the town intact. Getting major structures designated as landmarks and then historic sites. Going up through the ranks of government, from local Park Service rangers to county government leaders to get introduced to congressmen and eventually former U.S. senator Bob Dole to pass an act of Congress to formally recognize her small town. In some important sense, these are likely the only ways that a town like Nicodemus can be preserved and made somewhat economically viable through historic tax credits. The federal government and state historical commissions can defray and subsidize the costs of rehabilitating buildings. The town's hotel and post office, which once greeted countless newcomers, have been saved by this action—a stopgap between preservation and oblivion. Saving these structures has provided jobs to those who otherwise would watch these structures decay.

Life here has not always been fair: Bates shared dozens of war stories of disagreements with family members, of Park Service rangers who didn't request as much money as she wanted, who ultimately received less than they or Bates wanted. But there is no despair in Bates's voice. Rather, she looks back to this past as a source of strength.

While she giggles at the travails McCabe suffered as he entered the town from the Solomon Valley still smarting from food cooked over fires kindled by cow dung, she is pained by the fact that from the start of Nicodemus, its white founder planned its demise. With deft recollection, she told me that W. R. Hill was meant to have "brought the railroad into Nicodemus. They would have been on the north side." But with regret in her voice, as if she had discussed this with McCabe herself, she said, "Hill did not." In her estimation and in the estimation of surveyors of the time, bringing the railroad through Nicodemus made the most sense. But W. R. Hill, a town promoter, and Virgil Bogue, an engineer for the Union Pacific Railroad, schemed, in Bates's estimation, to ensure that the river flowed naturally through the south side, grating against the natural landscape to the towns founded after Nicodemus. Hill and Bogue, from Bates's perspective, were the first to pass them by, and Nicodemus's history was rooted in being bypassed—McCabe's, A. T. Hall, Jr.'s, and even Z. T. Fletcher's shared aspiration of a railroad to vitalize the town was doomed from the start. Like Langston's aspiration of becoming a booming urban town and maybe even the capital of the Black state of Oklahoma, these ambitions were hampered by the plans of those with power. Try as McCabe and Hall might to use the tools of colonization to build the Black future they wanted, colonization had already doomed their ambitions.

These towns were meant to be sentinels of Black success. But their ambitions would have to contend with an equally fervent desire to suppress them to the least number of Black people as possible. And therein lies the fatal flaw of the grand ambitions of McCabe and the ambitions of Bates and Boyles who follow him some 134 years later. They are left with the challenge of making sure their ambition is not forgotten.

What does this history have to do with us today?

Perhaps the struggles of Bates and the Boyleses not to let their towns fade into nonexistence are sufficient to convince you that this story matters. The greatest lessons of history can be found in our smallest totems—for Bates and the Boyleses, the mere existence of these towns serves as totems to ambition, and the inequity in our ability to chase and achieve these ambitions. It's not just these remote towns in the West. Other Black towns, settlements, and neighborhoods are suffering a fate similar to Langston and Nicodemus—serving as ground upon which the broader stories of American ambition and dreams are built. The dreams of Seneca Village's Black community were removed from Manhattan to make way for the dreams of what Central Park could become. Tulsa's modern downtown, vaunted for its excellence and rapid progress, is built atop the dead bodies and haunting dreams of Tulsa's Black Wall Street. The sprawling campus of Columbia University co-opted once thriving parts of the Harlem Renaissance. Boston's Roxbury, Mattapan, the Port, and Dorchester all face headwinds of economic progress today after witnessing massacres, raids, and urban renewal of yesterday.

These towns and neighborhoods are the remnants of the American Dream pursued by Black people, often without the assistance and support of their government. These towns and those who preserve their histories are not as concerned with preserving the extant structures of these communities. McCabe's story, like Angela Bates's story and the Boyleses' story, honors the willingness to try—that the trying offers its own kind of salvation. McCabe's dream might have appeared impossible from the start. But then and now, we strive to carve out homes in a country that wasn't built for most of us.

These towns' survival relies on the dream continuing today. The story of McCabe will forever be the tale of what could have been if Black dreams were as respected as the ambitions of any other people. Instead, we build over their stories and bypass them on our way to a different promised land.

People like Angela Bates and Michael Boyles, the people of Tulsa's Black Wall Street and those who built and remain in Blackdom in New Mexico, and those who blazed trails for Allensworth, California; Mattapan; Durham, North Carolina's Black Wall Street; and East St. Louis, and the Black cowboys who still gather today as they have since 1903 in Boley, Oklahoma—site of the first Black rodeo—are doing what McCabe and thousands of others did: They are deciding that every person is their own Moses now. All that is left for us to wonder and answer today is: Will we continue to bypass those who have been forced to begin again?

Acknowledgments

I love process—studying process, breaking down my less-than-linear life into discrete segmented parts and tasks makes me feel like I can control something. And despite that love of process, I chose as my vocation writing. There are dozens of people who have in some way made this otherwise opaque and byzantine process of making this book happen legible to me. Sadly, I cannot name every one of them—many of them I'll never meet: the people in production who have made material that which only existed digitally; the people who work in transporting this book from warehouses to bookstores; the sales team who called upon their collective talents of synthesis to help this book stand out from the thousands of other books also made this year; and the booksellers who gave and will continue to give this book space on their analog and digital shelves.

There are, however, people on whom I leaned directly to bring this story to you. First, to Charlotte Hinger, author of several works, chief among them *Nicodemus*, your willingness to share what archives you'd accessed, to, even at the height of the pandemic times, meet with me and answer my questions, this book is for you and because of you. The Open City Writing Group served as the first stop for reviewing much of what you've read. Fiction writers, poets, and memoirists in this group called upon their diverse perspectives to provide me meaningful feedback over the course of years. To the Watchdog Writers Group under the leadership of Christopher Leonard, your support of this work created a community of support, without which I would not have been able to complete this work. Much of this book was written while I was on sabbatical at the Radcliffe Institute for Advanced Study at Harvard University. As opulent as the setting of the Radcliffe is, its warmth was filled out by the staff and fellow members of my cohort—most notably, Christopher Muller, Francesca Mari, Elizabeth Maddock Dillon, and Leah Gose, who likewise found themselves just as obsessed with McCabe and invested in my career long after the conclusion of the fellowship. But even the pursuit of the fellowship at the Radcliffe would not have been possible without the chairs of my departments at Northeastern University, Jonathan Kaufman and Régine Jean-Charles, from whom I also received mentorship as a journalist and thinker. To Andrea Blatt, you helped *Black Moses* land at Riverhead Books. And Chris Parris-Lamb, you helped transform this from yet another book into a necessary and helpful pivot in my contribution to answering long-standing questions of belonging. To the team in marketing and publicity at Riverhead Books—namely Ashley Garland—you helped show the way of making the world care about this part of the country and the story of people's ambition in my first book, and it undoubtedly carried over to *Black Moses*. Whitney Peeling, and the team at Broadside PR, you helped to amplify both the book and also my understanding of how to reach varied publics with this story. To Ben Platt, your help while I was in the proverbial trenches of reshaping the book have likewise made this book what it has become. To Anna Colletto, thank you for your deft research assistance. Your curiosity and perspicacity made even more navigable the world of those who pursued this saga of ambition. I cannot wait to celebrate your work as a journalist, a thinker, and, likely, my future boss. To Bill Vourvoulias, your research support and fact-checking provided and continue to provide me with confidence about the way I rendered this tale for the reader.

To Jake Morrissey, you are the editor I wish more writers had in their lives. Your specified and painstaking review of my work adds dignity to the telling of stories. Your patience with me and my style and my fixations and my desires models what collaborative creative processes should be. And your encouragement made it possible for me to continue this work and complete it.

To my wife, this book would not have happened unless, years ago on our first date, you told me—before you even completed your training, before the way was straight, before we could afford much—to quit my job and write. The faith you have in me is unlike any feeling I have ever known. This book is a testimony to that faith. To my parents and siblings, your willingness to read this work before it was polished, and even your willingness to depart with the safe choice—continuing the journey in business—and recommend I pursue my wildest dreams, both abandons rational thought and embraces radical love. And so, I thank you.

And though it is presumptuous to thank you, the reader, for making it this far, I do. Your choice to read the undertold story enables more undertold stories to get the shine they deserve.

Notes

INTRODUCTION

1 **"We will have a new party"**: "Black State," *Chicago Tribune*, October 2, 1891, p. 10. This is a direct quote from McCabe as quoted in the *Tribune*. While this particular installment is useful and seemingly comprehensive, as it was the *Chicago Tribune*'s full feature on the question of Oklahoma becoming an all-Black state, I highly recommend also considering several additional sources if you would like to learn how other contemporary newspapers with less sympathy for the Black colonization movement covered it. Here are a few other examples to consider. John A. Cockerill, an intrepid reporter, chronicled McCabe's efforts to colonize the Oklahoma Territory for Black people against the backdrop of reports of the declining travails of people to constitute Liberia: John A. Cockerill, "Cockerill's Letter: Bishop Turner and Negro—Discouraging Reports from Liberia-Ex-Senator McCabe's Oklahoma Scheme," *Salt Lake Herald*, October 2, 1891, p. 14. Consider also the coverage around the same time by Lawrence, Kansas, newspapers the *Weekly Record* and *Lawrence Daily Gazette*, along with northeastern papers the *Morning Journal-Courier, Boston Evening Transcript, Times Union*, Davenport, Iowa's *Daily Leader*, and many others. The *Daily Picayune* coverage nuances the framing as a pitch McCabe and other Black elites were making to "work out there the colored problem." Each article weaves in local elements to color their varied views of McCabe's ambition.

1 **McCabe was known**: "Fixing for a Negro State: Oklahoma, the New Canaan of the Colored Race," *Milwaukee Journal*, March 8, 1890. The case is made in this article that McCabe might perhaps be believable—and Oklahoma is cast as a new Canaan, McCabe situated as the Moses who might lead them there.

2 **some twenty-five thousand people**: According to the Oklahoma Historical Society, this number is an estimate. The first land run recruited some fifty thousand to sixty thousand. This, the second land run, recruited estimates of as little as twenty thousand people, some topping over thirty thousand.

2 **harsh conditions of the Jim Crow South**: This, however, was not a sentiment held by all Black people, especially those who were deeply engaged in politicking in and around both the South and the country's capital. There are several examples, but chief among those covered in this work is Charles Henry James Taylor, a contemporary and short-term colleague of McCabe who argued that "Black people were

doing well" in the South. For more on that, consult both his once widely circulated document/pamphlet *Whites and Blacks, or The Question Settled*, in which he believed it critical for Black people in the South to develop greater comity with white southerners. An easier and quicker articulation of this can be found in "The Negro in the South: He Is Doing Well and Progressing Rapidly," *Kansas City Times*, July 21, 1890, p. 8.

2   **Citizens of Indigenous nations watched:** David A. Chang, "Living Under Allotment," part III of *The Color of the Land: Race, Nation, and the Politics of Landownership in Oklahoma, 1832–1929* (Chapel Hill: University of North Carolina Press, 2010), 107–204. Though there are many texts that articulate these varied collisions about land ownership and future along questions of race, ethnicity, and indigeneity, Chang's work perhaps best situates the conflict and its motivations.

2   **Miss Daisy:** "A RARE RACE: Men, Women and Children Enter a Vicious Scramble for Land," *Times-Picayune*, September 30, 1891, p. 2.

2   **carrying anxious Boomers:** "As Free as Air: Opening of the Indian Lands to Settlers," *Times-Democrat*, September 23, 1891, p. 4.

3   **were called "Exodusters":** Nell Irvin Painter, "Millenarian Aspects of the Exodus to Kansas of 1879," *Journal of Social History* 9, no. 3 (Spring 1976): 331–38.

3   **territory's governor as treasurer:** "Multum in Parvo," *The Appeal*, June 28, 1890, p. 1, www.newspapers.com/article/the-appeal-mccabe-makes-2k-per-year/1420675 35/. The reports of McCabe's wealth and earning potential have ranged through oral history accounts, but in this newspaper, specific mention is made of the wealth of the county he was treasurer for, called "one of the largest and richest counties of the new Territory." Of particular note should be that this update of McCabe's status is not his first and is seen by some, as is made clearer later, as part of the spite he incurs from contemporaries both Black and white.

3   **number of Black people to move:** "Making a Negro State: Black Men of the West Organizing in Oklahoma," *Oregonian*, March 8, 1890, p. 7. There was and still is much debate as to how many Black people entered Oklahoma. Scholars such as Daniel Littlefield have estimated that at this time there were less than ten thousand. Other contemporary news writers opined that there might be far less than even that. There were others, especially from the Northeast and West Coast, who estimated it would grow to some fifty thousand before the end of the 1891 land run.

4   **three cowboys who greeted McCabe:** "As Free as Air," p. 4.

5   **dubbed Edward P. McCabe as "Moses":** "Awaiting Harrison's Order. Negroes Massed on the Borders of New Oklahoma Lands," *Kansas City Times*, September 7, 1891.

6   **"But in a new country":** "Opposed to M'Cabe: The Citizens of Oklahoma Territory Openly Declare Negro Immigrants," *Rocky Mountain News*, March 3, 1890.

6   **trainloads of Black colonizers:** "The Race Question in Oklahoma," *Daily Picayune*, March 6, 1891, p. 2. The long and short of the challenges in coming into the state are covered in the chapters that follow. However, it is of note to mention that most came through the Atchison, Topeka and Santa Fe Railway and stopped in either what we now call Oklahoma City or just several miles away, at Guthrie. There is a fascinating and painful history about the damage these kinds of railways visited upon people. For more information on that, see the work of Frank J. Best of Oklahoma City from 1951 in which he describes the railway as itself a pioneer that ferried pioneers.

6   **"penalty for a black person":** "Additional Telegraph News, Correspondence and Miscellany," *Atchison Daily Globe*, July 25, 1891, p. 1.

6   **"this caste law":** "Few Kansas City Negroes Going. They Do Not Take," *Kansas City Times*, August 28, 1891, p. 9.

6 **unnamed one of three "prodigals"**: "This Is No Lie; Though It Be Nigger Talk," *Arkansas Democrat*, March 19, 1891. The aim of this article, among others, was to defame the purported success of the Black colonization of Oklahoma. So, too, did the *Minco Minstrel*, which does not make reference to the names of other Black people who supposedly had this experience. One of whom was named Tucker, it seems, the only Black person to speak on the record about his prodigal nature. However, it was in the *Little Rock Gazette* that Tucker's fuller statements make clear his true objection: that "Tucker had the appearance of going through rough times and two cent pieces were the extent of his fortune, he having squandered his little savings on a 'pleasure trip' to 'the promised land.'" The question, however, is not asked nor answered, just why Tucker had been made so impoverished. In several advertisements, McCabe made clear just how much people should be ready to work arduously to secure this promised land.

6 **Oklahoma an all-Black state**: "This Is No Lie; Though It Be Nigger Talk."

8 **"HO! For Kansas"**: This is a direct pull from the advertisements issued by Benjamin "Pap" Singleton. To get a better understanding of this effort at huckstering promotion of Black colonization efforts by the formerly enslaved, see Charlotte Hinger, *Nicodemus: Post-Reconstruction Politics and Racial Justice in Western Kansas*, vol. 11 of Race and Culture in the American West Series (Norman: University of Oklahoma Press, 2022).

8 **options of Black people**: This article presents the challenge to Black people to stay in or leave the South and how Kansas became an ideal location for potential opportunity: "KU-KLUX OR KANSAS!: The Only Alternative the Bull-dozers Have Left the Southern Negro," *St. Louis Globe-Democrat*, March 22, 1879, p. 8.

8 **headed to Liberia**: The efforts for crafting an African republic and the superimposition of white desires to recreate Black opportunity outside the United States is a well-chronicled body of work to which many have contributed in venerable ways. To explore it further, especially in relation to this work, consult the following texts:

Marie Tyler-McGraw, *An African Republic: Black and White Virginians in the Making of Liberia*, John Hope Franklin Series in African American History and Culture (Chapel Hill: University of North Carolina Press, 2007). In this text, according to Tyler-McGraw, "The founders of the American Colonization Society (ACS), all white men, had varied motives. Most hoped that African colonization would lead to general emancipation; some hoped to be rid only of free blacks. Northern free blacks suspected the all-white Society of wanting to deport them, but Chesapeake free blacks saw merit in the plan. It was, basically, the kind of impossible plan that would appeal to many Americans: aging Revolutionaries who felt uneasy over slavery, evangelicals, urban free black traders, emancipated slaves tutoring as teachers and missionaries, Quakers, and opportunistic politicians." What will be seen in my book is that the motivations of white promoters of Black colonization of the West are of a piece with other colonization schemes founded by white men and superimposed on Black people.

Allan E. Yarema, *The American Colonization Society: An Avenue to Freedom?* (Lanham, MD: University Press of America, 2006). In this work, a more general overview of the history of the movement to Liberia, the ACS's failure lies primarily in its willingness to directly deal with the persistence of slavery while trying to dispense with Black people in the effort to create their own democratic society thousands of miles away from the United States.

For a shorter review of this work, Charles Foster's "The Colonization of Free Negroes, in Liberia, 1816–1835," *Journal of Negro History* 38, no. 1 (January 1953): 41–66, can be a useful guide as well.

To see how Black people's fates, especially those of enslaved Black people, were bound in northern "charity," see the case study of Leonard Bacon, a Congregationalist. For that, consult Hugh Davis's "Northern Colonizationists and Free Blacks, 1823–1837: A Case Study of Leonard Bacon," *Journal of the Early Republic* 17, no. 4 (Winter 1997): 651–75.

8   **or Canada, or:** Likewise, the efforts at colonization of parts of Canada by Black people, especially formerly enslaved Black people, is deftly chronicled. For more, see the following works, which were considered in the rendering of this book:

Robin Winks, *The Blacks in Canada: A History*, 2nd ed., Carleton Library Series (Montreal: McGill–Queen's University Press, 2000). While not exclusively focused on colonization efforts, this book provides a comprehensive history of Black people in Canada, including discussions on early settlements, migration patterns, and the social, political, and economic challenges they encountered.

Robert W. O'Brien, "Victoria's Negro Colonists—1858–1866," *Phylon (1940–1956)* 3, no. 1 (1st Quarter 1942): 15–18. Consult this text to get a more robust understanding of the movement of Black people through the Pacific Northwest region of the North American continent, who in many cases saw themselves as colonists.

8   **"Our new government['s]":** Alexander H. Stephens's "Cornerstone Speech," March 21, 1861, Savannah, Georgia, from Henry Cleveland, *Alexander H. Stephens, in Public and Private: With Letters and Speeches, Before, During, and Since the War* (Philadelphia, 1886), 717–29. This excerpt is the tail end of a speech delivered by Stephens in Savannah, Georgia, toward the beginning of the Civil War.

9   **"But what shall we do with the negroes":** Taken from an excerpt recorded in Benjamin Butler's diary four days before Lincoln's murder, which, of course, came after Lincoln had more openly discussed moving the "whole colored race of the slave states into Texas." More can be learned by consulting Mark Neely, "Colonization and the Myth That Lincoln Prepared the People for Emancipation," in *Lincoln's Proclamation: Emancipation Reconsidered*, ed. William A. Blair and Karen Fisher Younger (Chapel Hill: University of North Carolina Press, 2009), 45–72; Phillip S. Paludan, "Lincoln and Colonization: Policy or Propaganda?," *Journal of the Abraham Lincoln Association* 25, no. 1 (2004): 23–37; and Phillip W. Magness, "Benjamin Butler's Colonization Testimony Revaluated," *Journal of the Abraham Lincoln Association* 29, no. 1 (2008): 1–28.

9   **unrelenting grip of Jim Crow:** There are many texts that illuminate this, but for the purposes of this book, the most applicable texts are Kidada E. Williams, *I Saw Death Coming: A History of Terror and Survival in the War Against Reconstruction* (New York: Bloomsbury, 2023); W. E. B. DuBois, *Black Reconstruction in America: An Essay Toward a History of the Part Which Black Folk Played in the Attempt to Reconstruct Democracy in America, 1860–1880* (New York: Harcourt, Brace & Co., 1935); and Eric Foner, *Reconstruction: America's Unfinished Revolution, 1863–1877* (New York: Harper Perennial, 1988). The first two texts are most consulted, especially as Williams's work inverts the usual consideration of centered voices.

9   **the Great Migration:** There are several canonical texts by both journalists and historians that were consulted in developing an understanding of the backdrop against which this book was created. Here are a few to consider:

Alferdteen Harrison, ed., *Black Exodus: The Great Migration from the American South* (Jackson: University Press of Mississippi, 1991).

Nicholas Lemann, *The Promised Land: The Great Black Migration and How It Changed America* (New York: Vintage, 1992).

Isabel Wilkerson, *The Warmth of Other Suns: The Epic Story of America's Great Migration* (New York: Random House, 2010).

10 **pick up all they had and move west:** This is far from the first book that has focused its attention on Black people who made the West or the "Old West" home. For a broader understanding of the reach of Black migration into the Old West, see the following texts:

William Loren Katz, *The Black West: A Documentary and Pictorial History of the African American Role in the Westward Expansion of the United States* (Chicago: Chicago Review Press / Fulcrum, 2019).

Timothy E. Nelson, *Blackdom, New Mexico: The Significance of the Afro-Frontier, 1900–1930* (Lubbock: Texas Tech University Press, 2023).

Quintard Taylor, *In Search of the Racial Frontier: African Americans in the American West 1528–1990* (New York: Norton, 1999).

Quintard Taylor and Shirley Ann Wilson, eds., *African American Women Confront the West, 1600–2000* (Norman: University of Oklahoma Press, 2003).

10 **an elusive survival:** To understand some of the complexities of understanding the at times conflicted, at other times harmonious, and at other times both Black and Indigenous interactions in the Old West, consider the following text as an introduction: Tiya Miles and Sharon Patricia Holland, *Crossing Waters, Crossing Worlds: The African Diaspora in Indian Country* (Durham, NC: Duke University Press, 2006).

CHAPTER 1

15 **"If you must bleed":** *Minutes of the National Convention of Colored Citizens: Held at Buffalo, on the 15th, 16th, 17th, 18th, and 19th of August, 1843. For the Purpose of Considering their Moral and Political Condition as American Citizens* (New York: Piercy & Reed, 1843 | Arno Press, 1969), 139.

16 **Convention of Colored Citizens:** *Minutes of the National Convention of Colored Citizens,* 4–7.

16 **leading voice of abolition:** *Minutes of the National Convention of Colored Citizens,* 7.

17 **average real estate wealth per:** *Minutes of the National Convention of Colored Citizens,* 35–38.

17 **convention offered a snapshot:** *Minutes of the National Convention of Colored Citizens,* 35–38.

17 **Douglass believed that there was still hope:** *Minutes of the National Convention of Colored Citizens,* 13–15.

17 **the Oneida Institute:** Milton C. Sernett, "Axe-Honing on the Western Reserve," in *Abolition's Axe: Beriah Green, Oneida Institute, and the Black Freedom Struggle* (Syracuse, NY: Syracuse University Press, 2004), 28–29.

18 **"The gross inconsistency":** *Minutes of the National Convention of Colored Citizens,* 5.

18 **"If hereditary bondmen would be free":** *Minutes of the National Convention of Colored Citizens,* 5.

19   **"responsible for the consequences"**: *Minutes of the National Convention of Colored Citizens*, 5.

19   **institution of slavery in the United States**: Thomas J. Weiss, "U.S. Labor Force Estimates and Economic Growth, 1800–1860," in *American Economic Growth and Standards of Living Before the Civil War*, ed. Robert E. Gallman and John Joseph Wallis (Chicago: University of Chicago Press, 1992), 24–26, 37–39.

20   **"go to their masters"**: *Minutes of the National Convention of Colored Citizens.*

21   **"Men of Color! To Arms!"**: Frederick Douglass, "Men of Color, to Arms!," *The North Star*, March 2, 1863, in Quintard Taylor, *The African American Experience: A History of Black Americans from 1619 to 1890.*

21   **"recommending a servile insurrection**: "NATIONAL ANTI-SLAVERY CONVENTION," *Niles National Register*, September 16, 1843, p. 15.

22   **"madness of fanaticism"**: "NATIONAL ANTI-SLAVERY CONVENTION," p. 15.

23   **McCabe was born in Troy**: Martin Dann, "From Sodom to the Promised Land: E.P. McCabe and the Movement for Oklahoma Colonization," *Kansas Historical Quarterly* 15, no. 3 (Autumn 1974): 370–78.

23   **"It touches one's sense of honor"**: Herman Melville, *Moby Dick* (1851), chapter 1.

24   **tenth-richest American in history:** "The All-Time Richest Americans," *Forbes*, July 17, 2012.

24   **Rensselaer's land, manor, and personal holdings**: Wes Turner, "Stephen Van Rensselaer III," *The Canadian Encyclopedia* (2011).

24   **Gradual Emancipation Act**: David Nathaniel Gellman, "Ambiguous Victory: Gradual Abolition Becomes Law," in *Emancipating New York: The Politics of Slavery and Freedom, 1777–1827* (Baton Rouge: Louisiana State University Press, 2006), 153–88.

CHAPTER 2

26   **Charles S. Weyman:** Weyman was a prominent anti-slavery journalist who for the *New York Tribune* wrote this poem to mark what became credited as the rallying cry of "Bleeding Kansas" among anti-slavery leaders, activists, and homesteaders. This is considered one of the first mentions of the term. This poem became a Republican campaign song in the state and it is for that reason that it is of particular note. For other contemporaneous mentions of "Bleeding Kansas" that have otherwise been noted as the first mentions of the term, see below:

G. Douglas Brewerton, "When Kansas Bleeds, Georgia Must Open Her Veins and Massachusetts, Too," in *War in Kansas: A Rough Trip to the Border, Among New Homes and a Strange People* (New York: Derby & Jackson, 1856), 395.

Governor Robert J. Walker's inaugural address at Lecompton, May 27, 1857, contains the statement "Does she want to be 'bleeding Kansas' for the benefit of political agitation within or without her limits?"

"Plea for Kansas," *Ohio State Journal*, August 9, 1856. The first verse reads: "Listen! hear ye not the sighing, / Of the Goddess, Freedom, dying, / On the fields of Kansas lying, / Weltering in her gore! / Hear ye not her mournful pleading? / See ye not her votaries bleeding? / Lo! their souls from earth receding, / Call for vengeance sore."

R. S. Peale, "Webb Scrap Book," in *The Home Library of R.S. Peale* (1883), poem "Our Country's Call." The first verse reads: "Hear the Nation's call, freemen, one and all, / Hear Poor Kansas' earnest cry: / See her bleeding land lift its beckoning hand; / Sons of freedom, come ye nigh." *Davenport Gazette* (Iowa), July 17, 1856.

"Freedom's Summons," poem, *Springfield Republican*, July 25, 1856. First verse: "Over Kansas' lovely plains, / Widely desolation reigns; / Dark her soil with many stains, / Stains from freeman's blood! / He who scorns to own a slave, / Finds, full soon a bloody grave; / Death and ruin meet the brave, Scorn and hate, the good."

Charles S. Weyman, "Fremont & Victory," *New York Tribune*, September 13, 1856.

Daniel Webster Wilder, *The Annals of Kansas*, New edition, *1541–1885* (Topeka: T. Dwight Thacher Kansas Publishing House, 1886).

26   **Alone, Charles Dow:** The tale of Charles Dow, a free-stater from Ohio, was most summarily captured nearly four decades after his murder in a feature article in the *Lawrence Daily World*. The article focuses on Dow's work as a martyr in the Tertullian sense that the "Blood of the Martyr is the Seed of the Church," which is to say Dow's murder accelerated the movement to make Kansas a "free state." "A Martyr's Grave," *Lawrence Daily World*, November 20, 1897, pp. 2–4.

27   **Dow turned to leave:** Dramatized versions of the Charles Dow story emerged both as fable and aspirational qualities of Kansas history. A robust serialized account of a play was carried in the *Topeka Daily Capital* nearly sixty years after. In a particular entry, this is seen in Act I of this play. "Baldwinites in Play Depict First Christmas in Palmyra," *Topeka Daily Capital*, December 26, 1915, p. 15.

28   **collect his bullet-shredded body:** There is however a scattershot of accounts contemporaneously about the Dow murder. A free-stater, G. W. Smith, less than a month after the incident, submitted a report through the *Kansas Free State* in which he recounted the Dow murder; the man who dealt the fatal shot at Dow is assumed to be a pro-slavery advocate named Buckley. However, in other accounts, the *Daily Kansas Tribune* places the blame speciously on another pro-slavery advocate named Frank Coleman. In any case, this was a signature moment for many in commencing the "bleeding" of Kansas.

For another account of how Dow was murdered, consider Isaac Tichenor Goodnow, who recounted for his colleagues in the New England Emigrant Aid Company numerous instances of violence, one of which was the attack on Charles Dow, and blames Frank Coleman. Consider that Goodnow was an avid abolitionist of the NEEAC variety and aligned strongly with the Republican Party. Additionally, he was apprising his colleagues to whom he and others in Kansas were advocating for greater levels of political and, most importantly, financial support (often for weaponry). Isaac Tichenor Goodnow, *Narrative, the Murder of Charles Dow* (Topeka: Maintained by the Kansas Historical Society, 1856).

28   **another toxic compromise:** At the beginning of 1854, Senator Stephen Douglas drafted and presented a bill that would divide an area west of Missouri into Kansas and Nebraska Territories. The bill reflected his interest in ensuring that a popular vote, not an act of Congress, would decide if slavery would be considered legal. This was for abolitionists and anti-slavery supporters considered an act of limited courage that incited many of them to move into the state en masse—likewise for the pro-slavery leaders. It passed on May 30, 1854. For more details on the act, see the following additional sources that I consulted in the rendering of the narrative for this section of the chapter:

An Act to Organize the Territories of Nebraska and Kansas. An act of Congress, Washington, D.C.: Statutes at Large of the United States of America, 33rd Cong., 1st sess., chap. 59, 1854.

Nicole Etcheson, *Bleeding Kansas: Contested Liberty in the Civil War Era* (Topeka: University Press of Kansas, 2004).

Michael A. Morrison, *Slavery and the American West: The Eclipse of Manifest Destiny* (Chapel Hill: University of North Carolina Press, 1997).

David M. Potter, *The Impending Crisis, 1848–1861* (New York: Harper & Row, 1976).

John R. Wunder and Joann M. Ross, eds., *The Nebraska-Kansas Act of 1854*, vol. 10 of Law in the American West (Lincoln: University of Nebraska Press; Illustrated edition, 2008).

29   **"Compromise Union Whigs"**: Amos Lawrence, "Letter from Amos Lawrence to His Uncle, Abbott Lawrence," in *Life of Amos A. Lawrence: With Extracts from His Diary and Correspondence, by His Son, William Lawrence* (Boston: Houghton Mifflin, 1888).
       In addition to this, see Amos Lawrence, "A Letter to a Friend in South Carolina," June 12, 1852, in *Extracts from the Diary and Correspondence of the Late Amos Lawrence; With a Brief Account of Some Incidents of His Life* (Boston: John Wilson & Son, 1855). In this brief letter to an unnamed friend in South Carolina, Lawrence makes clear his true belief in the colonization of Black people when he writes, "I have never countenanced these abolition movements at the North; and have lately lent a hand to the cause of Colonization, which is destined to make a greater change in the condition of the blacks than any event since the Christian era."

29   **New England Emigrant Aid Company (NEEAC)**: Louise Barry, "The New England Emigrant Aid Company Parties of 1855," *Kansas Historical Quarterly* 12, no. 3 (August 1943): 227–68.

29   **Founded by Eli Thayer**: Barry, "The New England Emigrant Aid Company Parties of 1855."

30   **"The negroes seem very happy here"**: Amos Lawrence, "A Journal Entry from South Carolina," January 20, 1837, *Amos Lawrence Papers 1814–1879, a Collection of the Massachusetts Historical Society*, Ms. N-1559, Massachusetts Historical Society.

30   **spring in New England was late**: "Culture of the Pie Plant," *Greenfield Democrat*, May 24, 1854, p. 2. While a seemingly innocuous point, the treachery of the trip made by Anthony Burns cannot be understated, given the uncharacteristic frost that had been visited upon the shores of Massachusetts upon his arrival.

31   **Burns's eventual trial**: *Boston Slave Riot, and Trial of Anthony Burns: Containing the Report of the Faneuil Hall Meeting; the Murder of Batchelder; Theodore Parker's Lesson for the Day; Speeches of Counsel on Both Sides, Corrected by Themselves; a Verbatim Report of Judge Loring's Decision; and Detailed Account of the Embarkation*, Fetridge and Co. from the Joseph Meredith Toner Collection from the Library of Congress & Harvard University's Libraries, 1854, pp. 15, 25, 31.
       Further details as to the nature of the trial for the following pages can be found in the citation above and in Charles Emery Stevens, *Anthony Burns: A History* (John P. Jewett and Co.—From the Book Collections of University of California, 1856).

32   **city's oldest Black churches**: "The Slave Case: Rumored Withdrawal of the Owner's

Proposition to Sell! Incidents of Saturday Night and Sunday," *Boston Evening Transcript*, May 29, 1854, p. 1.

32   **distance from the scourge of slavery:** Two invaluable resources, which describe this case in detail and were invaluable to my research and reporting, are:

Earl M. Maltz, *Fugitive Slave on Trial: The Anthony Burns Case and Abolitionist Outrage* (Topeka: University Press of Kansas, 2010).

Albert J. Von Frank, *The Trials of Anthony Burns: Freedom and Slavery in Emerson's Boston* (Cambridge, MA: Harvard University Press, 1999).

The details of the arrest can be most easily found in a collection of several newspaper clippings. However, perhaps the most illuminating of the varied sentiments can be found in the contemporaneous filings in "Arrest of Fugitive Slave in Boston!," *New England Farmer*, May 29, 1854.

34   **reckonings over race and racism:** In this section, I leverage several key texts to illustrate and reinterpret the motivations and moral impulses that animated the work of the New England Emigrant Aid Company—specifically as abolition adjacent:

Henry David Thoreau, "Slavery in Massachusetts, 1854," in *The Portable Thoreau*, ed. Carl Bode (New York: Penguin, 1982), 268–309.

Gunja Sen Gupta, *For God and Mammon: Evangelicals and Entrepreneurs, Masters and Slaves in Territorial Kansas, 1854–1860* (Athens: University of Georgia Press, 1996).

Eli Thayer, "New England Emigrant Aid Company, and Its Influence, Through the Kansas Contest, upon National History" (Worcester, MA: F. P. Rice—From the Collection of The Johns Hopkins University Sheridan Libraries, 1887).

Courtney Buchkoski, "'Luke-Warm Abolitionists': Eli Thayer and the Contest for Civil War Memory, 1853–1899," *Journal of the Civil War Era* 9, no. 2 (June 2019): 249–74.

Louise Barry, "The New England Emigrant Aid Company Parties of 1855," *Kansas Historical Quarterly* (August 1943): 227–68.

Earl M. Maltz, *Fugitive Slave on Trial: The Anthony Burns Case and Abolitionist Outrage* (Topeka: University Press of Kansas, 2010).

Michael A. Morrison, *Slavery and the American West: The Eclipse of Manifest Destiny* (Chapel Hill: University of North Carolina Press, 1997).

Charles Robinson, *The Kansas Conflict* (Lawrence, KS: Journal Pub. Co., 1898).

History of the New-England Emigrant Aid Company. With a Report on Its Future Operations (Boston: Press of J. Wilson & Son, 1862).

35   **Soon, letters came in:** Thousands of letters were pored over to render these three pages of dialogue. For a more extensive exploration of this, I recommend navigating the microfilm made available by the joint efforts of the University of Kansas and the Kansas Historical Society to compile this collection of correspondence, which serves as a companion to an even greater number of materials like financials, advertisements, billets, and more.

"Correspondence (on Microfilm)," New England Emigrant Aid Company Papers, 1854–1909, University of Kansas and Kansas Historical Society.

36   **November 29, 1854:** The consequential election was hotly covered in varied forms of
      press. To render the tension, I not only consulted the actual electoral outcomes by
      county, but I scanned several contemporary press stories on the election. Of partic-
      ular note are the articles from the *Kansas Herald of Freedom*, the newspaper run
      and funded almost entirely by the philanthropic efforts of the NEEAC. Their slant
      in favor of NEEAC efforts features quite prominently:

      "Song of the Kansas Emigrant," *Kansas Herald of Freedom*, January 6, 1855, p. 1.

      "The Election and Probable Population of Kansas Territory," *Kansas Weekly Her-
      ald*, December 1, 1854, p. 2.

      "Interesting Incident: Reception of Gov. Reeder," *Kansas City Enterprise*, October
      23, 1854.

      "Why Don't You Subscribe?," *Kansas Herald of Freedom*, January 20, 1855, p. 1. Of
      note in this entry is the contextualization of the election within the backdrop of a
      larger pull to get more men to move to Kansas to enhance the electoral power of
      free-staters.

36   **Comanche, the Pawnee and the Kiowa:** From the *Kansas Herald of Freedom*'s last
      few issues referenced above in which several articles attest to the need to either mor-
      alize or move the Indigenous who predated the advent of these NEEAC supporters.

37   **Whitfield, a racist, pro-slavery candidate:** "Whitfield's Vote," *Kansas Herald of
      Freedom*, October 20, 1855, p. 1.

37   **"the Kansas struggle":** This quote was collected in a speech, but in another speech
      given by U.S. senator David Atchison, he went further, as can be seen later in Eric
      Coder, "Kansas Is Slave Soil," in *Prelude to Civil War: Kansas-Missouri, 1854–1861*
      (New York: Crowell-Collier Press, 1970), 24: "You cannot watch your stables to pre-
      vent thieves from stealing your horses and mules; neither can you watch your negro
      quarters to prevent your neighbors from seducing away and stealing your negroes."

38   **2,905 eligible voters in Kansas:** We see the swelling of the Kansas population by pro-
      slavery forces in the *Kansas Free State*, but in the most comprehensive early work on
      this, we see Coder cover this even further in the previous citation.

CHAPTER 3

44   **New Orleans import-export broker and trader:** Bernard Kock, "To his excellency,
      Abraham Lincoln, President of the United States Washington, D.C.," letter, re-
      trieved from the Library of Congress, October 1, 1862.

44   **"your philanthropic ideas of Colonization":** See Phillip W. Magness and Sebas-
      tian N. Page, *Colonization After Emancipation: Lincoln and the Movement for
      Black Resettlement* (Columbia: University of Missouri Press, 2011), 164.

45   **"part of [Lincoln's] emancipation policy":** Gordon Welles, "Administration of Abra-
      ham Lincoln," *Galaxy* 24, no. 4 (1877): 440. On the 444th page of this journal, Welles
      continues to elucidate his concerns about how the historical record might remember
      Lincoln's notions of emancipation at the exclusion of remembering his strong favor-
      ing of colonization as a critical component. He writes, "Those who applaud [Lin-
      coln's] course omit to mention that colonization and deportation of the slaves when
      set free was deemed [by Lincoln to be] an essential part of his emancipation policy."

46   **Latrobe dangled wealth:** A voluminous collection of Latrobe's speeches have been
      noted over the years. The most recent one can be found here: John Hazlehurst Bone-
      val Latrobe, *African Colonization—Its Principles and Aims. An Address Delivered*

by John H. B. Latrobe, President of the American Colonization Society, at the An-niversary Meeting of the American Colonization Society Held in the Smithsonian Institute, Washington City, January 18, 1859 (Baltimore: Printed by John D. Toy, 1859).

47   **affectionately, "Freedom's Fort":** Luther P. Jackson, "The Origin of Hampton Insti-tute," *Journal of Negro History* 10, no. 2 (1925): 131–49.

47   **Île-à-Vache, or Cow Island:** Descriptions of the island can be found in the following documents: J. D. Lockett, "Abraham Lincoln and Colonization: An Episode That Ends in Tragedy at L'Ile à Vache, Haiti, 1863–1864." *Journal of Black Studies* 21, no. 4 (1991): 428–44.

Second, it can be found in the recently published book by Kock's direct ancestor: Boyce Thompson, *Lincoln's Lost Colony: The Black Emigration Scheme of Bernard Kock* (Jefferson, NC: McFarland, 2023).

Though Kock mentions that he obtains direct agreement in his Statement of Facts and his descendant Boyce Thompson attests to this, it is not clear that Haiti offers that explicitly. Perhaps Kock did not directly garner this agreement. How-ever, it was widely known that President Geffrard of Haiti did advertise the notion of immigrating to Haiti quite widely. John Baur writes, "On August 14, 1860, Gef-frard issued a decree whereby agents appointed in foreign lands to promote immi-gration and diffuse information would be welcomed. A building was to be placed at the disposal of each emigration office to receive the newcomers. Five ports of disem-barkation were established." John E. Baur, "The Presidency of Nicolas Geffrard of Haiti," *The Americas* 10, no. 4 (April 1954): 425–61.

48   **"the wants of free labor":** Kock, "To his excellency, Abraham Lincoln," p. 2.

48   **"Christian minister, and New England schoolteachers":** This particular quote is taken from Kock, "To his excellency, Abraham Lincoln," p. 3.

48   **"more especially cotton":** Kock, "To his excellency, Abraham Lincoln," pp. 4–5.

48   **political and financial returns:** References to return of capital can be found on page 3 of Kock's letter to the president, in which he writes, "All money thus expended, except for transportation and rations, as above, I propose to refund within two years, and as security for the same, I will give a deed of trust upon all my personal property upon the Island, upon my deed of concession of A'Vache, and I will place at your disposal so much of each of my semi-annual crops as may be agreed upon."

49   **$600,000 to defray Kock's expenses:** Willis E. Boyd, "The Île a Vache Colonization Venture, 1862–1864," *The Americas* 16, no. 1 (July 1959): 45–62.

49   **Charles K. Tuckerman:** Boyd, "The Île a Vache Colonization Venture," 50. The de-tails of the deal established can be found on pp. 50–52.

The following materials were consulted in rendering this section:

"An Agreement Between the United States of America and Bernard Kock of the Is-land of A'Vache Under the Republic of Hayti, 1862," translated contract between Bernard Kock and the Republic of Hayti, 1862.

Contract with attached empowering legislation between Charles K. Tuckerman, Paul S. Forbes, and the United States Government countersigned by John P. Usher, Secretary of the Interior, 1863.

39th Congress, 1st Sess., Senate Executive Document 55. Report on the Transporta-tion, Settlement, and Colonization of Persons of the African Race, n.d.

Caleb Smith to Robert Murphy, Sept. 16, 1862. 39th Congress, 1st Sess., Senate Ex-ecutive Document 55. Report on the Transportation, Settlement, and Colonization of Persons of the African Race, n.d.

Caleb Smith to Samuel Pomeroy, Sept. 20, 1862. 39th Congress, 1st Sess., Senate Exec. Doc. 55. Report on the Transportation, Settlement, and Colonization of Persons of the African Race, n.d.

"They demanded luxuries to which they were unaccustomed in this country": Charles K. Tuckerman, "Statement of Circumstances Attending the Experiment of Colonizing Free Negroes, at the Island of A'Vache, Hayti, W.I." (New York: Latin American pamphlet digital program at Harvard College Library, 1864).

50   **Senator James H. Lane of Kansas:** J. H. Lane, "Vindication of the Policy of the Administration, a Speech of Honorable J.H. Lane of Kansas on the Special Order being Senate Bill No. 45, to set apart a Portion of the State of Texas for the Use of Persons of African Descent" (speech), February 16, 1864, Senate of the United States, Washington, D.C.

Additional materials consulted for this section:

Mark E. Neely, "Abraham Lincoln and Black Colonization: Benjamin Butler's Spurious Testimony," *Civil War History* 25, no. 1 (March 1979): 77–83.

"What to Do with the Negro?," *Daily Green Mountain Freeman*, December 9, 1864, p. 2. The *Daily Green Mountain Freeman* was published by Charles Wesley Willard (a congressman), essentially asking what was the best path forward for "the Negro." Willard stated that colonization and relocation were the best options for "the Negro."

"The Negro Colonization Scheme," *Memphis Daily Appeal*, November 1, 1862, p. 1.

James Lane, *Senate Bill No. 45, 38th Congress, 1st Session, A Bill to Set Apart a Portion of the State of Texas for the Use of Persons of African Descent*, February 4, 1864.

Morton S. Wilkinson, *Senate Bill No. 169, 38th Congress, 1st Session, A Bill to Repeal all Acts Making Appropriations for the Colonization of Free Persons of African Descent*, March 15, 1864.

James H. Lane, "Remarks on the State of Negro Colonization," *Congressional Globe*, February 16, 1864, pp. 672–74.

Benjamin J. Butler, *Butler's Book: Autobiography and Personal Reminiscences of Major-General Benjamin Butler; a Review of His Legal, Political, and Military Career* (Boston: A.M. Thayer & Co. Book Publishers, 1892).

Bjorn F. Stillion Southard, "Abraham Lincoln's Second Annual Message to Congress and Public Policy Advocacy for African Colonization," *Rhetoric & Public Affairs* 21, no. 3 (2018): 387–416.

Walter Prichard, "The Effects of the Civil War on the Louisiana Sugar Industry," *Journal of Southern History* 5, no. 3 (August 1939): 315–32.

Samantha Seeley, "Beyond the American Colonization Society," *History Compass* 14, no. 3 (March 2016): 93–104.

William Lloyd Garrison, *Thoughts on African Colonization or an Impartial Exhibition of the Doctrines, Principles and Purposes of the American Colonization Society Together with the Resolutions, Addresses and Remonstrances of the Free People of Color* (Boston: Garrison & Knapp, 1832).

CHAPTER 4

52 **"The slave went free":** W. E. B. DuBois, "The Black Worker," in *Black Reconstruction in America: An Essay Toward a History of the Part Which Black Folk Played in the Attempt to Reconstruct Democracy in America, 1860–1880* (New York: Harcourt, Brace & Co., 1935), 30.

52 **As General Ulysses S. Grant wrote:** Ulysses S. Grant, "To Elihu Washburn," in *The Papers of Ulysses S. Grant*, vol. 9, *July 7–December 31, 1863*, ed. John Y. Simon (Carbondale: Southern Illinois University Press, 1982), 217–18.

53 **"A veritable reign of terror":** Carl Shurz, *Can the South Solve the Negro Problem?* (New York: African American Pamphlet Collection, 1903).

53 **For years after the Civil War:** I consulted Ari Hoogenboom, "Foreword," in *Rutherford B. Hayes: Warrior and President* (Topeka: University Press of Kansas, 1995), 536. In this section of Hoogenboom's book he chronicles what he casts Hayes's decision to withdraw troops, marking for many the end of the Reconstruction era, as an inevitable and unavoidable choice. The inevitability of this decision is, of course, debatable and debated.

53 **first iteration of the Ku Klux Klan:** The Enforcement Acts of 1870 and 1871 did have some success in temporarily reducing the activities of the Ku Klux Klan and other similar groups. Federal prosecutions and military intervention in certain areas helped to suppress Klan violence to some extent in the early 1870s. However, the effectiveness of the Enforcement Acts varied across different regions, and the Klan adapted its tactics in response to increased federal enforcement. Additionally, political shifts and changes in administration at the federal level impacted the enforcement of these acts. Over time, as Reconstruction policies were rolled back and federal troops were withdrawn from the South, Klan activity resurged. For more, consider the following:

United States, "An Act to amend an Act entitled 'An Act to enforce the Right of Citizens of the United States to vote in the several States of the Union, and for other Purposes,' passed May 31, 1870, and to enforce the Provisions of the Fourteenth Amendment."

United States, "An Act to enforce the Provisions of the Fourteenth Amendment to the Constitution of the United States, and for other Purposes," 17 Stat. 13 (1871).

United States, "An Act to enforce the Right of Citizens of the United States to vote in the several States of the Union, and for other Purposes," 16 Stat. 140 (1870).

William Watson Davis, "The Civil War and Reconstruction in Florida," *Annals of the American Academy of Political and Social Science* 52, no. 1 (March 1913).

53 **Grant's opinion of the Fifteenth Amendment:** This is a quoted mention from Hamilton Fish, Grant's secretary of state. It can be found in Allan Nevins, *Hamilton Fish: The Inner History of the Grant Administration* (New York: Dodd, Mead & Co., 1936).

54 **"I think the policy of the new":** Referenced in Eric Foner, *Reconstruction: America's Unfinished Revolution, 1863–1877*, updated edition (New York: HarperCollins, 2014), 581.

55 **"The wage of the Negro worker":** DuBois, *Black Reconstruction*, 599–600.

55 **548 cases of aggravated assault:** DuBois, *Black Reconstruction*, 603–5. For more details, DuBois references a report provided to Congress in 1872. For more, review: United States Congress, Joint Select Committee on the Condition of Affairs in the

Late Insurrectionary States, *Report of the Joint Select Committee Appointed to In-quire into the Condition of Affairs in the Late Insurrectionary States, So Far as Regards the Execution of Laws, and the Safety of the Lives and Property of the Citizens of the United States and Testimony* (Washington, DC: Luke P. Poland, John Scott, and Woodrow Wilson Collection, 1872).

55   **the KKK in South Carolina:** DuBois, *Black Reconstruction*, 605.

56   **"capitalists on this foundation":** DuBois, *Black Reconstruction*, 599.

56   **economic survival on the margins:** For a short overview of the referenced concept and the policy of home rule, see Eric Foner and Olivia Mahoney, "Preface," *America's Reconstruction: People and Politics After the Civil War* (Baton Rouge: LSU Press, 1995), 12.

      For more discussion of the actions of Hayes and the restoration of home rule and its impacts, see Allan Peskin, "Was There a Compromise of 1877?," *Journal of American History* 60, no. 1 (June 1973): 63–75. For a perspective on how the end of Reconstruction was inertial and focusing attention on the construction of power within parties as driving forces for the end of Reconstruction, see Keith Ian Pola-koff, *The Politics of Inertia: The Election of 1876 and the End of Reconstruction* (Baton Rouge: LSU Press, 1973).

57   **Henry Adams warned in 1877:** *Testimony of Henry Adams on the Negro Exodus Senate Report* (Washington DC: United States Senate, 1880).

PART II

59   **"After the reconstruction period":** Lulu Sadler Craig, *Manuscript on the History of Nicodemus Colony* (Kenneth Spencer Research Library at the University of Kansas, n.d.).

CHAPTER 5

61   **"With sad hearts and weeping eyes":** Elizabeth Comstock, "Letter from Elizabeth Leslie Rous Comstock to Catherine Hale, February 9, 1880," in *Life and Letters of Elizabeth L. Comstock* (Hansebooks GmbH, November 18, 2015). This is a collection among others from women members and organizers of both the Quaker movement and, more specifically, the temperance movement. Much of Comstock's treatment of the formerly enslaved is informed by the notion of improving the "refu-gee" status of Black people.

62   **His aim was seeing the next day:** This and much of the Curtis Pollard story can be found in "Curtis Pollard," *St. Louis Globe-Democrat*, March 22, 1879, p. 8.

62   **"They were forced to leave the South":** "Curtis Pollard."

62   **"muzzle of bull-dozers' muskets":** "KU KLUX OR KANSAS!: The Only Alternative the Bull-dozers Have Left the Southern Negro (and the) Terrible Sufferings of the Darkies Under the Reign of the Shot-gun," *St. Louis Globe-Democrat*, March 22, 1879, p. 8.

62   **and fled west:** The reference of thousands can be found in several masterful works on this. Aside from Nell Irvin Painter's excellent work on the Exoduster movement, as it relates to the initial stop in St. Louis, I consulted the tabulation included in Bryan M. Jack, *The St. Louis African American Community and the Exodusters* (Columbia: University of Missouri Press, 2008), 108.

62   **vote for Democrats or die:** The testimonies of Claurence Winn and Frederick Mar-shall can be found in the same feature article, "KU KLUX OR KANSAS." Addition-ally, it can be found in the amassing of affidavits compiled by Charlton Tandy, a

Black Missouri-based attorney and political activist who supported the Exoduster movement.

63 **"everlasting fire of slavery"**: Nell Irvin Painter, "Millenarian Aspects of the Exodus to Kansas of 1879," *Journal of Social History* 9, no. 3 (Spring 1976): 331.

63 **the idea of millenarism**: Painter, "Millenarian Aspects of the Exodus to Kansas of 1879," 336.

63 **Listen to James Brown**: James Brown's story can be found in "KU KLUX OR KANSAS!," p. 8.

63 **"I tell you, every black man"**: "THE NEGRO EXODUS: A Day and Evening Spent Among the Colored People. Information Gathered from Preachers, Politicians, Editors, Refugees, Etc.," *Chicago Tribune*, May 23, 1879, p. 9.

64 **stopped first in St. Louis**: The sentiment in St. Louis, however, among white residents of the city regarding the arrival of Black people was that the city wanted them nearly as little as the South did. Several publications from around the country covered this movement and the unsettling nature of the experience in St. Louis:

A Correspondent of the Cincinnati Commercial, "INDICATIONS," *St. Louis Post-Dispatch*, May 19, 1879, p. 2.

"THE NEGRO EXODUS: More Direct Testimony from Reliable Residents of the South | The Poor Negroes Deceived by Selfish Designing Rascals | Promises of Land, Money, and Mules in Kansas," *Boston Post*, May 2, 1879, p. 2.

"THE NEGRO EXODUS: A Day and Evening Spent Among the Colored People," p. 9.

J.B.R., a Memphis Correspondent, "The Negro Exodus: Conclusions from a Tour of Observation Through the South," *Chicago Tribune*, May 29, 1879, p. 9.

"Off for Wyandotte: A Large Band of Negroes Take Passage on the Joe Kinney," *St. Louis Globe-Democrat*, March 23, 1879, p. 12.

Wendell Phillips, "THE REPUBLICAN PARTY: What Wendell Phillips Thinks of It," *Cincinnati Enquirer*, September 13, 1879, p. 9.

64 **Arkansas or northern Texas**: The dire straits of their passage from the South are captured in the testimonies included in both "THE NEGRO EXODUS: A Day and Evening Spent Among the Colored People," p. 9, and "KU KLUX OR KANSAS!," p. 8.

The passages included thereafter are an amalgam/composite of dozens of testimonies from news reports, affidavits, and congressional testimonies.

64 **McCabe had never been enslaved**: Martin Dann, "From Sodom to the Promised Land: E.P. McCabe and the Movement for Oklahoma Colonization," *Kansas Historical Quarterly* 15, no. 3 (Autumn 1974): 370–78.

65 **a newer version of power and prestige**: Brian Luskey, "What Is My Prospects?," in *On the Make: Clerks and the Quest for Capital in Nineteenth-Century America* (New York: NYU Press, 2010), 21–53.

66 **between State and Wabash Streets**: William Cronon, *Nature's Metropolis: Chicago and the Great West* (New York: Norton, 2009), 328.

66 **one-way ticket to Chicago, customers**: Cronon, *Nature's Metropolis*, 329.

67 **built their own world**: Charlotte Hinger, "'The Colored People Hold the Key': Abram Thompson Hall, Jr.'s Campaign to Organize Graham County," *Kansas History: A Journal of the Central Plains* 31, no. 1 (Spring 2008): 33–34.

67 **set their eyes on Kansas**: Hinger, "'The Colored People Hold the Key,'" 34.

68   **build nice lives for themselves:** Angela Bates, interview by Caleb Gayle, edited by Anna Colletto, Bogue, KS, November 1, 2023.

68   **But chief among their interests:** Hinger, "'The Colored People Hold the Key,'" 34.

CHAPTER 6

69   **Hickman was eager to find her new home:** Dorothy Sterling, "New Beginnings," chapter 17 in *We Are Your Sisters: Black Women in the Nineteenth Century* (New York: Norton, 1997), 375.

69   **Another formerly enslaved woman:** Angela Bates, interview by Caleb Gayle, edited by Anna Colletto, November 15, 2023.

70   **Nicodemus was not what she envisioned:** Lulu Sadler Craig, *Manuscript on the History of Nicodemus Colony* (Kenneth Spencer Research Library at the University of Kansas, n.d.).

70   **buffalo grass browned:** Richard Craig, "The Cultural Landscape of the Pawnees: Native Americans, Dispossession, and Resettlement & Environmental Problems," in *Kansas and the West: New Perspectives*, ed. Rita Napier (Topeka: University Press of Kansas, 2008), 68–69.

70   **"I don't see it":** Nicodemus Historical Society, "1878 Settlers: March 1878, Scott County Group. Review of the Settler Groups Who Moved to Nicodemus from the South" (Nicodemus, KS: Nicodemus National Historic Site, n.d.).

70   **"That is Nicodemus":** "1878 Settlers." For more color, Willina recounted being "very sick" and that at the initial siting she "hailed this news with gladness." It was not until she saw the dugouts—seeming anthills—that she became despondent and began to cry.

70   **human-built dugouts:** Cassie Branstetter, interview by Caleb Gayle, edited by Anna Colletto, November 2, 2023.

70   **"The scenery was not at all inviting":** "1878 Settlers."

71   **The town had been founded:** Bruce G. Harvey and Deborah E. Harvey, "Chapter 1: Historic Background," in *Nicodemus on the Great Plains: Administrative History of Nicodemus National Historic Site Kansas*, National Park Service (Omaha, NE: U.S. Department of the Interior, 2023).

71   **fields were lush and fertile:** Craig, *Manuscript on the History of Nicodemus Colony*.

71   **alleviated by the Native Potawatomi:** Angela Bates, interview by Caleb Gayle, edited by Anna Colletto, Bogue, KS, November 1, 2023.

72   **"most tormenting of insect pests":** Craig, *Manuscript on the History of Nicodemus Colony*, 23.

72   **The Wimms family:** Craig, *Manuscript on the History of Nicodemus Colony*, 23. Craig goes on to mention that the Wimmses as well as other families found that they could "control" but not exterminate these pests by "wetting the floors." However, even after Mrs. Wimms did this, "It was found that the fleas could live in the wet dirt."

72   **about John Wayne Niles:** W. L. Chambers, *Niles of Nicodemus: Exploiter of Kansas Exoduster, Negro Indemnity and Equality of Black with Whites His Obsession, Beats Bankers, Bench and Barristers; Counter League to Post-War K.K.K. Riots and Finally Prison* (1925).

72   **After being pardoned:** E. Merton Coulter, *William G. Brownlow: Fighting Parson of the Southern Highlands* (Knoxville: University of Tennessee Press, 1937), 308. In this section of the book, Coulter explains that Brownlow "became the President's chief adviser concerning the granting of pardons to Tennesseans and during the early part of Johnson's term all pardons went through Brownlow's hands. As has

appeared the Governor and the President worked together in the early development of the Brownlow regime to the extent of the President's promise of the United States army if it should be needed."

72   **the title "Shrewd Scoundrel":** "A Shrewd Scoundrel," *Stockton Review and Rooks County Record*, May 19, 1882, p. 5.

72   **as history has recorded:** William A. Darity, "John Wayne Niles," in *Four Hundred Souls: A Community History of African America, 1619–2019*, ed. Ibram X. Kendi and Keisha N. Blain (New York: Random House, 2021), 244–48.

72   **"ponies and a shining buggy":** "Niles the Busy Borrow" and "Financing by Finesse," in Chambers, *Niles of Nicodemus*. The questionable nature of his financial management is captured not only by Chambers but is also chronicled significantly in the *Russell Record, Stockton Record*, and *Western Cyclone*. In some cases, Niles would defend himself under pseudonyms in other newspapers around the state.

CHAPTER 7

74   **"I am to be punished":** W. L. Chambers, *Niles of Nicodemus: Exploiter of Kansas Exoduster, Negro Indemnity and Equality of Black with Whites His Obsession, Beats Bankers, Bench and Barristers; Counter League to Post-War K.K.K. Riots and Finally Prison* (1925).

75   **His colleague, William D. Matthews:** Matthews was a noted abolitionist and former Black soldier and officer during the Civil War who had been involved in helping people escape through the Underground Railroad. For more on him, see Roger D. Cunningham, "Douglas's Battery at Fort Leavenworth: The Issue of Black Officers," *Kansas History: A Journal of the Central Plains* 23, no. 4 (Winter 2000–2001): 204–16. However, for even more biographical details of William D. Matthews one can look at an article referenced thoroughly by Charlotte Hinger's "'The Colored People Hold the Key'" in the same journal, which I used to verify the identification of Matthews as a noted abolitionist: "Capt. Matthews, Pioneer Colored Kansan Is Dead," *Leavenworth Times*, March 3, 1906. In addition, however, I also consulted the Kansas Historical Society's material items, which they have digitized through their Kansas Memory Project: A. C. Nichols, "A sepia-colored carte-de-visite of First Lieutenant William Dominick Matthews," Kansas Historical Society, Kansas Memory Project, Topeka, n.d.

75   **"Here was a human interest story":** Hinger, "'The Colored People Hold the Key,'" 35.

75   **Niles's murky reputation:** Brent M. S. Campney, "W. B. Townsend and the Struggle Against Racist Violence in Leavenworth," *Kansas History: A Journal of the Central Plains* 31, no. 4 (Winter 2008–2009): 260–73.

76   **The trip to Nicodemus:** Charlotte Hinger, "'The Colored People Hold the Key': Abram Thompson Hall, Jr.'s Campaign to Organize Graham County," *Kansas History: A Journal of the Central Plains* 31, no. 1 (Spring 2008).

77   **town's disbursing clerk:** Lulu Sadler Craig, *Manuscript on the History of Nicodemus Colony* (Kenneth Spencer Research Library at the University of Kansas, n.d.).

77   **Hall became the clerk of Nicodemus:** Hinger, "'The Colored People Hold the Key,'" 37.

77   **According to Craig, "The":** Lulu Sadler Craig, "Culture of Colonists," in Craig Manuscript Collection (Hill City: Graham County Historical Archives & Kenneth Spencer Research Library, n.d.), 9–11.

77   **"journey to the District Land Office":** Charlotte Hinger, *Nicodemus: Post-Reconstruction Politics and Racial Justice in Western Kansas*, vol. 11 of Race and

Culture in the American West Series (Norman: University of Oklahoma Press, 2022).

78 Now all residents of the county: Hinger, "'The Colored People Hold the Key,'" 36–37.

79 "The summers of 1878 and 1879": Craig, *Manuscript on the History of Nicodemus Colony.*

79 more than fifteen hundred land claims: Hinger, "'The Colored People Hold the Key,'" 36–37.

79 the territory's governor, John Pierce St. John: Hinger, "'The Colored People Hold the Key,'" 39. Their exact mention is: "We desire to refresh your memory relative to your promise to us, at an interview held with you at your office [on January 13, 1879], during the month of January. The promise was that, when Graham County applied for organization, if in any manner consistent with your position you could further the interests of Nicodemus you would do so . . . What we ask of you is, to use your option, thus given you by the signers, and declare Nicodemus as temporary County Seat."

80 a Black town the power base: The mention of the power of the perfunctory and quotidian is built upon the ideas conveyed in Walter Johnson, "On Agency," *Journal of Social History* 37, no. 1 (Autumn 2003): 113–24. In short, Johnson writes, "It suggests to me that the statement 'give them back their agency' is a 'white' form of address which originally served the purpose of admitting the speaker to a 'Black' conversation. It was, that is, a form of address which had embedded in it a politics which inter-related the past and the present in a way that was genuinely political: in a climate of overt discrimination and intellectual segregation making these historical gestures of alignment with slaves and, through them, with Black scholars, served a purpose and had a cost, even if that cost was only a little ridicule over dinner at the faculty club. I suppose what I am suggesting is that the present has changed and with it have the implications of our form of address to the past." Put another way, perhaps exegetically reading out of, but not into, the lives of the formerly enslaved amidst the afterlife of slavery might provide the best insight into an agency we do not have to conjure and then assign in a way to ameliorate retroactively the sins committed against them. This is a theme recurrent in this book by enabling their actions and their voices to leap off the page as opposed to my present-day reading into their lives an agency they never needed me to assign.

80 shaping their own Black nationalism: This notion of Black nationalism is a reference to the pragmatic Black nationalism referred to by Tommie Shelby. See Tommie Shelby, *We Who Are Dark: The Philosophical Foundations of Black Solidarity* (Cambridge, MA: Harvard University Press, 2007).

80 they were world-building: The distinction of world-building builds upon the notions articulated in Tiya Miles and Sharon P. Holland, "Seeing Red: Native America in the African American Imaginary," in *Crossing Waters, Crossing Worlds: The African Diaspora in Indian Country* (Durham, NC: Duke University Press, 2006), 13. The quote in particular that animates this is, "Dispersed from their countries of origin and perpetually homeless on this continent, African Americans have *imagined* into being a Promised Land that is located both within and outside the national boundaries of the United States. In the realm of the black imaginary . . ."

81 solidify its imperial footprint: Tonia Compton, "Challenging Imperial Expectations: Black and White Female Homesteaders in Kansas," *Great Plains Quarterly* 33, no. 1 (Winter 2013): 49–61.

81 Hayden was an unlikely "colonizer": Compton, "Challenging Imperial Expectations," 55–61.

CHAPTER 8

83   **"idea of freedom was too high":** James Lewis, "Letter from James Lewis writing from Kosciusko, Attalie County, Miss. to Governor John Pierce St. John," September 3, 1879, *Transcriptions of Governor St. John's Exoduster Correspondence.*

84   **"I am a native of [Texas]":** Stephen Hackworth, "Letter from Stephen Hackworth on the 'Colored exodus,'" May 9, 1879, *Transcriptions of Governor St. John's Exoduster Correspondence.* In this very long letter, Hackworth describes himself as someone who can advise the governor on how to both manage and take advantage of what he called the "exodus fever" and how to extract the greatest gains from Black migration into the state.

85   **"read with lively and painful interest":** Elizabeth Rous Comstock, "A Letter from Elizabeth Rous Comstock to Governor John Pierce St. John of Kansas," August, 31, 1879, *Transcriptions of Governor St. John's Exoduster Correspondence.*

85   **Agricultural and Industrial Institute for Refugees:** Robert Athearn, "The Afterglow," in *In Search of Canaan: Black Migration to Kansas, 1879–80* (Topeka: University Press of Kansas, 1978), 267.

85   **needed Christian education:** This is a reference to the charitable fundraising Comstock had done. Athearn, "The Afterglow."

86   **divided into three classes:** Hackworth letter.

91   **solution to the overwhelming number:** James H. McKay, "Letter from James H. McKay, General Manager of the Pacific Coast Immigration Bureau to Governor St. John on the Matter of Exodusters and their Availability," August 12, 1879, *Transcriptions of Governor St. John's Exoduster Correspondence.*

92   **Kansas Freedmen's Relief Association (KFRA):** *Second Report of the Kansas Freedmen's Relief Association,* Kansas Freedmen's Relief Association (Topeka, KS: Daily Capital Steam Printing House, 1880), 3–4.

92   **"Our enterprise is not political":** J. E. Gilbert, "Report of the President to the Board of Directors of the Kansas Freedman's Relief Association," Topeka, 1880, pp. 7–9.

92   **"1380 packages comprising":** John D. Knox, "Statement of Contributions Received by the K.F.R. Association from October 13, 1879 to March 31, 1880, Inclusive," Topeka, 1880, pp. 12–23.

CHAPTER 9

94   **McCabe reached out to a local minister:** Lulu Sadler Craig, "Vignette: E.P. McCabe," in Craig Manuscript Collection, n.d., 91.

94   **what she called "Mac's place":** Craig, "Vignette." McCabe was routinely referred to throughout this document and others as "Mac," usually colloquially or between friends/peers.

95   **churches were far from formal:** Ella Johnson Bridges, "History of the First Baptist Church of Nicodemus, Kansas," in Craig Manuscript Collection, n.d., 81.

96   **McCabe was no longer just a notary:** Details of McCabe and Hall's appointments can be found in Charlotte Hinger, "'The Colored People Hold the Key': Abram Thompson Hall, Jr.'s Campaign to Organize Graham County," *Kansas History: A Journal of the Central Plains* 31, no. 1 (Spring 2008): 36.

96   **people like Z. T. Fletcher:** Lulu Sadler Craig, "Vignette: ZT Fletcher," in Craig Manuscript Collection, n.d., 86.

96   **White men, too:** The white town boosters of Nicodemus—S. G. Wilson, C. H. Newth, William Green—can be found in Claire O'Brien, "With One Mighty Pull:

Interracial Town Boosting in Nicodemus, Kansas," *Great Plains Quarterly* 16, no. 2 (Spring 1996): 117–30.

97   **"no new debts, but pay as we go":** John Pierce St. John, "Biennial Message of John P. St. John, Governor, to the Legislature of Kansas, 1881. Governor's Message" (Geo. W. Martin, Kansas Publishing House, January 1881).

98   **"a state of small businessmen":** Scott McNall, *The Road to Rebellion: Class Formation and Kansas Populism, 1865–1900* (Chicago: University of Chicago Press, 1988), 99.

CHAPTER 10

99   **"If the Southern whites":** This is part of an exhaustive report by the *St. Louis Globe-Democrat* on the activities of the Voorhees Committee. Digs are being taken at the committee specifically for not being (a) exhaustive and (b) for not fastidiously minding the "people's money." "The Exodus Report," *St. Louis Globe-Democrat*, June 3, 1880, p. 4.

100 **mocked the motivation for the investigation:** "The Astonishment of Voorhees," *New York Times*, December 23, 1879, p. 4.

100 **"The benevolent Mr. Voorhees":** "The Astonishment of Voorhees."

100 **The committee's witness list:** Daniel W. Voorhees, Chairman, Zebulon B. Vance, William Windom, and Henry W. Blair, *Report and Testimony of the Select Committee of the United States Senate to Investigate the Causes of the Removal of the Negroes from the Southern States to the Northern States in Three Parts*, 46th Congress, 2nd Session, Report No. 693 (Washington, DC: Government Printing Office, 1880), 3.

101 **five times the salary of each senator:** "The Query Answered: Senator Voorhees' Exodus Investigation Will Cost the People a Round Sum of Money," *Princeton Clarion-Leader*, February 5, 1880, p. 1.

101 **Kansas was an indictment:** "The Exodus Report." The notion of Voorhees trying to pinpoint the cause of this removal from the South among Black people is articulated in the majority's report found on the first several pages of his report.

102 **carving out the outline:** Roy Garvin, "Benjamin, or 'Pap,' Singleton and His Followers," *Journal of Negro History* 33, no. 1 (1948): 7–23. Additionally, for specific consideration, see Benjamin "Pap" Singleton, "Ho for Kansas!," Real Estate and Homestead Association in Nashville, Tennessee & Courtesy of Kansas Historical Society, March 18, 1878.

102 **Singleton's testimony ran counter:** *Report and Testimony* (Voorhees Committee).

102 **"and learn the South a lesson":** *Report and Testimony* (Voorhees Committee).

103 **Charlton Tandy, a Black man:** Robert G. Athearn, "And Walk into Jordan's Tide," chapter 1 in *In Search of Canaan: Black Migration to Kansas* (Lawrence: University of Kansas Press, 1978), 11.

103 **letter addended with select affidavits:** "The Negro Exodus: Memorial to Congress from St. Louis," *National Republican*, April 8, 1879, p. 4.

103 **survived the "vilest atrocities":** "The Negro Exodus."

103 **Tandy, whose mild-mannered:** Tandy's stature in the St. Louis community, as well as his nature and physical attributes, can be found in Elinor Mondale Gersman, "The Development of Public Education for Blacks in Nineteenth Century St. Louis, Missouri," *Journal of Negro Education* 41, no. 1 (Winter 1972): 35–47.

103 **"fawning sycophant" of the Republicans:** "Fred Douglass," *Niles Democrat*, May 24, 1879, p. 2.

103 **Missouri Equal Rights League:** Christopher K. Hays, "Charlton W. Tandy," *Dictio-*

nary of Missouri Biography, ed. Lawrence O. Christensen, William E. Foley, Gary R. Kremer, and Kenneth H. Winn (Columbia: State Historical Society of Missouri, 1999).

104 **bad weather would not deter them:** Bryan M. Jack, *The St. Louis African American Community and the Exodusters* (Columbia: University of Missouri Press, 2008), 32–36. Bryan Jack discusses the significance of the weather that greeted the Exodusters in St. Louis. In one instance, he mentions how Tandy happens upon people trudging through the snow with little by the way of provisions.

104 **Not "a single kind remembrance":** "The Negro Exodus."

106 **emerged as a political leader in Kansas:** Mentions of McCabe and his career ascent, as well as appointments referenced by Hinger, but more thoroughly and directly, can be found in "Secretary of State—Second Biennial Report," in *Public Documents: Kansas, 1879–1880* (Topeka: Geo. W. Martin, Kansas Publishing House, 1881).

106 **voted against the Thirteenth Amendment:** George Pendleton's opposition to the Thirteenth Amendment can be found in Thomas Mach, "From Victory Came Defeat & Pendleton and Party Unity," in *"Gentleman George" Hunt Pendleton: Party Politics and Ideological Identity in Nineteenth-Century America* (Kent, OH: Kent State University Press, 2007), 100, 106–10.

106 **vested interest in recasting North Carolina:** Zebulon Vance discussed his perspectives on North Carolina and the South and its treatment politically in "A Difference," *Democrat & Chronicle*, September 27, 1880, p. 2. The interests of his state and the indifference to the plight of Black people and the threat their departure posed is covered in "No Cause for Fear," *Charlotte Democrat*, October 24, 1879, p. 3.

106 **"friendship of their white neighbors":** "The Negro Exodus," p. 8.

106 **already "civilized" on their own:** This is a paraphrasing of the direct quote on the same page, which reads, "the sooner they will gain that friendship; and that friendship and harmony once fully attained, there is nothing to bar the way to their speedy civilization and advancement in wealth and prosperity, except such as hinder all people in that great work."

107 **The goal of the entire investigation:** From Senator William Windom's report of the minority. *Report and Testimony* (Voorhees Committee), p. 9.

CHAPTER 11

109 **"sold out my people":** Edward Preston McCabe, "Letter from Graham," *Herald of Kansas*, April 30, 1880, p. 1.

109 **"prevented [Black Kansans]":** "The Convention of Colored Men: Our Report of the Same," *Herald of Kansas*, April 16, 1880, pp. 1–2.

110 **the Kansas Convention of Colored Men:** "The Convention of Colored Men," p. 2.

110 **"rust until another election":** "The Convention of Colored Men," p. 2.

111 **amelioration of the condition of the race:** Abram T. Hall, Z. T. Fletcher, E. P. McCabe, and Granville Lewis, "Letter to the Gentlemen of the Convention [of Colored Men]," *Herald of Kansas*, April 16, 1880, p. 2.

112 **Known as W.B.:** Brent M. S. Campney, "W. B. Townsend and the Struggle Against Racist Violence in Leavenworth," *Kansas History: A Journal of the Central Plains* 31, no. 4 (Winter 2008–2009): 260–73.

112 **the "Afro-American Diplomat":** Campney, "W. B. Townsend," 262. He was given this title by a collection of newspapers and political observers. As Campney recounted, "Known for his dapper attire, he established himself as a force among

Republicans . . . wielding significant influence over many aspects of black political life in the state . . . several times elected congressional and state-at-large representative to National Republican nominating conventions."

113 **McCabe took it upon himself:** W. B. Townsend, "An Explanation," *Herald of Kansas*, April 23, 1880, p. 1.

113 **"while there [I] strove hard":** The sordid details of the failure of nominating Townsend are referenced in "Letter to the Gentlemen of the Convention." Additionally, see Campney's article entry cited above for the estimation of the number of votes by which he lost, which Campney recalls as "a few votes."

114 **evidence of "envy or spleen":** Townsend, "An Explanation."

CHAPTER 12

116 **"The anti–St. John faction":** "E.P. McCabe's Candidacy," *Garnett Journal*, September 23, 1882, p. 1.

116 **draw Black votes to the Republicans:** This is derived by reports, especially the *Burlington Independent* report, which examined statements by St. John and lodged complaints that his placing McCabe on the ballot was nothing but trying to gin up support among Black voters. "Sensible Advice to Colored Men in Kansas," *Burlington Independent*, November 3, 1882, p. 2.

117 **"was too heavy a load":** "E.P. McCabe's Candidacy."

117 **owner and publisher of the *Colored Citizen*:** Biographical information on William L. Eagleson was found in Mary M. Cronin, "A Chance to Build for Our Selves: Black Press Boosterism in Oklahoma, 1891–1915," *Journalism History* 26, no. 2 (2000): 71–80. In this work by Cronin, not only do we get an understanding of the basic biographical details of Eagleson, but she places into context his work as a journalist, which doubled as a booster for what could become of the Black towns and areas that he covered.

119 **1880 was both the year:** Edward Preston McCabe, "Letter from Graham," *Herald of Kansas*, April 30, 1880, p. 1.

119 **year of McCabe's own defenestration:** "The Convention of Colored Men: Our Report of the Same," *Herald of Kansas*, April 16, 1880: "Night Session," pp. 1–2.

119 **State Senator Perry Hutchinson:** Perry Hutchinson was a well-regarded, wealthy Republican politician with significant contacts across the state, especially as a banker for numerous farmers and farming companies. For more on Hutchinson, see "Perry Hutchinson" in Frank Blackmar, *Kansas: A Cyclopedia of State History, Embracing Events, Institutions, Industries, Counties, Cities, Towns, Prominent Persons, Etc.* (Chicago: Standard Publishing Co., 1912), 312–14.

120 ***Whose Black Politics?*:** The differences associated with a generation of Black political leaders (and aspirants) is described in depth in Andra Gillespie, "Meet the New Class, Theorizing Young Black Leadership in a 'Postracial' Era," chapter 1 in *Whose Black Politics? Cases in Post Racial Black Leadership*, ed. Andra Gillespie (New York: Routledge, 2010), 9–16. While it may seem anachronistic to include Gillespie's analysis, there are similarities in the push to be post-racial. Post-racial desires are not and have never been in America a matter of inertia but rather a push-pull exercise—a desire for the dominant group in American society and politics to push out and racial analysis and the tension that is produced by the Black populace to pull America back to a more grounded understanding of itself, one that includes fundamentally a consideration of race. At the time of Reconstruction and in its aftermath (during McCabe's rise) this, too, was the case—a desire and distinct effort had been

made at trying to ablute race as a consideration of repair. McCabe's actions and the blowback he received reflect the well-worn traditions of Black politicians.

120 **bona fides of "Blackness":** Barack Obama being painted as not Black enough and "out of touch" was explored in Lorrie Frasure, "The Burden of Jekyll and Hyde, Barack Obama, Racial Identity, and Black Political Behavior," chapter 6 in Gillespie, *Whose Black Politics?*, 140, 143.

120 a **"sink-hole of iniquity":** Brent M. S. Campney, "A Day More Dreadful Than Any That We Have Yet Experienced," in *This Is Not Dixie: Racist Violence in Kansas, 1861–1927* (Champaign: University of Illinois Press, 2017), 97.

122 **"A large proportion":** Augustus Wilson, "Speech by Mr. Augustus Wilson," *Proceedings of the Convention of Colored Men* (Parsons, KS: W.B. Avery, April 27–28, 1882), 2.

122 **did "not possess the requisite teams":** "Address of W.B. Avery Before the Convention," *Proceedings of the Convention of Colored Men*, 4–5.

122 **"Some of the best white friends":** "Address of W.B. Avery," 5.

123 **"capable, trustworthy and deserving":** "E.P. McCabe," *Atchison Daily Globe*, April 24, 1882, p. 4.

123 **The accumulation of endorsements:** The *Millbrook Herald* listed over a dozen endorsements from the western part of Kansas, including making McCabe the titular head of the headlines on that paper above candidates they were supporting for Congress (arguably more important positions). John H. Currie, ed., "Our Candidate for Auditor," *Millbrook Herald*, August 8, 1882, p. 2.

124 *Abilene Gazette* **and the** *Leavenworth Times*: The first endorsement can be found in "E.P. McCabe," *Abilene Gazette*, August 25, 1882, p. 1, while the second can be found in "LOCAL POLITICAL NOTES: Speakers to Stump the County—A Card from Mr. McCabe," *Leavenworth Times*, October 25, 1882, p. 1.

124 **The** *Beloit Gazette*: W. W. Abercrombie, "McCabe Got There," *Beloit Gazette*, November 18, 1882, p. 2.

124 **"a smoked Irishman":** "Republican Nominations," *Stockton Record* referenced in *Stockton Review and Rooks County Record*, August 18, 1882, p. 4.

125 **as much as it was gaining support:** St. John's popularity within the Black community was injured by the treatment of McCabe during his run for state auditor in Kansas, as evidenced by "The Negro in Politics Kansas and Iowa," *Negro History Bulletin* 25, no. 5 (February 1962): 110–11, 113.

125 **"bossism" and "third termism":** "Sensible Advice to Colored Men in Kansas," *Burlington Independent*, November 3, 1882, p. 2, and "The Negro in Politics Kansas and Iowa," *Garnett Journal*, November 3, 1882, p. 113.

126 **"happiest day of my life!":** "A Scene in the Convention," *Daily Eclipse*, August 12, 1882, p. 1.

126 **"the most hilarious nomination":** "A Scene in the Convention."

CHAPTER 13

129 **"Are the colored people satisfied":** "A Colored Stateman's Views," *Parsons Daily Sun*, December 1883, p. 1.

130 **soundly beaten by his challenger:** Overall McCabe did receive more votes, but for purposes of driving this point that much further, see "Election Results," *Parsons Weekly Eclipse*, November 9, 1882, p. 3.

130 **proponent of good governance:** Governor Glick, in the estimation of some, could be said to speak out of both sides of his mouth. However, he was known for his public,

vocal support (often only vocally, but not in terms of policy) of the "Society for Total Abstinence from Intoxicating Liquors." However, he was known as the leader of the "wet Democrats" but espoused "good moral suasion." Jonathan Zimmerman, "'A Little Brief Authority': Mary H. Hunt, the Woman's Christian Temperance Union, and the Birth of Scientific Temperance Instruction," in *Distilling Democracy: Alcohol Education in America's Public Schools, 1880–1925* (Lawrence: University Press of Kansas, 1999), 24.

130 **actively pushed for women's suffrage:** Mary Meyers, "George Glick, Farmer, Lawyer and Man of His Time," *Atchison Globe*, February 28, 2014.

CHAPTER 14

143 **covered wagons drawn by teams:** The mention of these come from a report by the *St. Louis Globe-Democrat* that reads, "There are camping about 1000 homeseekers within a radius five miles of this city . . . Along the roads leading here white covered wagons are crawling in from almost every part of the Union." "Among the Boomers' Camps," *St. Louis Globe-Democrat*, August 22, 1893, p. 2.

143 **Indigenous nations exiled from the East:** This is in specific reference to the five largest Indigenous nations (Choctaw, Cherokee, Muscogee Creek, Chickasaw, and Seminole), who in large swaths had been removed from predominantly what we now call the southeastern United States due to the Indian Removal Act of 1830: United States Congress, *An Act to provide for the removal of the Winnebago Indians from the lands ceded to the United States by the treaty of October twenty-sixth, eighteen hundred and thirty-two, and for their location west of the Mississippi River* (Washington, DC: Gales & Seaton, May 26, 1830).

143 **the territory *appeared* empty:** The "appearance" of emptiness is a very clear sleight of hand to demonstrate that it was not actually empty. It had been declared "unassigned" through the actions, first, of Representative William M. Springer, who added Section 13 to the annual "Indian Appropriations Act," which greenlit the president (at that time, Benjamin Harrison) to open lands to settlement through a proclamation in 1890: Dianna Everett, "Springer Amendment," in *The Encyclopedia of Oklahoma History and Culture*, Oklahoma Historical Society, okhistory .org, published January 15, 2010.

144 **This expansion of public lands:** Benjamin Harrison, Presidential Proclamation 288—Opening to Settlement Certain Lands in the Indian Territory, Washington, D.C., March 23, 1889.

145 **Mythmaking grew as quickly:** The mythmaking can be seen in a variety of ways, and its enablement was powered by a variety of forces and will be covered in depth later on. But informing the contemporary and near-after moments of the myths being made at the time, see William Willard Howard, "The Rush to Oklahoma," *Harper's Weekly*, May 18, 1889, pp. 391–94. In this article, Howard captures the beat-by-beat actions to establish the myth of what Oklahoma might become. For instance, he cynically writes, "Unlike Rome, the city of Guthrie was built in a day."

145 **Chilocco Indian Agricultural School:** To better understand the nature of the Chilocco Indian Agricultural School and set this scene in this section, I consulted K. Tsianina Lomawaima, "Oral Histories from Chilocco Indian Agricultural School 1920–1940," *American Indian Quarterly* 11, no. 3 (Summer 1987): 241–54.

In addition, I consulted Lomawaima's additional work: K. Tsianina Lomawaima, "Domesticity in the Federal Indian Schools: The Power of Authority over Mind and Body," *Journal of the American Ethnological Society* 20, no. 2 (May 1993): 227–40.

Last, consider, for greater context on the ways in which schools like Chilocco embedded further hardship and discrimination toward Indigenous people in America, Eve Ewing, *Original Sins: The (Mis)education of Black and Native Children and the Construction of American Racism* (New York: One World Books, 2025).

146 **white families looking toward Oklahoma Territory:** David A. Chang discusses the way in which "poverty brutalized the tenant farmers," many of whom were white migrants who came wanting to become farmers, but ended up as simply tenants having to contend with the "delicate soils of the prairie": David A. Chang, *The Color of Land: Race, Nation, and the Politics of Landownership in Oklahoma, 1832–1929* (Chapel Hill: University of North Carolina Press, 2010), 3, 187, 200.

147 **Many fell ill and died:** For a more specified estimate of the mortality rate along Indian removal, consider that the collective rate, according to Patrick Minges, is 50 percent: Patrick Minges, "Beneath the Underdog: Race, Religion, and the Trail of Tears," *American Indian Quarterly* 25, no. 3 (Summer 2001): 469.

147 **It lasted only five decades:** What tribal autonomy there may have been in these lands faded most abruptly with the introduction of the actions of the Dawes Commission. However, during and after the Civil War, the forced renegotiations of the peace treaties of 1866 with the Five Tribes also represented a significant end to an assumed cessation of interference and incursion. For more, consider the following works:

Kent Carter, *The Dawes Commission: And the Allotment of the Five Civilized Tribes, 1893–1914* (Orem, UT: Ancestry Publishing, 1999).

Claudio Saunt, *Unworthy Republic: The Dispossession of Native Americans and the Road to Indian Territory* (New York: Norton, 2020).

147 **which was often held communally:** Kenneth H. Bobroff, "Retelling Allotment: Indian Property Rights and the Myth of Common Ownership," *Vanderbilt Law Review* 54, no. 4 (2001): 1557.

147 **own ways of determining citizenship:** For the ways in which Indigenous sovereignty enabled more creative pathways to citizenship, consult the following:

Alaina Roberts, *I've Been Here All the While: Black Freedom on Native Land*, America in Nineteenth Century Series (Philadelphia: University of Pennsylvania Press, 2021).

Claudio Saunt, *Black, White, and Indian: Race and the Unmaking of an American Family* (Oxford: Oxford University Press, 2005).

Tiya Miles and Sharon Holland, *Crossing Waters, Crossing Worlds: The African Diaspora in Indian Country* (Durham, NC: Duke University Press, 2006).

Tiya Miles, *Ties That Bind: The Story of an Afro-Cherokee Family in Slavery and Freedom* (Berkeley: University of California Press, 2015).

Caleb Gayle, *We Refuse to Forget: A True Story of Black Creeks, American Identity, and Power* (New York: Riverhead, 2022).

148 **loss of over 1.8 million acres:** Dwanna L. McKay, "Oklahoma Is—and Always Has Been—Native Land," *The Conversation*, July 16, 2020. McKay makes painfully clear the degree of land loss in her piece when she writes, "The Muscogee lost nearly half their lands in an 1866 Reconstruction-era treaty. And in 1889, almost 2 million acres in western Oklahoma were redesignated as 'Unassigned Lands' and opened to white settlement. By 1890, the U.S. Census showed that only 28% of people in Indian Territory were actually 'Indian.'"

148 **Senator Preston B. Plumb:** Plumb's support of McCabe and Black people writ large is considered dubious, as is found in the work of Mary F. Berry. Plumb was quoted as saying that instead of pensioning Black people who were formerly enslaved (an opportunity at reparations), whom Plumb uniformly called "able bodied people who are quite capable of making a living," they should instead spend their time as "pension disabled soldiers." Even more, he said, "for every damage done, it would be too much of a burden on tax payers." This shows that Plumb saw Black people as a white man's burden but one too large to bear sufficiently. So, of course, he would soon encourage McCabe to abandon Kansas and depart for Oklahoma Territory: Mary F. Berry, "Reparations for Freedmen, 1890–1916: Fraudulent Practices or Justice Deferred?," *Journal of Negro History* 57, no. 3 (June 1972): 219–230.

148 **newspaperman in his native Ohio:** Preston Plumb and his short biographical details can be found in William Elsey Connelley, *The Life of Preston B. Plumb, 1837–1891, United States Senator from Kansas for the Fourteen Years from 1877 to 1891, "A Pioneer of the Progressive Movement in America"* (Chicago: Browne & Howell Co., 1913).

148 **same possibilities for Oklahoma Territory:** Plumb's interest in the Oklahoma Territory was not just a public but also a matter of well-documented involvement in the background: "A Negro Commonwealth," *San Francisco Examiner*, March 3, 1890, p. 1. In addition, in particular reference to "public lands" and Oklahoma, see the following two chapters in his biography, which chronicle his time in the 1880s as chairman of the U.S. Senate Committee on Public Lands.

"Chapter LV: Oklahoma," in Connelley, *The Life of Preston B. Plumb*, 327–33. On the last two pages of this brief chapter, Elsey makes painfully clear Plumb's lack of interest in giving Oklahoma to "the town-site boomers," preferring that the "lands of Oklahoma were reserved to the settlers."

"Chapter LVIII: Public Lands," *The Life of Preston B. Plumb.*

149 **Conference of Friends of the Indian:** Henry L. Dawes, "Conference of Friends of the Indian, 2nd Day of the Conference Proceedings," *Proceedings of the Twelfth Annual Meeting of the Lake Mohonk Conference* (Lake Mohonk, NY: The Lake Mohonk Conference, 1884).

149 **"fix the Indian problem":** Further thoughts as expressed by Dawes beyond legislation and speeches can be found in Henry L. Dawes, "Have We Failed with the Indian?," *Atlantic Monthly*, August 1899: "To permit him to be a roving savage was unendurable, and therefore the task of fitting him for civilized life was undertaken."

150 **wrest control of Indigenous land:** Dawes, "Have We Failed with the Indian?"

150 **The tragedies of this "help" are numerous:** I critique the desire to "help" the Indigenous in ". . . And Oklahoma Became the South," in *We Refuse to Forget*, 81–90. The details of how the tragedies of help turned out can be found in the General Allotment Act of 1887, 24 Stat. 388. Washington, D.C.: United States Congress, 1887.

150 **The enactment of the Dawes Act:** United States Congress, General Allotment Act of 1887.

CHAPTER 15

152 **"There never was a more favorable time":** Initially this was carried in the *Colored Citizen*, which is difficult to track down in physical form. However, it was also carried thoroughly in several papers: W. L. Eagleson, "To Colonize Oklahoma," *Topeka Daily Press*, July 8, 1889, p. 8.

153 **an influential booster:** "Pioneering Editor Fought for Rights Years Before Brown," *Los Angeles Sentinel*, February 22, 1996, pp. A11, A13.

153 **"You will be free":** Eagleson, "To Colonize Oklahoma."

153 **might have been a true believer:** Early biographical details about Eagleson's life in Missouri can be found in "'From Labor to Reward': William Lewis Eagleson (Obituary)," *Topeka Plaindealer*, June 30, 1899, p. 2.

154 **"We would not advise an affiliation":** "'From Labor to Reward.'"

154 **The *Colored Citizen* became the nexus:** "'From Labor to Reward.'"

154 **"targets of white men":** Charlotte Hinger, "William Lewis Eagleson (1835–1899)," Blackpast.org, January 13, 2014.

154 **affiliation with the Republican Party:** His rejection of forced affiliation was displayed in his support of T. W. Henderson for lieutenant governor of Kansas, a direct repudiation of dominant Republican politics in Kansas: Hinger, "William Lewis Eagleson."

154 **the "Coveted Prize":** Eagleson claimed (exaggerated) in this article that there were twenty-two thousand Negroes and estimated that there would be fifty thousand: "The Coveted Prize: The Ambition of the Colored Topekans to Found a State," *Topeka Daily Press*, January 16, 1890, p. 4.

155 **"the land of promise":** For more on Eagleson's warnings and compulsion to move west for Black people, see Nudie E. Williams, "Black Newspapers and the Exodusters of 1879," *Kansas History: A Journal of the Central Plains* 8, no. 4 (Winter 1985–1986): 217–25.

155 **Appoint a Moses:** The reference here comes from "Awaiting Harrison's Order: Negroes Massed on the Borders of New Oklahoma Lands," *Kansas City Times*, September 7, 1891, p. 5. The reporters from *Kansas City Times* wrote, "In the eyes of the southern darkies McCabe is figuring now as a modern Moses leading his people to a land of 'milk and honey.'"

155 **Sarah needed a medical procedure:** "Updates," *Washington Bee*, June 15, 1889, p. 2.

156 **namely the Oklahoma Immigration Association:** "On to Oklahoma: A Colored Immigration Company Organized Last Night—An Address to the Colored People," *Topeka Daily Press*, July 18, 1889, p. 8. In this article, we see Eagleson as the business manager, corresponding secretary, and McCabe is the titular head as they sell Black people on the notion of immigrating to establish their own homestead.

156 **gathering enough Republican bona fides:** For more on McCabe's crumbling bona fides with local Kansas Republicans and their repudiation of his presentation of them with national Republicans toward the end of the Cleveland presidency (first term), see "McCabe Slaughtered," *Topeka Daily Press*, May 3, 1888, p. 2.

156 **He set up his family in the District:** For more on McCabe moving to Washington, see "Personal Mention," *Topeka State Journal*, March 15, 1889, p. 1.

157 **S. H. Scott moved to Oklahoma:** "The Arkansas Contribution," *Parsons Daily Eclipse*, April 16, 1889, p. 1.

157 **John Young and D. B. Garrett:** "NOT DISAPPOINTED: The Colored Colonists at Red Fork and Turkey Creek, Oklahoma," *Topeka Daily Capital*, April 30, 1889, p. 3. (In some instances, D.B. is written in newspapers as "P.S. Garrett.")

158 **"the neutral Strip":** "McCabe's Candidacy, Special to the News," *Rocky Mountain News*, April 2, 1890, p. 2.

158 **notion of a Black state:** For more on Plumb and Ingalls's support of McCabe and a Black state, see "NEGRO STATE: What the Colored People Propose to Have in Oklahoma. Senators Ingalls and Plumb Lending Their Influence to the Movement. The Negroes Organized," *Fort Worth Daily Gazette*, March 3, 1890, p. 1.

158 the solution to the "Colored Problem": "The Race Question," *Garnett Journal*, February 21, 1890, p. 2.

159 in his meeting with Harrison: "Opposed to M'Cabe: The Citizens of Oklahoma Territory Openly Declare Against Negro Immigrants. President Harrison Pressed to Appoint McCabe Governor to Encourage the Negro State," *Rocky Mountain News*, March 3, 1890.

159 "broke down the barriers of slavery": "Opposed to M'Cabe."

159 reputation as a modern Moses: "FIXING FOR A NEGRO STATE: Oklahoma, the New Canaan of the Colored Race, and its Future Status. ONE WHO WOULD BE MOSES: Colored Applicant for Governorship of the Territory—An Indiana White Republican Politician in the Way," *Milwaukee Journal*, March 8, 1890.

160 "Come Prepared or Not at All": "IN OKLAHOMA: A Talk with W.L. Eagleson, The First Negro to Urge Settling There," *Topeka Daily Capital*, October 27, 1892, p. 5.

CHAPTER 16

162 the prospect of a Negro state: "Why Not McCabe?," *New York Age*, November 7, 1891.

163 "Give the blacks a chance": "Why Not McCabe?"

163 William Waldorf Astor promised: "NEGRO STATE: What the Colored People Propose to Have in Oklahoma. Senators Ingalls and Plumb Lending Their Influence to the Movement. The Negroes Organized," *Fort Worth Daily Gazette*, March 3, 1890, p. 1.

163 The Black population of Oklahoma reported: The population numbers and estimations by McCabe and his acolytes appear more fabulation than verified numbers. As an example, see the following news articles reporting on the variances of the Black Oklahoma population, which often did not account for the Black citizens of the various Indigenous nations:

"A KANSAN INTERVIEWED: Hon. E.P. McCabe Talks About the Policy of the President Toward the Colored Republicans," *Capper's Weekly*, May 23, 1889, p. 5.

"Special Correspondence: A Colored Politician," *North American*, July 15, 1892, p. 2.

"FOR GOVERNOR OF OKLAHOMA: Ex-State Auditor McCabe of Kansas Strongly Endorsed in the West," *New York Age* carried in *Spokane Falls Capital*, March 15, 1890.

"McCabe's Candidacy, Special to the News," *Rocky Mountain News*, April 2, 1890, p. 2.

163 "greatest states in the Union": "The Coveted Prize: The Ambition of the Colored Topekans to Found a State," *Topeka Daily Press*, January 16, 1890, p. 4.

164 until the train got to "The Elbow": Michael Boyles and Mary Boyles, interview by Caleb Gayle at Langston City Hall, Langston, OK, edited by Anna Colletto, August 25, 2023.

165 "barrel of money out of his scheme": "TO BOOM NEGRO TOWNS: McCabe and His Cohorts to Soon Begin Operations," *Guthrie Daily Leader*, October 18, 1893, p. 3.

166 Its oil was first discovered in 1859: Kenny A. Ranks, "Petroleum Industry," *The Encyclopedia of Oklahoma History and Culture*, Oklahoma Historical Society, okhistory.org, published January 15, 2010.

166 The Osage despised the new Black people: On Osage and Black interaction with McCabe's early involvement and town settlement, see "Heading for Perry," *Guthrie Daily Leader*, November 8, 1893, p. 3.

167 "When we got up a colony": "OKLAHOMA: The Negro Colonization Scheme Pronounced a Myth. Hon. John Paul Jones Gives Expression to His Views. Bitterly Opposed to McCabe's Candidacy for Governor," *Atchison Daily Champion*, December 8, 1890, p. 1.

168 "It became necessary for Republicans": "OKLAHOMA: The Negro Colonization Scheme Pronounced a Myth."

168 "For months [McCabe] hung by the eyebrows": *Atchison Globe*, March 10, 1890.

169 "demand the secretaryship of the territory": *Atchison Globe*, March 10, 1890.

169 "It would be unwise to recognize": "Will He Get It?," *Galveston Daily News*, March 6, 1890.

169 "simply idle gossip": "Will He Get It?"

169 "If I should be appointed Governor": "Will He Get It?"

170 accusations of Negro Supremacy: "MCCABE for GOVERNOR: Republican Says if McCabe Is Governor, He Would Not Give [Support] for His Life," *Arkansas Democrat*, March 4, 1890, p. 1.

170 That line in the proverbial sand: "FIXING FOR A NEGRO STATE: Oklahoma, the New Canaan of the Colored Race, and its Future Status. ONE WHO WOULD BE MOSES: Colored Applicant for Governorship of the Territory—An Indiana White Republican Politician in the Way," *Milwaukee Journal*, March 8, 1890.

171 one hundred thousand Black people: "The Story of Oklahoma," *Buffalo Weekly Express*, April 11, 1889, p. 3.
       He started initially with estimates closer to fifty thousand: "Coveted Prize."

173 mockingly solemn headline: "Poor Kansans," *Kansas Democrat*, May 12, 1890.

173 "This is the first and only time": "PRACTICAL DEMONSTRATION," *Fort Scott Daily Tribune* and *Fort Scott Daily Monitor*, May 9, 1890, p. 4.

CHAPTER 17

175 "For the master's tools": Audre Lorde, "The Master's Tools Will Never Dismantle the Master's House," in *Sister Outsider: Essays and Speeches* (Berkeley, CA: Crossing Press, 2007), 110–14.

175 "Each day's crowd of arrivals": "A FREE-FOR-ALL, THE GREAT RACE TODAY FOR HOMES IN OKLAHOMA: The Excitement at Fever Heat Among the Boomers Along the Borders of the Reservations," *Wichita Eagle*, September 22, 1891, p. 1.

176 an encampment of these newcomers' dreams: For information on the scenes of people gathering in Guthrie and the store closures, etc., see "READY TO RAID: Homeseekers Crowd the Border of the Newly Opened Indian Lands, Preparatory to the Great Grab for Homes on Tuesday. The Bitter Contest for Choice Lands May Lead to Bloodshed," *Times-Picayune*, September 21, 1891, p. 2.

176 homesteads could be established: "A FREE-FOR-ALL."

177 "surveyors are suffering for water": "The Home Grabbers in the Territory," *Times-Picayune*, September 26, 1891, p. 2.

177 "Black and white and Indian will participate": See John A. Cockerill, "Cockerill's Letter: Bishop Turner and Negro—Discouraging Reports from Liberia-Ex-Senator McCabe's Oklahoma Scheme," *Salt Lake Herald*, October 2, 1891, p. 14.

177 "Gamblers are here with their outfits": "Among the Boomers' Camps," *St. Louis Globe-Democrat*, August 22, 1893, p. 2.

177 "Everything is wide open": "THE DAY AT GUTHRIE," *Wichita Eagle*, September 22, 1891, p. 1.

178 "Sooners," rushing into the land: Mary Ann Blochowiak, "Sooner," *The Encyclopedia of Oklahoma History and Culture*, Oklahoma Historical Society, okhistory .org, published January 15, 2010.

178 "timber of the finest quality": "THE NEW LANDS, Guthrie, O.T.," *Wichita Eagle*, September 22, 1891, p. 1.

178 "a never-failing supply of water": "THE NEW LANDS."

179 "swearing they would return": "War Between Negroes and Cowboys in the Indian Territory," *Times-Picayune*, September 19, 1891, p. 2.

180 by Gooseneck Bend: The scenes of Gooseneck are supported by "WAR IN THE TERRITORY: NEGROES FORTIFIED AGAINST THE CHEROKEES, War in Indian Territory," *Pratt Union*, May 7, 1891, p. 2.

183 "poverty-stricken negroes": Term coined by the *Daily Picayune* in "DESTITUTION AND STARVATION: Negro Colonists in Oklahoma Suffering Greatly," May 12, 1892.

184 Impassioned pleas rang out: "Prodigal Son": "This Is No Lie; Though It Be Nigger Talk," *Arkansas Democrat*, March 19, 1891. The aim of this article, among others, was to defame the purported success of the Black colonization of Oklahoma. So, too, did the *Minco Minstrel*, which did not make reference to the names of other Black people who supposedly had this experience. One of whom was named Tucker, it seems, the only Black person to speak on the record about his prodigal nature. However, it was in the *Little Rock Gazette* that Tucker's fuller statements make clear his true objection: that "Tucker had the appearance of going through rough times and two cent pieces were the extent of his fortune, he having squandered his little savings on a 'pleasure trip' to "the promised land." The question, however, is not asked nor answered, just why Tucker had been made so impoverished. In several advertisements, McCabe makes clear just how much people should be ready to work arduously to secure the promise in this promised land.

184 "five cents for his life": "This Is No Lie; Though It Be Nigger Talk."

184 cowboys who greeted McCabe were white: Scenes from the gunfight between McCabe and the cowboys are supported by Daniel F. Littlefield and Lonnie E. Underhill, "Black Dreams and 'Free' Homes: The Oklahoma Territory, 1891–1894," *Phylon* 34, no. 4 (4th Quarter 1973): 342–57.

CHAPTER 18

186 "At present the Oklahoma blacks": "Black State," *Chicago Tribune*, October 2, 1891, p. 10. This is a direct quote from McCabe as quoted in the *Tribune*. While this particular installment is useful and seemingly comprehensive, as it was the *Chicago Tribune*'s full feature on the question of Oklahoma becoming an all-Black state, I highly recommend also considering several additional sources to learn how other contemporary newspapers with less sympathy for the Black colonization movement covered it. For that nuanced approach, see John A. Cockerill, "Cockerill's Letter: Bishop Turner and Negro—Discouraging Reports from Liberia-Ex-Senator McCabe's Oklahoma Scheme," *Salt Lake Herald*, October 2, 1891, p. 14. Consider also the coverage around the same time by Lawrence, Kansas, newspapers, the *Weekly Record* and *Lawrence Daily Gazette*, along with northeastern papers: the *Morning Journal-Courier, Boston Evening Transcript, Times Union*, Davenport, Iowa's *Daily Leader*, among many others. The *Daily Picayune* coverage nuanced the fram-

ing as a pitch McCabe and other Black elites were making to "work out there the colored problem." Each article wove in local elements to color their varied level of ambition about McCabe's ambition.

187 **"A hotel, dry goods store":** Larry O'Dell, "Langston," *The Encyclopedia of Oklahoma History and Culture*, Oklahoma Historical Society, okhistory.org, published January 15, 2010, last modified July 29, 2024. Additionally, McCabe boasted of it in his own newspaper, the *Langston City Herald*: Edward McCabe, "FREEDOM: Peace, Happiness and Prosperity. Do You Want all These? Then Cast Your Lot With Us & Make Your Home," *Langston City Herald*, November 17, 1892, p. 3. Littlefield discusses it further in Daniel F. Littlefield and Lonnie E. Underhill, "Black Dreams and 'Free' Homes: The Oklahoma Territory, 1891–1894," *Phylon* 34, no. 4 (4th Quarter 1973): 342–57.

187 **"McCabe professes to be thoroughly well satisfied":** "A Black State," *Times-Picayune* (published as the *Daily Picayune*), October 6, 1891, p. 4.

187 **"outnumber the whites two to one":** Though numerous reports have been provided as references, the "Negro population" is an incredibly difficult estimate. What McCabe professed to be the tally of Black people in those lands, some scholars have made significant attempts to better estimate. In Taylor's work, he uses U.S. Census Bureau data on the "Negro Population in the United States" and combines it with the Population Statistics of Nineteenth Century Indian Territory for the 1900 census. That number is 55,684. For Indian Territory that share is 18,831, and for the Oklahoma Territory, it is 36,853. Quintard Taylor, "Migration and Settlement, 1875–1920," in *In Search of the Racial Frontier: African Americans in the American West, 1528–1990* (New York: Norton, 1998), 134–63.

However, it is important to mention that census-taking during the implementation of the Dawes Commission's enrollment system often utilized scant and informal, non-scientific, non-genealogical methodologies to record the racial categorization of people. There are several accounts, which can be found in Claudio Saunt, *Black, White, and Indian: Race and the Unmaking of an American Family* (Oxford: Oxford University Press, 2005) and Caleb Gayle, ". . . And Oklahoma Became the South," in *We Refuse to Forget: A True Story of Black Creeks, American Identity, and Power* (New York: Riverhead, 2022), 81–90, in which we see people being miscategorized and mislabeled. Additionally, for more context, see a contemporary analysis of chronic enumeration and census efforts during the late 1800s and early 1900s: Kelly Miller, "Enumeration Errors in Negro Population," *Scientific Monthly* 14, no. 2 (February 1922): 168–77.

187 **ballooned to over ten thousand people:** Guthrie was said to have "sprang into existence on the day." It was also the sole location for a train depot for quite some time at a location called Deer Creek: Linda D. Wilson, "Guthrie," *The Encyclopedia of Oklahoma History and Culture*, published January 15, 2010, last modified February 7, 2024.

187 **two thousand agents to proselytize:** "A Black State."

188 **"the white people living in Oklahoma:** "A Black State."

188 **"Another Hayti in the heart":** "A Black State."

188 **"necessary as an object lesson":** "A Black State."

189 **"Why Not McCabe?":** "Why Not McCabe?," *New York Age*, November 7, 1891.

190 **activities of the Logan County Republican Convention:** "Logan County Platform," *Kingfisher Times*, September 22, 1892, p. 1.

191 **creation of "mixed schools":** "Issues of Mixed Schools," *Kingfisher Times*, September 29, 1892, p. 4.

191 **"The negroes ran the whole concern":** "Issues of Mixed Schools."

192 **Fusion was simply an agreement:** "Death of Fusion," *Oklahoma State Capital*, April 15, 1893, p. 4.
192 **"It also brings forward":** "Issues of Mixed Schools."
192 **"domination of blacks of the whites":** And the other mentions of Negro supremacy: "Difference Between Voting for a Negro and Voting for the Man the Negro Controls," *Kingfisher Times*, September 22, 1892, p. 1.
193 **quiet threats of a supposed departure:** "Republican, of Course," *Oklahoma State Capital*, September 24, 1892, p. 6.
194 **struck defensive postures:** For scenes from the bolting of several Black people from the Republican Party in Oklahoma, see "OKLAHOMA NEGROES TO BOLT: Can't Stand Republican Domination—Riot in a County Convention," *Industrial Free Press*, September 22, 1892, p. 1.
194 **tussling scrum did break out:** Martin Dann, "From Sodom to the Promised Land: E. P. McCabe and the Movement for Oklahoma Colonization," *Kansas Historical Quarterly* 40, no. 3 (Autumn 1974): 370–78.

CHAPTER 19

195 **The railway was the highway:** Frank Best wrote about the railway as a character—a pioneer—in the creation of the state from its status as a territory. Frank J. Best, "Early Day Account," *The Santa Fe Railway as an Oklahoma Pioneer* (Oklahoma Historical Society—held and maintained by the Ardmore Public Library, 1951). Additionally, in a less opiniated fashion, the Oklahoma Historical Society has an account of Santa Fe: Augustus J. Veenendaal, "Atchison, Topeka and Santa Fe Railway," *The Encyclopedia of Oklahoma History and Culture*, Oklahoma Historical Society, okhistory.org, published January 15, 2010.
196 **"JIM CROW CARS":** "JIM CROW CARS: Railroads Are Preparing for Separate Accommodation of Races," *Norman Democrat-Topic*, December 20, 1907, p. 2.
196 **"General Laws of the State of Kansas":** *General Laws of the State of Kansas, Passed at the Third Session of the Legislature, Commenced at the Capital January 13, 1863, to Which Are Appended Lists of State Officers and Members and Officers of Both Branches of the Legislature* (Lawrence: *Kansas State Journal*, Steam Press Print, January 13, 1863).
196 **Texas spent its first years in the Union:** *Constitution of the State of Texas, Adopted in Convention, at the City of Austin 1845*, State of Texas (Austin: *New Era* [newspaper], 1845).
198 **who suffered a flesh wound:** "NEGROES ATTACK TRAIN ENROUTE TO MUSKOGEE: Throw Coal Through Windows and Scatter Glass over Delegates," *Shawnee News-Herald*, February 22, 1908, p. 1.
198 **the *Boley Beacon*:** The satirical *Boley Beacon* wrote about the "goodness" of the laws, specifically the Jim Crow "Separate Car" law: "Good Laws," *The Beacon*, February 27, 1908, p. 4.
198 **"[hearty] applause from the citizens":** "The Royal Train," *The Beacon*, February 27, 1908, p. 4.
199 **Hart had descended on Oklahoma:** "Will Argue Jim Crow," *Shawnee-News Herald*, February 26, 1908, p. 5.
199 **all the way to Guthrie:** "Will Argue Jim Crow."
199 **Roosevelt urging Judge John H. Cotteral:** "Will Argue Jim Crow."
199 **"fighting the constitutionality of the law":** "Will Argue Jim Crow."
200 **Samuel Robert Cassius wrote:** S. R. Cassius, "Jim Crow as I Saw It," *The Western Age*, February 28, 1908, p. 4.

201 **A. C. Hamlin, Oklahoma's first Black state legislator:** For information on A. C. Hamlin's defeat due to the grandfathering process, see Michael L. Bruce, "Hamlin, Albert Comstock," *The Encyclopedia of Oklahoma History and Culture*, published January 15, 2010, last modified July 29, 2024.

201 **Republicans and the Black Oklahomans:** Logan County's Black and Republican population was debated at the time. Democrats would at times downplay the number of Black people, in hopes of discouraging further Black migration into the state. In other instances, Democrat-affiliated papers would overplay it as a mentioned threat. "State Capital on Population," *Norman Democrat-Topic*, August 12, 1904, p. 1. Another example of that downplaying is of the "danger" of the Jim Crow and its deleterious effects on Oklahoma's population, leading a newspaper to write that "there is no Negro population" in Oklahoma: "NOT GENERALLY NEEDED: Many Oklahoma Counties Have No Negro Population," *Wagoner Record-Democrat*, February 6, 1908. However, in *The Western Age*, we see a countervailing opinion about the size of the population: "Oklahoma Figures," *The Western Age*, January 3, 1908, p. 1.

202 **Tate Brady Hotel in Tulsa:** Scott Carter, "The Capital War: Haskell's Secret Plan to Move the Government," *Epic News Network*, June 15, 2020.

202 **As above reproach as Haskell presented himself:** Carter, "The Capital War.

202 **incentive to move the state's capital:** For more on Haskell's plan, see Carter, "The Capital War."

202 **"PASSING OF E.P. M'CABE":** "PASSING OF E.P. M'CABE: Story of Negro Politician Which Is Full of Human Interest," *McAlester Capital*, August 27, 1908, p. 4.

203 **"M'Cabe Soldier of Fortune:** "M'CABE, SOLDIER OF FORTUNE KICKS DUST OF OKLAHOMA FROM FEET AFTER VARIED CAREER, VICTIM OF TREACHERY AND BROKEN PROMISES: After Long Years' of Service in Republican Party He Is Turned Down," *Guthrie Daily Leader*, August 19, 1908, p. 1.

203 **"Appointed by President McKinley":** "M'CABE, SOLDIER OF FORTUNE."

203 **"appointed assistant auditor of Oklahoma":** "M'CABE, SOLDIER OF FORTUNE."

203 **"effort to embed his ambitions":** "M'CABE, SOLDIER OF FORTUNE."

203 **Sarah, his wife, waited by her side:** "PASSING OF E.P. M'CABE."

204 **the debts he had accumulated:** "M'CABE, SOLDIER OF FORTUNE."

204 **"I must seek other fields":** "M'CABE, SOLDIER OF FORTUNE."

204 **"cannot depend on Republican promises":** "M'CABE, SOLDIER OF FORTUNE."

CHAPTER 20

205 **"It is most gratifying to note":** "BOOKER WASHINGTON SPEAKS ELOQUENTLY, NOTED EDUCATOR APPEARS BEFORE A LARGE SOUTH MCALESTER AUDIENCE: Advises His Race to Become Home Owners and Says Large Per Cent of Crimes by Negroes Comes from the Homeless Class," *McAlester Capital*, November 23, 1905, p. 3.

205 **popular Royal Hotel in downtown Guthrie:** "Booker T. Washington in Guthrie," *The Boley Progress*, November 23, 1905.

206 **An estimated five thousand waited outside:** "Booker T. Washington in Guthrie."

206 **"In order for us to grow":** Selected quotes from Washington's speech are found in "BOOKER WASHINGTON SPEAKS."

207 **"the tendency of Negroes":** "BOOKER WASHINGTON SPEAKS."

207 **feted by Oklahoma's leading mayors:** "BOOKER T. WASHINGTON: Received in Capitol City, Greeted by Greatest Crowd of Whole Trip. Speaks at Opera House Was Banqueted at City Hall," *Oklahoma Safeguard*, November 24, 1908, First ed.

207 **A Pullman car:** "BOOKER T. WASHINGTON."

207 oyster soup, fresh radishes and pickles: "BOOKER T. WASHINGTON."

208 "Oklahoma is the best country": Colored Townsite Board of Ferguson, Oklahoma,
     "Watonga News," *The Western Age*, July 26, 1907, p. 1.

208 granted citizenship in 1866: Info on the Creeks and their dispensation of citizenship
     for Black members can be found in "Article 2," *U.S. Treaty with the Creek Nation*,
     June 14, 1866, Ratified July 19, 1866, Proclaimed Aug. 11, 1866 (Washington, DC:
     Government Printing Office, June 14, 1866).
        Info on Seminoles and dispensation of citizenship for Black members: "Article
     2," *U.S. Treaty with the Seminole Nation*, Mar. 21, 1866, 14 Stats. 755, Ratified July
     19, 1866, Proclaimed Aug. 16, 1866 (Washington, DC: Government Printing Office,
     March 21, 1866).
        Info on Cherokees and dispensation of citizenship for Black members: "Article
     4," *U.S. Treaty with the Cherokee Nation*, July 19, 1866, 14 Stats. 799, Ratified July
     27, 1866, Proclaimed Aug. 11, 1866 (Washington, DC: Government Printing Office,
     July 9, 1866).

209 deputy auditor of Oklahoma Territory: McCabe's initial appointment is documented
     in "McCABE DEPUTY AUDITOR," *Daily Enterprise-Times*, July 1, 1897, p. 2.

209 for nearly a decade: McCabe held his position as a deputy auditor for ten years
     under four different gubernatorial administrations (under Governors Barnes, Jen-
     kins, Ferguson, and Frantz), as noted in "McCabe Considered a Worthy Man," *The
     Western Age*, November 22, 1907, p. 2.

210 leaders from all over the Indian Territory: The details of the Sequoyah Constitu-
     tional Convention are found in Amos DeZell Maxwell, "Sequoyah Constitutional
     Convention" (Masters thesis, Oklahoma Agricultural and Mechanical College,
     April 24, 1950).

212 At the time of the 1900 Territorial Census: Quintard Taylor, *In Search of the Racial
     Frontier: African Americans in the American West 1528–1990* (New York: Norton,
     1999), 135.

212 Blacks were far outnumbered by white people: "NOT GENERALLY NEEDED:
     Many Oklahoma Counties Have No Negro Population," *Wagoner Record-
     Democrat*, February 6, 1908; "State Capital on Population," *Norman Democrat-
     Topic*, August 12, 1904, p. 1.

213 "is liable to do queer things": "McCABE AND DYCHE," *Vinita Leader*, September
     5, 1907, p. 2.

213 "Negro McCabe today": "The Republican Speakers," *Norman Democrat-Topic*,
     August 23, 1907, p. 1.

213 eighteen Black men protested: "A Coarse Democratic Trick," *Muskogee Cimeter*,
     February 1, 1907, p. 4.

CHAPTER 21

214 "a sense of Gargantuan humor": "WEST DEFENDS LAW, COMPLETES BRIEF
     IN JIM CROW SUITS IN SUPREME COURT, ACTION WAS AGAINST SANTA
     FE: Negroes Claim There Is a Distinction Between White and Black Races as to
     Comfort and Many Conveniences," *Morning Examiner* (Bartlesville), November
     21, 1913, pp. 1, 6.

215 Eighth Circuit Court of Appeals agreed: "HEARING OF RATE CASES IN ST.
     PAUL COURT," *Muskogee Daily Phoenix* and *Times-Democrat*, May 8, 1910, p. 3.

215 judges was William C. Hook: Background information on Hook is found in "PRESI-
     DENT TAFT AND THE NEGROES," *Lexington Herald-Leader*, March 27, 1912,
     p. 4.

215 **McCabe and the other three plaintiffs:** "DECISION MAY AFFECT JIM CROW SUPREME COURT'S VIEW AWAITED," *Daily Ardmoreite*, April 7, 1911, p. 4.

215 **Hook dismissed these Black men's claims:** "PRESIDENT TAFT AND THE NE-GROES," *Lexington Herald-Leader*.

216 **Justice John Marshall Harlan:** Harlan's death is documented in "JUST HARLAN IS DEAD, THE END CAME IN WASHINGTON HOME THIS MORNING: An Attack of Bronchitis Fatal to the Venerable Justice, Who Was Older in Age and in Service Than Any Other Member of the Supreme Court," *Kansas City Star*, October 14, 1911, p. 2.

216 **a dissenter-in-chief:** Harlan's dissents were highlighted in the same publication under a different headline: "WAS THE DISSENTING JUSTICE: Harlan's Opinions Were Often Not Those of the Supreme Court," *Kansas City Star*, October 14, 1911, p. 2.

216 **looked enviously toward the Supreme Court:** For President Taft's legal career and record before the Supreme Court and activities as U.S. solicitor general, see Walter Stahr, "William Howard Taft as Solicitor General," *Journal of Supreme Court History* 48, no. 3 (2023): 317–31.

217 **elevated Edward White:** Jeffrey B. Morris, "Chief Justice Edward Douglass White and President Taft's Court," *Yearbook 1982: Supreme Court Historical Society* (Washington D.C.: Supreme Court Historical Society, 1982): 27–45.

217 **"weakest presidents the country has ever had":** "Bishop Walters Says Taft One of Weakest Presidents," *The Butte Miner*, August 30, 1911, p. 1.

218 **the relative silence of President Taft:** "Taft and Lynchings," *Messenger-Inquirer* (Owensboro, KY), August 30, 1911, p. 4.

218 **His bona fides were clear:** More information on William C. Hook is found in the *Daily Ardmoreite*.

219 **"ugly" race relations:** Brent M. S. Campney, "W. B. Townsend and the Struggle Against Racist Violence in Leavenworth," *Kansas History: A Journal of the Central Plains* 31, no. 4 (Winter 2008–2009): 260–73.

219 **"Negroes are opposed to the Hook appointment":** "Negroes Opposed to Appointment of Hook," *Washington Bee*, January 27, 1912, p. 1.

219 **a letter from Kelly Miller:** "Negroes Opposed to Appointment of Hook."

219 **"opposite directions at the same time":** "Negroes Opposed to Appointment of Hook."

219 **"The Evangelical Ministerial Alliance, embracing":** "MINISTERS' ALLIANCE: Protest Against the Appointment of Judge Hook," *Washington Bee*, January 27, 1912, p. 1.

220 **dissuade Black Republicans from bolting:** *Lexington Leader*.

220 **"We have no statistics at hand":** *Lexington Leader*.

CHAPTER 22

222 **"One by one, that brilliant group":** "Untitled," *The Black Dispatch*, October 13, 1921, p. 2.

223 **the Victoria colonization effort:** "M'CABE, SOLDIER OF FORTUNE KICKS DUST OF OKLAHOMA FROM FEET AFTER VARIED CAREER, VICTIM OF TREACHERY AND BROKEN PROMISES: After Long Years' of Service in Republican Party He Is Turned Down," *Guthrie Daily Leader*, August 19, 1908, p. 1; "E.P. McCabe," *The Searchlight* (Guthrie), August 21, 1908, p. 9.

223 **McCabe was spotted in a place:** "E.P. MCCABE FORMER ASSISTANT NEGRO STATE AUDITOR NOW WAITER," *Oklahoma State Register*, August 31, 1911, p. 2.

224 **Sam's program the imprimatur:** Larry O'Dell, "Chief Alfred Sam," *The Encyclopedia of Oklahoma History and Culture*, Oklahoma Historical Society, okhistory .org, published January 15, 2010, last modified July 24, 2024.

For a deeper dive into Chief Alfred Sam's work, see William E. Bittle and Gilbert Geis, *The Longest Way Home: Chief Alfred Sam's Back-to-Africa Movement* (Detroit: Wayne State University Press, 1964).

224 **Sam managed to engage a ship:** "Untitled: E.P. McCabe and Chief Alfred Sams," *Weekly Eagle* (Wichita), February 20, 1914, p. 8.

225 **"He never bartered":** "THE SAD ENDING OF HON. E.P. M'CABE: Former Auditor of Kansas Dies Penniless in an Alms House at Chicago," *Topeka Plaindealer*, March 19, 1920, p. 1.

225 **Luckily, he had bought a family plot:** Details on the death of McCabe's children are found in "Miss Edna McCabe Died in Chicago Tuesday Evening," *Oklahoma State Capital*, March 8, 1907, p. 6.

226 **"This should serve as an object lesson":** "THE SAD ENDING OF HON. E.P. M'CABE."

226 **Lowell Manis could be found:** Details on Lowell Manis's background as part of the Topeka Cemetery staff are found in "Obituary of Lowell Burnes Manis," Davidson Funeral Home, August 4, 2020.

227 **A pancake feed:** "Curtis Gravesite Fixed Up," *Manhattan Mercury* (Associated Press), April 29, 2002, p. 3.

228 **"a committal service":** Michael Hooper, "Black Leader to Have Formal Burial Service," *Topeka Capital-Journal*, September 21, 2000.

228 **McCabe Family Monument Fund:** "Curtis Gravesite Fixed Up."

Index

Ingalls, John J., 158, 269*n*158
Interior Department, U.S., 181–82

Jack, Bryan M., 256*n*62, 263*n*104
Jackson, Andrew, 63, 147
Jackson, W. C., xiv, 35
James, Horace, xiv, 35
Jerome, Leonard, xiv
"Jim Crow as I Saw It" (Cassius), 200
Jim Crow South, 2, 138, 243*n*2
Johnson, Walter, 260*n*80
Johnston, Douglas, 211
Johnston, Henry, 198
Jones, John Paul, xv, 167–68
Jones, Samuel J., 39–40

Kansas, 36, 41–42, 85–87, 98–99, 251*n*35,
    252*n*38
  Arkansas City in, 150–51
  "Bleeding," 26, 118, 248*n*26
  Colored Convention (1880) in, 111–15
  Eagleson doubting, 117–18
  Exodusters in, 101–3
  Graham County in, 78
  Hickory Point in, 27
  as indictment of the narrative about
      Black life, 101
  Lawrence in, 243*n*1
  political leadership of, 118
  Republican Party in, 112–13, 118,
      123–24, 158
  Rooks County in, 78
  see also Nicodemus; St. John, John
      Pierce
Kansas and Texas railway, 197
Kansas Black Farmers Association,
    69, 96
Kansas City Times (newspaper), 6, 132,
    269*n*155
Kansas Democrat (newspaper), 154, 173
Kansas Freedmen's Relief Association
    (KFRA), 92–93, 97
Kansas Free State (newspaper), 40
Kansas Herald of Freedom (newspaper),
    39–40
Kansas Historical Society, 251*n*35
Kansas-Nebraska Act, 29, 30–31
Kansas State Republican Convention,
    McCabe, E. P., attending, 112–13
Kansas Territory, 27, 29
Kelley, Harrison P., 126
Kellogg, William P., 63

KFRA. *See* Kansas Freedmen's Relief
    Association
Kingfisher (Oklahoma), 190
Kingfisher Times (newspaper), 190–92
Kirwin Chief (newspaper), 123
Kock, Bernard, xiv, 44–45, 47–50,
    253*nn*47–48
Ku Klux Klan, 53, 202, 255*n*53, 256*n*62

land runs, in Oklahoma, 2–4, 175–78, 180,
    184, 243*n*2
Lane, James Henry, xii, 50–51
Langston (Oklahoma), 3–4, 162–65, 187,
    231–33
Langston, Charles Henry, xii, 110
Langston, John Mercer, xii, 110, 118
Latrobe, John Hazlehurst Boneval, 45–47,
    252*n*46
Lawrence (Kansas), 243*n*1
Lawrence, Amos, xiv, 29–30, 33–35,
    250*n*29
Lawrence Daily Journal (newspaper), 177
Leavenworth Times (newspaper), 124
Lee, Jonathan, xiv, 35
Lewis, James M., 83
Lewis County Journal (newspaper), 184
Lexington Herald-Leader (newspaper), 49
Lexington Leader (newspaper), 220
Liberia, 45–47, 57, 245*n*8
Liberty (Oklahoma), McCabe, E. P.,
    founding, 165–66
Liberty Street Presbyterian Church, 23
Lincoln, Abraham, xiii, 8, 43, 44–45,
    48, 50
Littlefield, Daniel, 143, 187
Little Rock Gazette (newspaper), 245*n*6,
    272*n*184
Logan County (Oklahoma), 191, 201
Logan County Republican Convention, 190
Logan Enterprise (newspaper), 124
Lorde, Audre, 175
Los Angeles Sentinel (newspaper), 153
Luskey, Brian, 65
Lynwood, Ernest D., 198

Manis, Lowell, 226–29
*Manuscript on the History of Nicodemus
    Colony* (Craig), 59
Marshall, Frederick, 62, 256*n*62
Martin, John A., 54, 119, 133
Matthews, William D., 75, 259*n*75
Mayes, Joel B., 181–82

Victoria colonization effort, by Singleton,
  Benjamin "Pap," 223
Vinita Leader (newspaper), 213
Voorhees, Daniel, xiii, 100–101, 104–6
Voorhees Committee, 101, 262*n*99

Walker, Robert J., 248*n*26
Walters, Alexander, 217
Warmoth, Henry C., 63
Washington, Booker T., 196, 205–8
Washington, D.C., McCabe, E. P., in,
  155–56
Washington Bee (newspaper), 219
Welles, Gideon, 44
Welles, Gordon, 252*n*45

We Who Are Dark (Shelby), 109
Weyman, Charles S., 26, 248*n*26
White, Edward, 217
white settlement, of Indian Territory,
  267*n*148
Whitfield, John, xiii, 37
Whose Black Politics? (Gillespie), 120
Wichita Eagle (newspaper), 137, 175, 176
Willard, Charles Wesley, 255*n*50
Williams, Emma, xv, 69–70
Windom, William, 107–8
Winn, Claurence, 62, 256*n*62
Wood, Fernando, 92

Young, John, 157